The Rape
of the Great Plains

Also by K. Ross Toole

The Rape of the Great Plains

Northwest America, Cattle and Coal

K. Ross Toole

An Atlantic Monthly Press Book
Little, Brown and Company—Boston—Toronto

Second Printing

T 03/76

ATLANTIC–LITTLE, BROWN BOOKS
ARE PUBLISHED BY
LITTLE, BROWN AND COMPANY
IN ASSOCIATION WITH
THE ATLANTIC MONTHLY PRESS

LIBRARY OF CONGRESS CATALOGING IN PUBLICATION DATA

Toole, Kenneth Ross, 1920–
    The rape of the Great Plains.

    "An Atlantic monthly press book."
    Bibliography: p. ✦✦✦.
    Includes index.
    1. Strip mining — Environmental aspects — Montana   2. Elec-
tric power-plants — Environmental aspects — Montana.   3. Mon-
tana — Economic conditions.   4. Environmental protection —
Montana.   I. Title.
TD195.S75T66   333.7′6   75-31927
ISBN 0-316-84990-1

Designed by Susan Windheim

Published simultaneously in Canada
by Little, Brown & Company (Canada) Limited

PRINTED IN THE UNITED STATES OF AMERICA

To the dedicated and knowledgeable environmentalists
in the Great Plains states upon whose persistence
the fate of a great land depends

Acknowledgments

IN THIS KIND OF BOOK, dealing with a subject that is fiercely controversial, it is particularly important to assert that those who have helped me are in no way responsible for my conclusions or my point of view. I have been given much help by many people but it has been confined, in most cases, to the correction of egregious errors in figures, statistics, dates, names, and places. Others have helped with stylistic lapses or garbled expressions. None bears the slightest responsibility for my judgments, conclusions, or tone.

My debt is particularly great to Kit Muller of the Northern Plains Resource Council and to Tom France of the same organization. My boundless debt to John (Bud) Redding and his family will be obvious to anyone who reads this book. The same must be said of Wally McRae and of all the ranchers quoted herein.

In the actual process of research I owe much to Kevin O'Neil, Mary Lenihan, Peter Langdorf, Steve Lenchner, and Frank Grant.

To those members of the staffs of the several environmental agencies of the State of Montana I am very grateful for unfailing courtesy and cooperation. They are, in particular, Ted Clack, John Gore, Roger Tippy, Richard Hargesheimer, and Lieutenant Governor William Christiansen.

I must also thank collectively the legislative interns, aides and lobbyists, and students from the University of Montana, who have provided me with much information and have been unstinting with their time, their interest — and their friendship. They are, happily, too numerous to name individually, except for the several who have been run ragged by my requests: Bruce Nelson, Garry South, and Ed Smith, who is chief clerk of the Montana House of Representatives.

Several Montana legislators have been of enormous help. They are Majority Leader John Driscoll, Speaker of the House Patrick McKittrick, Senator Thomas Towe, Representatives Miles Romney and Richard Colberg.

To the members of my seminar in the history of Montana and the West I must say that they have sharpened their fangs on me and on every chapter in this book — and they have left a long trail of blood that is my own — but all of us are the better for it. At least I am.

My thanks to Phil and Robin Tawney and William Bryant of the Environmental Information Center.

My thanks, also, to George O'Connor, until recently the president of the Montana Power Company. The letters I have received from Mr. O'Connor have been stimulating and thought-provoking. Mr. O'Connor and I disagree on many fundamental matters, but he has been unfailingly courteous and I respect his views highly.

My thanks to my wife, Joan, who has lived patiently and cheerfully with coal dust for a long time and will now spend months shoveling it out of the house.

Good editors have always amazed me with their capacity to cut away blubber, see forests instead of trees, to keep a writer's seat planted firmly on his chair, and all the while remain cheerful and patient about the gory obstetrics of the birth of a book. They do not come any better than Peter Davison, director of the Atlantic Monthly Press, Mrs. Esther S. Yntema, senior editor, and Natalie Greenberg, administrative editor.

K. Ross Toole
June 15, 1975
University of Montana, Missoula

Contents

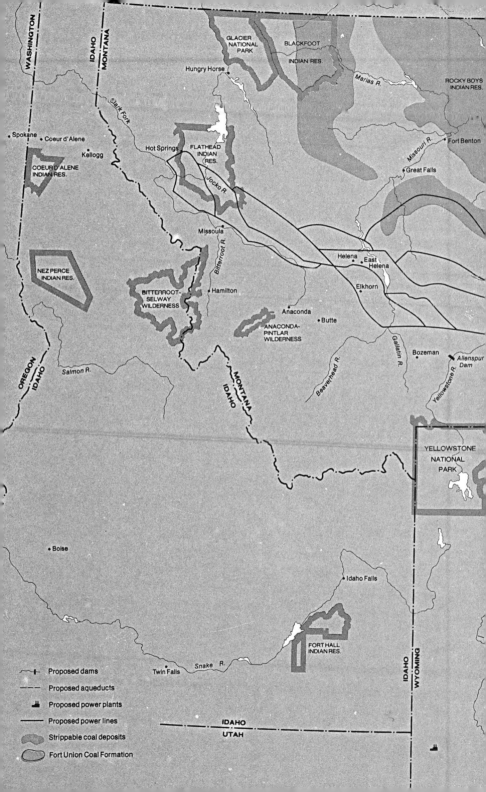

The Rape
of the Great Plains

Introduction

DISTANCES IN THE WEST have always been deceptive, especially on the plains. It has long been a favorite pastime of "natives" (pointing to a range of mountains sharply etched against the western sky) to ask a "pilgrim" how far away the mountains are. The answers usually range from ten to twenty miles. The native smiles. The mountains are almost sixty miles away.

As on the sea, depth perception is difficult to come by because there are no objects with which to gauge relativity — and the plains are awesome in their hugeness.

When the plans to strip-mine vast areas of the Northern Plains were announced, not even plains dwellers themselves could comprehend them. Nor, for quite some time, could they believe that the plans were other than some easterners' pipe dream even when coal companies and government reports converted those plans into acres, square miles, million acre-feet of water, and megawatts of power to be generated from plains coal in power plants located on the plains themselves.

It was not merely mind-boggling; it simply made no sense. After all, what kind of machines could tear up more than 250,000 square miles? What kind of machines could do that, having to rip down through 100 or 150 feet of "overburden" even to uncover the coal veins? What kind of power plants could possibly use up more water than flowed in the massive Great Plains rivers? What kind of power were they talking about here? It had to be nonsense. But it was not.

People were used to talking about watts. A big light bulb, after all, was 100 watts. But what was a megawatt? People were used to talking about water, but for irrigation the measurement was a miner's inch. How much water *was* 4.4 million acre-feet per year? People were used to power lines on telephone poles. But now they were talking about power lines of 500 to 1,000 kilovolts — and all they knew about such lines was that the right-of-way for these monsters was wider than a football field is long.

The way to believe it, and comprehend it, was to see it. So, after stripping had begun in various areas in Montana, Wyoming and North Dakota, the ranchers and the farmers and the people from the nearby small towns came to see. More and more came to see — and they saw not only that it could be done but that it was being done. And that is how the environmental movement began. If it was delayed, it was delayed by the paralysis of shock.

There is a reason for the emphasis on Montana. In 1972 the state adopted a new and remarkably streamlined constitution while North Dakota's proposed new constitution went down to ignominious defeat. The new Montana document contained a strong environmental article, and in implementation of the article a new and fractious legislature passed some startlingly tough and radical legislation in both the 1974 and 1975 sessions: a Utility Siting Act which had sharp teeth, a Reclamation Act with truly significant innovations, and a number of lesser environmental regulations. The legislature had already passed a Clean Air Act which put federal standards to shame. While Wyoming's course, under the aegis of Governor Stanley Hathaway (later nominated to be Secretary of the Interior), has been passively pro-development, Montana's reaction has been just the opposite. North Dakota is in almost all respects similar to Montana. Governor Arthur Link of North Dakota and Governor Thomas Judge of Montana have been in complete accord. But the Montana legislature has been far more aggressive than North Dakota's, largely because of the new constitution. Montana thus has a base for federal court action which would seem to be lacking in North Dakota. For whatever reasons, while Montanans and North Dakotans are strikingly similar in attitudes, Montana is far ahead of North Dakota in the strength of its constitutional and legislative counterattack. This is not to say that strong and dedicated private environmental groups are not active in North Dakota. They are. It is to say that *governmentally* Montana is in the vanguard.

Let us visit a typical, indeed, a rather small, strip mine near Sarpy Creek, Montana. It is owned by the Westmoreland Coal Company — small as such companies go.

The mine is surrounded by a high steel fence. You approach the guardhouse at gate number 2. A bulky guard informs you that you will have to come back for the regular tour ten days hence. You turn your car around and start to drive away. Suddenly there is a tremendous explosion. You slam on the brakes and look back. Good God! An acre of yellow-brown earth is hanging in the sky. As you watch it, it begins to disintegrate, spread outward, and drift across the land. The dust falls everywhere. They are breaking up the overburden so the dragline can begin its work. Overburden means everything between the coal seam and the sky: sometimes hundreds of feet deep. Rock, earth, grass. Trees, too, maybe; maybe roads, houses, and barns. Anything between the dragline and the coal. Yes, you will come back in ten days.

When you do, your first sight of the dragline is not terribly impressive. It looks like a big steam shovel. But you are a mile away. It is a Marion 8200 — a rather small outfit. But as you approach it you begin to crane your neck. It is, after all, 365 feet high; its boom extends out for 215 feet; its bucket holds 75 cubic yards of earth and the bucket scoops out a full load every minute.

All around you are two-story trucks, so huge that the drivers seem like dwarfs. And these trucks move up and out of the pit fully loaded at expressway speeds. The sound is deafening.

Your mind turns to a *big* dragline, called Big Musky, hard at work in Ohio. Big Musky is the prototype for the dragline to come. Like all draglines, it is electric, and it uses enough electricity to fully power a city of 50,000 people. It is sixteen stories high. Its scoop can easily accommodate three Greyhound buses at once.

Until the power plants and transmission lines are completed, the coal ripped from far beneath the fragile soil of the plains is transported by rail. The system is standardized and highly efficient. The giant trucks dump their coal from huge ramps into 100-car coal trains. Each hopper carries 100 tons of coal. Under usual circumstances it takes just a few minutes to fill a 100-car coal train and send it on its way.

But this is merely the stripping process. It is just the beginning. For if the nearly one hundred coal and energy companies — and the Department of the Interior — now deeply involved in the exploitation of plains coal have their way, the huge area known as the Northern Great Plains will have to be renamed — "A National Sacrifice Area" might be appropriate.

What the hell, says the rancher, is a megawatt? And what does a 10,000-megawatt coal-fired power plant mean? How big *is* it and what will it do to us? Again, the answer is hard to comprehend.

One way to begin to understand its implications is to recall that as the last group of astronauts was returning from the moon to the earth, and when they were still several thousand miles out in space, the only man-created thing they could see was a yellowish smudge emanating from the coal-fired power plants near Farmington, New Mexico — the Four Corners power plants. Together, this complex constitutes 2,085 megawatts. The plans of the coal companies and the Department of the Interior call for the construction in Montana alone of coal-fired generating plants totaling 200,000 megawatts. If one includes the plans for Wyoming and North Dakota (though figures are not yet definitive), the plants on the drawing boards would increase that megawattage three- to fourfold. In Wyoming, ten such plants, each five times the size of the New Mexico plants, are planned for the area near Gillette alone.

There is no longer any way to controvert the abundant scientific evidence that these plants, even when operating with the most sophisticated antipollution devices which technology can devise, are massive polluters. The New Mexico plants have pollution control equipment which removes 99.5 percent of all the particulate matter from the smoke — and 40 percent of the sulfur. But the stacks still put out 10 tons of particulate per day and 240 tons of sulfur. All of which is deadly to crops — and humans.

Coal-fired generating plants burn coal to convert water to steam to power turbines which generate electricity. Coal-gasification plants burn coal to convert coal into gas for the same purpose. Both processes use enormous quantities of water.

The plains and what can be grown on them and grazed on them are utterly dependent on water. The area is almost wholly agriculturally oriented. The margin of available water is very narrow — and always has been.

Yet these gargantuan power plants consume huge quantities of water. How much? What *is* a million acre-feet of water? Again, it is difficult to comprehend. Let us approach it in just one area and concern ourselves with just one river.

Let us stand on the banks of Yellowstone River at Sidney, Montana, close to the border of North Dakota. Here the historic river, turbulent and beautifully clear, runs an *average* of 8.8 million acre-feet a year. But averages are deceiving, especially on the Great Plains. In the dry year of 1961, the river's annual flow was only a little over four million acre-feet. Evidence exists that during the cyclical periods of deep drought on the plains the average annual flow of the Yellowstone probably dropped to about three million acre-feet.

Yet, as of 1974 the Bureau of Reclamation calculated that the drainoff of water for upstream coal-fired generating plants would be 2.6 million acre-feet — and that calculation goes back to 1974. The water used by these huge plants, both "generating" and "gasification," is not simply "used" and returned to the river. It is converted into steam and dissipated into the atmosphere. Industrial applications continue to pour in. What of downstream agriculture? How do you irrigate? How do the townspeople drink? What do the cattle do? What happens to the plains? And that is only one river, one case in point, one example of devastation — and incalculable loss of plains water for any and all agricultural purpose.

These 500-kilovolt transmission lines, now planned, routed, and on the maps — what do they mean to us? Just how big are they? Where will they go?

It does not help much to say that 500 kilovolts equals 500,000 volts. So let us approach it another way. Let us examine just one line of the many that will radiate like a giant spiderweb from the single power plant complex at Colstrip, Montana. And let us bear in mind that power plants numbers 1 and 2 at Colstrip are nearing completion and permits for plants numbers 3 and 4 have been applied for and that formal hearings are now being conducted on them. Each is 700 megawatts in size. Eighty percent of the power generated by these plants will be exported to Washington and Oregon by *twin* 500-kilovolt transmission lines.

The lines will run for 430 miles from southeastern Montana through western Montana. They run straight and totally ignore topography — because it is very expensive to turn or bend such a line. These twin lines will be constructed with cranes that weigh sixty tons. There will be a mile and a half of access road built for every mile of right-of-way.

Once they have crossed the plains the towering lines pass

through some of the wildest and most pristine mountain areas of the West, opening up vast areas to jeeps, snowmobiles, machines, and people of all kinds. They will cross winter and summer game ranges indiscriminately — and no living fish and game expert foresees other than violent disruption of game habitats, accustomed ranges, and migration routes. The last mountain goat in the last mountain pasture is by no means immune.

The utilities companies building these lines have the power of eminent domain — they can condemn private property. Thus far, they have met no significant opposition from either the Forest Service or the Bureau of Land Management. Yet there is abundant evidence that "roading" in any of the steep mountain areas causes massive erosion, a harrowing change in the ecosystem for miles around, and effectively destroys the entire nature of wilderness areas.

Moreover, where these lines pass near farms, ranches, or small communities, they endanger human and animal life, blank out television sets, attract lightning, and, if upped to 765 kilovolts in carrying capacity, shrivel crops, inhibit the germination of seeds, prevent corn from reaching fruition. Metal irrigation systems can become deadly electrocutors. Fences and metal buildings can become charged with dangerous static electricity. And studies indicate the utilities now have on the drawing boards lines of 1,000 and even 1,500 kilovolts.

It can be said, of course, and constantly is said, that America is in a critical energy situation and that whether we like it or not these things *must* be done or awesomely dire consequences will follow. We will go back to the cave; we will become military weaklings and hence prey for aggressors. Our economy will wither and our greatness as a nation will quickly end.

No thoughtful student of the matter argues that we do not have an energy crisis or that it is a short-term affair. No thoughtful student argues that the mining and burning of America's huge reserves of coal is other than necessary until solar, wind, atomic, and alternate sources of power come on the line.

But the westward rush for strippable coal is the surest kind of folly, the greatest kind of waste, and, as I propose to demonstrate, it is unnecessary. The energy and utility companies have massive resources for propaganda. What they have in mind is quick profits. Quick indeed: they have the capability of exhausting all the coal under the Northern Great Plains in a mere *thirty years*. To them it is of no concern that this vast region, in many respects the breadbasket of America, will be virtually destroyed in the process.

There is another way. Our country can keep moving and yet stay *whole*.

I am reminded of a story I read many years ago, perhaps in a *New Yorker* Profile, of a famous woman anthropologist who had been working for years with a certain remote southwestern Indian tribe. She loved them (and they her), understood them, and lived with them. Year after year she meticulously took down their stories and folklore. And they held nothing back.

In due course they said to her, "Now we have told you all our old stories which reveal why we are what we are. Now it is your turn. Tell us the greatest story that your people have." She underwent a moment of panic, but then, hesitantly at first but with growing vigor, she told the story of Beowulf. They were enormously pleased and said that it was indeed a great story.

Many years later the anthropologist was most intrigued to read a lengthy and very scholarly article in a professional journal by another anthropologist meticulously analyzing the fact that at the very root of the folklore of this Indian tribe was the pure story of Beowulf. Were these Indians, then, of ancient European origin? I don't know that the anthropologist ever answered the question.

Most researchers are academics. At the risk of alienating my colleagues in history, sociology, and political science, I am deeply suspicious of the capacity of academics to get inside anyone's head except their own — or those of people of like inclination and intellectual bent.

I can think of few mind-sets more inherently at odds than that of the average academic and the average rancher or farmer. This book, being about a region, and a conflict about a region, is about people too. I have concentrated on Montana because that is where the threat is greatest and where the issues are most clearly defined. And because I am a part of Montana, this book is about my own people, some of whom are not on my side.

Looking northward through the window in the room in which I now write, I cannot quite see the ranch my great-grandfather established one hundred and fifteen years ago. Montana was not yet even a territory. The gold rush was yet to come. Since then, some members of my family have always been ranchers.

For six years I ran a thousand head of yearlings in the remote foothills of the Beartooth Mountains of southwestern Montana. It is on those great, rolling, heaving foothills that the Great Plains begin. And this book deals with the Northern Great Plains. I do not feel a stranger there.

If I look southward through the window of this room, I can see my eleven-year-old son on a fractious Appaloosa horse, headed fast for the neighboring ranch. True, this is western Montana now, and I commute to the ivy halls where, in fact, I do *not* feel at home.

Quite obviously, I do not approach this subject objectively. I feel no guilt about that. The great coal and energy companies now descending upon the land I love are hardly defenseless. It is infuriating to hear them cry so piteously that they are misunderstood while their monstrous machines are eating at our vitals. It is deeply angering to hear them daily asserting that what they are doing to us is good for us — while every shred of historical (and scientific) evidence available demonstrates the contrary.

They have their forum. Their resources for "giving their side" are inexhaustible, and they are using those resources for blatant propaganda all over America.

Give me this small bow and this small arrow and let me fire just once in the name of the eternity they are about to steal from us.

PEOPLE AND EXPLOITERS

I

The Northern Great Plains

THIS VAST, BROWN MIDRIFF of America, which gave manifest destiny its longest pause and its gravest doubts, does not lend itself easily to generalization. It is true that the Great Plains constitutes a "region." From Alberta to Mexico and from the 98th meridian to the foothills of the Rocky Mountains it has more that binds it together than pulls it asunder. However, behind and beneath everything else that can be said about it lie three abiding facts: it is relatively level, relatively treeless, and it is, above all, semiarid. Yet what can be said of the Southwest can hardly be said of southeastern Montana's rolling, fertile hills.

This book concerns only the Northern Great Plains and its focus is, in fact, much narrower than that. It is a book about coal mining, strip mining, and so, presumably, the focus should be determined by where the coal is — southern Saskatchewan, eastern Montana, western North Dakota and northeastern Wyoming. But still the lens narrows. Not all the coal is readily strippable, not all the area is under leasing pressure by the coal companies — and the real contest is where stripping has already begun.

An enormous quantity of coal — technically low in sulfur, close to the surface, easily and cheaply mined — lies beneath what is called the Fort Union Coal Formation, which corresponds to the geographical area just delineated. It is probably the largest coal basin in the world. It contains an estimated 1.3 trillion tons. Strippable reserves in Montana alone are estimated at between 40 and 50 billion tons.

This enormous area is sparsely settled. One could spend years traversing it, talking to miners, ranchers, bartenders in sweltering little towns, housewives, sheepmen, farmers, and Indians. As of today, the stripping operations are rather widely separated — and in all essential respects they are the same.

And the people on the land are the same. Or, to proffer a seeming contradiction, they differ similarly. There are those ranchers — north, east, south and west — who will resist the strippers to their last breath; there are those who have already sold or leased; there are those who wish to sell but cannot do so because the holdouts (standing astride the run of the richest veins) forestall them. And among these groups resentments run dangerously and sometimes violently high.

In the larger towns there are few bloodied heads and the language may be cooler, but the conflict is there. It is mitigated, perhaps, by their more diversified economies. They will be affected by strip mining, but they will not be rendered different in totality. But the small places will live or die with stripping. Some say they will grow and boom and prosper as they never can with cattle on their thousand hills. But others say they will lose not only their land but their souls. They say their towns will be ravaged and when the miners are gone (in an estimated thirty years) there will be no going back because there will be no land and, hence, no cattle, no wheat — and nothing left of the town but a hot, gray wind blowing the tumbleweeds against the falling fences and empty buildings.

And so the argument goes on in Bighorn, Roundup, Arvada, Recluse, Wyola, Kirby, Birney, Forsyth, and Hardin. These have always been tough towns, full of tough men and women. They are palpably dangerous now.

The Indians, the Northern Cheyenne and the Crow: under their reservations lies nearly 30 percent of the coal. Here, again, there is disagreement. For one thing, they deal in leases on tribal lands only through the "filter" of the Department of the Interior and the Bureau of Indian Affairs, "the BIA," an agency of government which many of them hate and few of them trust. Their tribal councils, though elected, often seem not to reflect their constituents. They are in almost all respects a poor people. Income from coal leases and from royalties may be attractive to some — but the process of stripping is anathema to others.

Indian "identity" is rooted in the land and many of them feel that if the land is lost, they are lost. In the past decade or so the Indian people have engaged in a concerted drive for identity. They have sought their own ethnic roots; they have revived old religious and social ceremonies; they have demanded and received special Indian studies in the schools; they have concertedly set about to relearn their languages and their ancient arts and crafts. But all this depends on a stable tribal structure, on self-determination and, in the final analysis, on the land.

There is, too, far from universal agreement between the young and the old. The older Indians grew up under the ever-present aegis of the Bureau of Indian Affairs. They were the sons and daughters of a defeated and demoralized people. Their only recourse was the BIA. They were stoic, patient, tough and resilient. But they were not militant.

The younger Indians, most with a good deal more schooling, most with a growing sense of militancy, reflect a new attitude. They are outspoken. They want not merely to find out who they are, they want restitution. They want, also, somewhat anomalously, to go their own way but with government help. It will not do to take the militant leader Russell Means lightly when he says that in 1973 the American Indian Movement made its point at Wounded Knee; next it will be where the strip miners are tearing up their land.

The Bureau of Indian Affairs, once the arbiter of everything Indian, once the great power, has changed drastically under severe pressures in the past few years. But it is still damned if it does and damned if it doesn't. If it backs off from decision-making because of the almost constant Indian accusations that it is paternalistic, it is accused of sitting on its hands and doing nothing. And the BIA is now caught dead center in the middle of the stripping controversy on Indian lands.

It would be a serious mistake to set aside all these categories of people and feelings in separate simplistic pigeonholes. Often "antagonists" are not separated by brick walls but rather by semipermeable membranes of confusion. They don't *know* whether stripping is good or bad, necessary or unnecessary.

While it may be true that the business sector *tends* toward a benign if not an eagerly solicitous attitude toward the giant coal and power companies now moving swiftly westward, some businessmen are frightened, angry, and appalled. They do not buy the standard economic argument that this is progress; that a generally poor and sparsely settled region desperately needs the income and growth and the larger tax base. They are afraid of the old plains boom-and-bust pattern. And they are afraid that the social cost of a sudden and massive impaction of a fragile area will far outrun profits to that area. Yet it is generally true that chambers of commerce, taxpayers' associations, realtors, bankers, and developers strongly favor strip mining.

In short, a stranger running around asking questions in, say, eastern Montana may well have certain preconceptions shattered. He may approach a third-generation, leather-faced rancher only to find an ardent supporter of stripping agricultural land. Or he may approach a "glittery"-suited banker in Billings only to find that he is a charter member of Friends of the Earth and that he is spending all his free time fighting strip mining.

The lines are, indeed, drawn, but one must be careful about where they run and who is behind what barricade. This diversification or lack of "consensus" is, of course, of great value to the enormously powerful coal and power companies now turning to the West. They do not have to divide and conquer. The divisions are already there. They merely need exploiting. Yet the companies have thus far demonstrated that they do not understand the nature of those divisions and their blunders have often been egregious. This is not Appalachia. Moreover, they are facing a new phenomenon, imperfectly understood by economists, sociologists, historians and psychologists. And *very* imperfectly understood by governments. Vast numbers of Americans no longer believe that growth and good are inevitably symbiotically intertwined. And no longer believing that, they have turned with great passion to challenge old and time-honored economic verities. In doing so they are challenging great powers, great conglomerations of capital, and deeply entrenched institutions.

One manifestation, of course, is the rise of the "environmentalists." The word should (however new) be expunged from our lexicon. It means too little and too much. It is too specific and too general; it is too inclusive and too exclusive. But it is with us to stay. However inexplicit the movement may be, it, too, rises from sources essentially simple. Our resources are finite, not infinite; we are fouling our own nest to a dangerous extent; rampant materialism does not produce happiness; no nation can grow fat while its neighbors are starving; we cannot ravage our land without ravaging ourselves.

It is peculiarly significant that the young, and the brightest among them, are so deeply involved in so many environmental causes. Contrary to the assertions of many Americans, it is no fad with them. If, in the paneled boardrooms of the great "energy" companies, the men who make policy hear no whispering of the wind outside, they are not listening. They should; it is an angry murmuring now. It could become very dangerous to them, indeed.

This book has no ending — only a beginning and a middle. Because it is a book about a fight, that is a distressing circumstance.

What merit, then, is there in writing such a book at all? One reason is that I am an historian, and as such I recognize that when a long fight is over (and this will be a long one) people often forget how it started — and why. I suppose that I subscribe to the old aphorism, "A people that forgets its history is doomed to repeat it." I wish my grandchildren a better fate than that.

Yet there are great hazards (at least for historians) in writing about contemporary events. We are, after all, worshipers of documents — and the older they are the more comfortable we feel with them. Then we feel ourselves to be "objective." But the documents I am dealing with are very new, indeed. How, then, when I am finished, can I feel that I have been "objective"? The answer is simple: I cannot, and I lay no claim to it. The risk, however, is mine, not the reader's. I *have* to write this book because the land I am writing about is mine; I live on it and I love it.

Those "documents" need a few words of explication, for their nature is critical to this study. The coal beneath the Northern Great Plains has lain there for millions of years. But though its presence was never much of a mystery, no one cared about it. America had enormous energy resources — inexhaustible.

Though an energy crisis had long been predicted, no one, particularly the government, took heed of those predictions. Americans have never been an apocalyptic people; rather, perhaps more than any nation in the world, we have been a people of ebullient optimism. All the harbingers of an end to our "inexhaustible" resources were there long ago. We took no heed.

It was not really until the Arabs turned off the spigot that the average American gave even a passing thought to what had, in fact, long since become a critical situation.

A few others had — a very few others. In the broadest sense what was planned was first called "Project Independence" by President Nixon and subsequently by President Ford. But "Project Independence" was specific only in the assertion that the United

States was to be independent of the reliance on imported fuel sources by 1985. Even before the formal announcement of this national policy (and before the Arab oil embargo) a few people were hard at work on specifics. One of the results of concerns in very narrow circles was a document entitled the *North Central Power Study*, published in October 1971. It was this document that sent shock waves through knowledgeable environmentalists in the Northern Great Plains.

The study was conducted under the aegis of Assistant Secretary of the Interior James R. Smith and it was produced by the representatives of "19 investor-owned public utilities, six cooperatives, two public power districts, one Federal, and eight municipal representatives." It drew on the "technical expertise and the views of practically all bulk power suppliers in the 1,000,000 square mile area."* It concerned itself entirely with coal and proposed the stripping of vast coal reserves on the Northern Great Plains as well as the construction of unbelievably massive mine-mouth generating plants. In Montana alone the study proposed the construction of twenty-one such plants with a total production capacity of 69,000 megawatts. When one considers that a 700-megawatt plant is an enormous power plant, it is small wonder that concern began to rise in eastern Montana, especially since the study projected the production of 200,000 megawatts by the year 2000.

Moreover, since these huge plants, two of which were 10,000 megawatts in size and seven of which were 5,000 megawatts in size, were to be mine-mouth generating plants, the *North Central Power Study* suggested a massive network of transmission lines, radiating outward like a huge spiderweb in all directions from the plants. These transmission lines, it suggested further, should be 765-kilovolt lines, "for best economy." A 765-kilovolt line carries 765,000 volts. As we shall see, such gargantuan lines are massively

* See *North Central Power Study*, October 1971, Report of Phase I, Vol. I, prepared under the direction of the Coordination Committee, North Central Power Study, 1971.

destructive of the environment and may be very dangerous in many other respects.

After the initial shock of the *North Central Power Study* wore off a bit, all the states involved began reacting with their own reports. Montana reacted most violently since twenty-one of the proposed forty-two power plants were in eastern Montana. Only four were proposed for North Dakota, one each in South Dakota and Colorado, but fifteen in Wyoming.

Until 1971, and the release of the *North Central Power Study*, none of the states involved had done, or had had cause to do, any basic kind of research which could now be applied to the problems posed by the study.

But between 1972 and 1975 scores of groups formed, state and private. Acronyms proliferated until one enterprising man prepared a glossary of acronyms. Legislatures met, frantically passed laws or frantically passed no laws. The Bureau of Land Management, under whose land much of the coal lies, issued hasty reports. State boards of natural resources issued more reports; university hydrologists, geologists, botanists, sociologists, and ichthyologists rushed into the area and issued reports. Coal and utility companies issued more reports. Engineers, foresters, and soil scientists issued still more reports. Hearings were held; debates were conducted; reporters flocked in from the East. Politicians ranging from county commissioners to U.S. senators made speeches and circulated copies. The tonnage of reports grew immense — and all in four short years. At this writing massive new and "definitive" reports are on the verge of publication.

Once he is through with the background, it is these reports the historian must deal with. It is comfortable enough to relate how and why men and their animals and their plants did or did not adapt to the semiarid Northern Plains. That is not, in any event, a new story. It has been superbly done by the great Walter Prescott Webb. It has been very well done by many other historians and rural sociologists. But then what? What of adaptation now?

Must we adapt at all (again) — and if we must, *can* we — and still survive with some semblance of our life-style intact?

If from all the tonnage of recent reports one could draw a reasonable number of statistics, assertions or denials that fell within the range of a common pattern, it would be possible to deal with those areas with some confidence. But in many cases figures are wildly discrepant or misleading or simply unascertainable.

What to do then? Well, one might use Mark Twain's approach. Twain had a supreme contempt for statistics. In *Life on the Mississippi* he wrote:

In the space of one hundred and seventy-six years the Lower Mississippi has shortened itself two hundred and forty-two miles. That is an average of a trifle over one mile and a third per year. Therefore, any calm person, who is not blind or idiotic . . . can see that seven hundred and forty-two years from now the Lower Mississippi will be only a mile and three quarters long, and Cairo and New Orleans will have joined their streets together, and be plodding along comfortably under a single mayor and a mutual board of aldermen. There is something fascinating about science. One gets such wholesale returns of conjecture out of such a trifling investment of fact.

Though this is not a statistical book, tonnages, depths, percentages, acre-feet of water, taxes, some chemistry and other figures simply cannot be avoided. I have chosen them and used them with care. Where I have found wild discrepancies in statistics I have simply eschewed them. But these documents are still pouring forth and figures are constantly changing.

Laws, of course, are only as good or as bad as those who implement them, and whether any state law can take precedence over federal action is problematical if not doubtful. The fact remains that the great power and energy companies are not now moving into a state devoid of an unusually strong legal structure to deal with them. Whether, in the face of the Brobdingnagian powers now moving into Montana, the legal structures of state govern-

ment can resist them is much in doubt. Some of the new agencies
are understaffed, short of money — and long only in terms of
determination. Others are better equipped.

Throughout this book I shall continue to use the term "the environmentalists" because there is no other yet coined. It is a very
unsatisfactory term because everyone is an "environmentalist,"
including those most busily engaged in polluting everything in
sight — and out of sight. Were we to believe the officials of the
great oil companies, as they present their case on television, their
refinery lagoons are the only things preventing the extinction of
at least a dozen bird species.

The fact is that the environmentalists to whom I shall refer in
Montana have served their apprenticeship, which I hope to make
clear. They do not want to stop the world and get off nor do they
wish to build a wall around Montana. For the most part they are
hard pragmatists, skilled bargainers, very well informed, and many
of them are young and vigorous, though some of the most powerful are ranchers in their sixties and seventies.

The central theme in this work is, then, this: Can a state with a
population of less than a million people, a huge state of 147,000
square miles with only 4.7 persons per square mile, deal with this
enormous power now descending upon us? Can such a state and
such a people, so richly endowed with a vast reserve of an energy
resource for which America is so voraciously hungry, stand up in
the face of these myriad pressures?

It must be said at the beginning that the *North Central Power
Study* of 1971, the proposals of which run through this book like
a long night of nausea, has been termed by government agencies,
power and energy companies, and some environmentalists as "inoperative." I submit that it is not. It is the essence of "Project Independence." It is momentarily somnolent, but, as I hope I shall
indicate, it is not "inoperative" by any means.

If Montana — which is, in many essential respects, a pristine area
— cannot control the headlong, unnecessary rush toward devastat-

ing exploitation, then perhaps all Americans had better ask the question: Can it ever be stopped anywhere?

One of the notable things about the plains is that they have rarely been what people thought they were — neither as bad nor as good, as rich or as poor, as beautiful or as ugly, as wet or as dry, as cold or as hot. The region has almost always been underestimated or overestimated.

It is, and always has been, man's misunderstanding of what the plains were, or were not, that has resulted in periodic tragedies. That is not to say that no one understands the plains or that no one ever has. Those who have and who do understand them have adapted to them. It has never been the plains that adapted to man.

From the explorations of Lewis and Clark to the late 1870s or early 1880s it was a national assumption that the whole area was uninhabitable and uncultivatable. Only the Indians could live there. The plains were a giant and awesome barricade to the westward movement. To humid-area men emerging from the lush, wet, timbered country east of the 98th meridian (which is an arbitrary, but for our purposes satisfactory, line of demarcation), the flat, treeless, dry expanse of the Great Plains constituted a desert — dangerous, unpredictable, utterly strange. Crossing it in order to reach the lush, wet, timbered regions of the Pacific slope was an ordeal. Indeed, Stephen H. Long, exploring for the government in 1820, officially labeled the area "The Great American Desert" and thus it appeared on subsequent maps, a great blank slash across America. The object of westering Americans was to cross it as fast and as painlessly as possible. They ordinarily prepared for their journey grimly and in quasi-military fashion.

Though a very substantial literature developed about the plains at an early date, some of it, such as John Wesley Powell's, filled with great insight, real analysis of the area was very slow in coming. Indeed, it was not until 1931 that *the* classic book appeared. This was Walter Prescott Webb's *The Great Plains*. In spite of many fine studies of the area written in subsequent years, none surpasses Webb's book in significance, depth or insight. Any consideration of the plains must begin with Webb's work and, as tribute to its excellence, wherever one begins and however far one wanders afield, one returns to Webb.

That is not to say that research subsequent to Webb's work has turned up no errors therein. For instance, Webb says: "The plains are barren of minerals, especially metals, because the surface is fluvial in origin. The oil found in the region lies for the most part below the fluvial soil, under the surface of the marine rock foundation." He did not know about the coal — or perhaps, then, it did not seem to matter. That Webb's work is more detailed on the Southern Great Plains than on the Northern is a criticism often leveled, and there is considerable legitimacy to it. He was, after all, a Texan. In some instances he did, indeed, generalize for the whole region on the basis of his more intimate knowledge of the southern section. But the basic validity of his work remains unchallenged.

What Webb did was to explain that certain abiding characteristics of the plains made the area unique, and man either adapted to these characteristics or perished or left the plains alone. One characteristic Webb dwelt upon was "a deficiency in the most essential climatic element — water. Within this area there are humid spots due to local causes of elevation, but there is a deficiency in the average amount of rainfall for the entire region."

Webb pointed out that not only was there a deficiency of precipitation, but that its seasonal distribution and the rate of evaporation are of "vital importance." These combined factors mean that humid-area agricultural concepts — including the acreage normal for an economic agricultural unit—simply will not work in the plains area.

Though, in retrospect, it would seem that this should have been self-evident, the federal government, beginning with the Homestead Act of 1862 and running up into the second decade of the twentieth century, passed legislation for the free disposal of the public domain which was totally unworkable on the plains. Beginning with the humid-area concept that 160 acres was an economic farming unit, the government had made so little progress in any understanding of vast areas of the West that even as late as 1909 the acreage that could be filed on for homestead purposes was confined to 320.

Congress was equally ignorant, as we shall see, of what could be done on the plains in terms of reclamation. Congress, and Americans in general, were abysmally ignorant of the plains Indian who, indeed, was the only human being (until very recently) ever to adapt successfully to the plains. If it be said (as it often is) that he had thousands of years to do so, the assertion is quite incorrect. Prior to the year 1600 none of the Indians we refer to today as the Northern Plains Indians resided there. In a kind of domino or marbles-in-a-tube effect, they had been pushed westward by the pressures exerted by whites along the Atlantic seaboard. Their adaptation remains one of the most remarkable examples of human ingenuity and resiliency in American history.

Meriwether Lewis was a thoughtful and observant man. On June 25, 1805, he climbed a hill near the juncture of the Yellowstone and Missouri rivers and wrote of "a most pleasing view of the country, particularly of the wide and fertile valleys formed by the Missouri and Yellowstone rivers." Lewis referred to "these delightful tracts of country."

At the mouth of the Marias River he wrote of the country as "one of the most beautifully picturesque countries that I have ever beheld, through the wide expanse of which innumerable herds of living animals are seen." He spoke of the grass as giving the plains "the appearance throughout its whole extent of a beautiful bowling green . . . this scenery already rich and pleasing and beautiful was still further heightened by immense herds of buffaloe, deer, elk and antelope which we saw in every direction feeding on the hills and plains."

Zebulon Montgomery Pike set out from St. Louis on July 15,

1806, but it must be remarked that Pike did not see the Northern
Great Plains as Lewis had. He reached the source of the Arkansas
River and then turned southward into the Rio Grande Valley.
This is, though an integral part of the Great Plains, a profoundly
different kind of country and Pike's observations are not essentially
applicable.

Stephen H. Long's expedition is another matter. Though he was
a later entrant (1819–1820) and though he, too, explored south
of the Missouri, up the Platte, southwestward to the Arkansas and
returned, it was the Long Expedition that gave rise to the concept
of the Great American Desert. All we have left of Long's account
is the running narrative of Dr. Edwin James, who, in addition to
being a physician, was something of a botanist and geologist. But
Long made a very significant final report. Long's expedition was
widely heralded, as was this description of the plains:

> I do not hesitate in giving the opinion that it is almost wholly unfit
> for cultivation, and of course uninhabitable by a people depending
> upon agriculture for their subsistence. Although tracts of fertile land
> considerably extensive are occasionally to be met with yet the sparsity
> of wood and water almost uniformly prevalent will prove an insuper-
> able obstacle in the way of settling the country. This objection rests
> not only against the section immediately under consideration but ap-
> plies with equal propriety to a much larger portion of the country.
> . . . The whole of this region seems peculiarly adapted as a range for
> buffaloes, wild goats, and other wild game, incalculable multitudes of
> which find ample pasturage and subsistence upon it.

Now this is a mixed sort of business because if "incalculable
multitudes" of "buffaloes, wild goats, and other wild game" find
"ample pasturage," it is a somewhat strange and perhaps parochial
view of agriculture that the region is "wholly unfit" for a "people
depending upon agriculture for their subsistence."

But there is not only peculiar significance (and a confusion
which was to last for more than half a century) in that famous

statement, there is perhaps even greater significance in its peroration:

> This region, however, viewed as a frontier may prove of infinite importance to the United States inasmuch as it is calculated to serve as a barrier to prevent too great an extension of our population westward, and serve us against the machinations or incursions of an enemy that might otherwise be disposed to annoy us in that part of our frontier.

Long, of course, meant Europeans. There is a certain irony in the fact that the "enemy" was already there, the plains Indian, perhaps the world's finest light cavalry, completely at home on that "desert" and superbly equipped to fight there.

But others, later, had still other perceptions of this land. The artist George Catlin, viewing the Missouri in 1832 which Lewis had found so beautiful in 1805, thought it like no other river in the world. "There is terror in its manner. . . . Its water is always turbid and opaque." Catlin thought it a "hell of waters" and thought it should be called the "River Styx."

Still another artist, Alfred Jacob Miller, in 1837 found the plains awesome and very beautiful but "no primrose road of dalliance."

There were, of course, descriptions galore once the immigrants came in the 1840s and 1850s. They were as varied as the eyes of the beholders. The majority of them were superficial; some were not. Walt Whitman, after a trip to California in 1879, wrote, "I am not so sure that the prairies and the plains while less stunning at first sight, last longer, fill the esthetic sense fuller, preclude all the rest, and make North America's characteristic landscape."

William Gilpin, territorial governor of Colorado in 1868, wrote, "The semi-arid plains between the 100th meridian and the Rockies . . . were no desert, nor even a semi-desert, but a pastoral Canaan."

John Wesley Powell, quite legitimately still called "the father of reclamation," would, and did, most positively disagree with Gilpin's "Canaan."

As early as 1868 Powell was expressing a mixture of enthusiasm and dubiety about the Great Plains. In a way, however, he was to become a singular kind of prophet. As his principal biographer, Wallace Stegner, wrote, "Major John Wesley Powell was . . . working against the current of popular optimism in the policies he developed, and decades ahead of it in his vision." In 1893 Powell was invited to address the International Irrigation Congress at Los Angeles.

He came to the Congress as a towering figure — but as he sat and listened to what the "experts" had to say, he tore up his prepared speech and instead simply told the delegates that they were mad. Into the hecklers' rising clamor he shouted, "You are piling up a heritage of conflict and litigation over water rights for there is not sufficient water to supply the land." As with Mr. Webb, we shall return to Mr. Powell.

Among the very few men who understood the Great Plains and could articulate that understanding was the artist Charles M. Russell. Russell was singularly endowed because he had not only lived on the plains, in perfect concert with the plains Indians, but he could both paint and write. But he deserves attention for a more compelling reason. Contrary to a nearly universal view of Russell as a "Cowboy Artist," a "hail fellow well met," and a gregarious jokester, he was in fact a man who saw the land he loved being abused and, in his estimation, destroyed.

He was once introduced at a boosters' meeting in Great Falls as a "pioneer." This was his speech:

I have been called a pioneer. In my book a pioneer is a man who comes to a virgin country, traps off all the fur, kills off all the wild meat, cuts down all the trees, grazes off all the grass, plows the roots up, and strings ten million miles of bob wire. A pioneer destroys things and calls it civilization. I wish to God that this country was just like it was when I first saw it and none of you folk were here at all.

All through the books of his illustrated letters, his short stories and his poetry, Russell is talking about the plains. And of the some three to four thousand of his paintings (because he was enormously prolific) the majority picture the plains — but as they were, not as they are. Except for memory and his very early paintings, almost all the rest of his work is pervaded with sadness.

One of the genuine trail-herd cowboys was Andy Adams, whose book *The Log of a Cowboy* says of Wyoming in 1882:

We were bearing almost due north and passing through a delightful country. To our left ran a range of mountains [the Bighorns], while on the other hand sloped off the apparently limitless plains. The scarcity of water was beginning to be felt for the streams which had not a source in the mountains to our left had dried up weeks before our arrival. There was a gradual change of air noticeable too for we were rapidly gaining altitude, the heat of summer now being confined to a few hours at noon-day, while the nights were almost too cool for our comfort.

There is significance in this comment, too: "A horse, having reached the years of maturity in a southern climate, will grow half a hand taller and carry two hundred pounds more flesh when he has undergone the rigors of several northern winters."

What Adams did not add was that this was as true of cattle as of horses and it was due to the very high protein of the nutritious native grasses of the plains of Montana.

The range country produced a horse suitable to range needs, hardy and a good forager, which, when not over-worked under the saddle, met every requirement of his calling, as well as being self sustaining. The horses, in fact, were in better flesh when we crossed the Missouri than they were on the day we received the herd on the Rio Grande.

Another genuine trail-herd cowboy was Teddy Blue Abbott, who, in a book meticulously edited by Helena Huntington Smith, *We Pointed Them North*, lends further credence to the fact that

the men who trailed cattle more than a thousand miles across the
Great Plains, from Texas to Montana, understood the land — one
aspect of it.

"What kind of climate is it in Montana we asked him and he
gave the best answer I ever heard. 'I'll tell you what kind of
climate it is. You want a buffalo overcoat, a linen duster, and a
slicker with you at all times' "; or "It was a cowman's paradise —
big grass, all kinds of game except buffalo, and we had it all to ourselves."

Like all his fellow cattlemen who knew the open range, and those
who lived long enough to see the homesteader flock onto the
plains, Abbott was appalled:

In 1919 and 1920 every foot of that country back from the Missouri
on the south side was taken up for dry farms which was a crime, because that is grazing country, not farming country and all those bohunk
farmers did was to carve up good range for nothing but starvation in
the end. There is not a sign of them today. They've all gone; even the
empty houses have gone. . . . But the hills are still there. And this
summer, 1938, the grass came back the way it used to be, and waved
in the wind, and oh boy but it was a beautiful sight.

Here, of course, Abbott is referring to the homestead era on
the plains, which lasted roughly from 1909 to 1925 — an era we
shall consider in due course. His comments, like those of so many
who thought of the plains in terms only of their own utilization of
them, were at once right and wrong. It is true that the "bohunks,"
"honyockers," or, more accurately, the homesteaders, flooded onto
the plains, plowed the earth, met devastation, and then flooded
out. But not all of them. Some of them are still there — those who
adapted. It is true, too, that in some areas the grass returned — but
in vast areas it did not. It is not there today.

It is also true that the Northern Great Plains was superb cattle
country. But only up to a point and only sometimes and only
under certain circumstances.

It seems to have been an article of faith with the old-time cattle-men that the wondrous "open range" was suited only for cattle and that it was the farmer who brought that empire crashing down with his plow and his misunderstanding of the land. The fact is, the empire had crashed before the homesteader put up a single strand of wire or put the first plow into the earth. Close as he lived to it, much as he loved it, the cattleman himself underesti-mated and overestimated that vast land he thought he knew so well.

Let us for a moment return to Walter Prescott Webb, this time to an analysis of the plains in an article in *Harper's Magazine* en-titled "The American West: Perpetual Mirage." It is fruitless to paraphrase Webb. Listen to him:

The desert is the guest that came to dinner never to go away. . . . It is the great designer of the American West, painting the landscape with color, chiseling the mesas and pinnacles, building the plains with soil washed down from the perishing rivers. . . . If we do not under-stand the West it is because we perversely refuse to recognize this fact; we do not want the desert to be there. We prefer to loiter on its edges, skirt it, avoid it, and even deny it. . . . Its radius varies because the desert expands and contracts, at its enemy — rain — retreats or ad-vances. . . . When the desert pokes a hot finger into the border re-gions, the people speak of drought; when it pulls the finger back, they say "the country is getting more seasonable. . . ."

For a million years a fire of low intensity has been burning, and is still burning in the West. It is broader and more intense in the south, narrower and somewhat cooler in the north. . . .

As we look at the West with its dry center and rims of less dryness, we see that the desert is the unifying force. True, the people have moved into the oases, some of them man made, but for the most part they dwell around its moist edges where they struggle for water with all their ingenuity.

Webb's article, published in 1957, caused a furor in the states he called the desert and the "desert rim" states. *Harper's* was inun-dated with indignant letters from chambers of commerce, mayors, governors and newspapers. Most vehement were those from the eight "desert" states: New Mexico, Arizona, Nevada, Utah, Wyoming, Colorado, Idaho and Montana.

In a gentle rebuttal which appeared in *Montana: The Magazine of Western History*, Webb argued on.

It's extremely difficult to change the focus with which people are accustomed to viewing their history or their land. The conventional view of the West is from the East, the direction from which the viewers approached it. *The West should not be looked at from the outside, but from the inside, from the center.* The West is concentric, a series of moisture circles extending outward from the arid, to the semi-arid, to sub-humid and finally to the humid land. . . . The Great Plains to the east of the mountains are the burnt right flank of the desert. . . . Once the desert has been recognized and accepted as the dominant force in the West, what goes on there among animals, plants, and men makes sense.

It is desert influence that makes water more important than land in the West. . . . Nothing was further from my mind than to malign it. It is my country . . . and I have spent my whole adult life trying to understand it. [Italics mine.]

In that context, what happened to the explorers, the trappers, the cattlemen, the homesteaders, to governments and to settlements on the Northern Great Plains *does* make sense. And in that context what is happening to it now makes no sense at all. For the key to generating power from coal is water. And in that context, too, perhaps only the plains Indian would have completely understood what Walter Prescott Webb was talking about. They had lived in the "desert" for three hundred years.

But if the Indians fully understood their land, other Americans almost never did. With a kind of blind persistence, often, indeed, with the evidence and the reality of the plains literally staring them in the face, they moved out onto that abidingly different land full of ignorance often mixed with arrogance — a dangerous combination of attitudes.

2

The Indians:
The Cheyenne and the Crow

AMERICANS, as Vance Packard points out so poignantly in *A Nation of Strangers*, have become the most mobile people on earth. Families move across our land almost like nomads. We are a people who have been extraordinarily diligent in erasing both our past and our traditions. The latter word is fraught with peril. What *are* "traditions"? A better word perhaps is "continuity." A vast number of Americans have lost a sense of being an integral part of a continuous *something* or *anything*. It is as if one were to say, "I am the product only of my own years and my own time. Nothing else influences me, nor do I pay obeisance to any other influence."

That is why it is so difficult, perhaps, for so many Americans to understand that no man is the product merely of his own years or of his own time. He is the creature of accumulation. It is equally difficult for Americans to understand that all peoples and nations are also such long-term products.

Crow Agency and Lame Deer, Montana, are headquarters for the Crow and for the Northern Cheyenne tribes and are only slightly over thirty miles apart. The two reservations abut each other in southeastern Montana and the tourist passing through the area somewhat naturally assumes that these two Indian tribes are "cousins" and certainly have a common heritage. They are not "cousins" and the commonality of their heritage is in most respects superficial and recent. They are profoundly different peoples.

As has been pointed out, the Indians whom the white man called the Northern Plains Indians were not ancient dwellers of the region. The domino effect worked with startling rapidity. The first white settlements on the Atlantic seaboard very quickly put pressure on the contiguous Indian population which in turn put pressure on the next people to the westward, and the result was that an eastern, humid-area people were pushed onto the Great Plains with great rapidity.

We do not know precisely where the Cheyennes originated, but educated guesses by anthropologists put them as of the early sixteenth century on the Canadian side of the Great Lakes. They were Algonquian in origin and had undoubtedly lived still farther eastward at an earlier date. The first French explorers found them situated in south-central Minnesota and noted then that a great southern migration was very much a part of their tradition. In their migration, however, this rather small Algonquian-speaking group of people penetrated and were immersed in a great and rather diverse Siouan culture and thus their fate became linked much more closely to the Sioux than to their actual eastern cousins. Their continued movement was swift. By 1680, when La Salle first encountered them near present-day Peoria, Illinois, they were already about three hundred or more miles from the area they had occupied a scant seven years previously.

It is important to note that the Cheyenne were a small group of people who did not speak the Siouan language but who were nonetheless moving rapidly and aggressively into a very hostile country, for the Siouan people not only vastly outnumbered them but were a particularly ferocious and warlike people — especially the Dakotas. The Minnesota River Valley, presided over by the Dakotas, was not a very hospitable place for the Algonquian-speaking, utterly alien Cheyennes. Even the enemies of the Dakota were more closely tied to them by language and by blood than the Cheyenne. The Crow, ancient enemies of the Dakota, were at least Siouan in origin.

The current view of the Cheyenne and Dakota as "cousins" reflects only a short period of a common plains existence, one of latter-day exigency only. What is important is that a people with an eastern, forest-oriented, semihorticultural tradition could and did move through the domain of a vastly more numerous enemy and then move on and adapt very swiftly to the nomadic buffalo-hunting environment of the Great Plains. Like all other tribes ultimately pushed onto the plains, the coming of the horse (the date varies from tribe to tribe, but 1750 is an acceptable point of reference) made a tremendous difference in life-style and economy.

The horse, which wandered up from the Spanish in the south, converted the plains Indian into an entirely different kind of human being. It is possible if not probable that the Cheyenne got horses before the animal had become common among the Sioux, and undoubtedly they were equestrian before the Crow. Indeed, American cavalrymen were referring to the "Horse Indians" quite some time before the Crow had achieved that status. If true (and precisely when each tribe actually became equestrian is still a matter of speculation and considerable disagreement), the early acquisition of the horse by the Cheyenne, particularly vis-à-vis the Crow, may have had substantial bearing on the different subsequent attitudes of the two peoples. For the moment, suffice it to remark that the Cheyenne were a fierce and feared people, implacable enemies of the whites and of the Crow, and that they remained so until their ultimate defeat by the whites. They were withdrawn, suspicious, and aloof. Their remarkable migration doubtless made them what they were — and, in some respects, what they are.

The Crow, too, underwent a vastly complex and long migra-

tion. But if the task of tracing the origins of the Cheyenne is a
difficult one, it is impossible with the Crow — at least from 1500
to 1700. Let us place the Crow in the vicinity of the Mandan
villages on the upper Missouri in about 1750, somewhere near the
Heart River confluence. The Crow are indisputably Siouan and
not Algonquian, and while this does not preclude migration from
very far to the north, it does controvert any contention that, like
the Cheyenne, they emigrated from the Northeast. But there are
mysteries galore here. Since the tribes of Siouan origin migrated
into the Minnesota valley largely from the Southeast, where were
the Crow? The legends of those tribes make no reference to them.
Worse, some anthropologists believe that the Crow are related to
the Kiowa of the Southwest. The shadows will have to remain.
Let it suffice that they moved westward, but later than the
Cheyenne, and we may presume that while the Cheyenne were
already equestrian-buffalo-hunting plainsmen, the Crow were
pedestrian-semihorticulturists on the Missouri.

By the early years of the nineteenth century, the transition and
adaptation of both the Crow and the Cheyenne were complete.
They were both horse-dependent, nomadic hunters, living essentially the same kind of life. But that fact does not obliterate
another. The two tribes were different with respect to social
organization, religion, recreation, and government. They differed
in their concepts of warfare and commerce. They differed profoundly in their attitudes toward white men. Let a thoughtful
student of these two tribes put it his way:

With the advent of the nineteenth century and the ever increasing
flow of whites into the plains country, I believe we shall see that, because they were two totally different peoples, their reactions to a
rapidly changing environment which both understood was none of
their own making, were fundamentally diverse; with virtually no kin-
ship in emotional and mental response being found. Although there is
admittedly little affinity between the plains Indian of 1800 and the
Indian of the present day in either case of the Crow or Cheyenne, I am

convinced that we shall further see that these deep-seated variances as regards the two nations may very well pervade the profound Indian subconscious which, in my opinion, lies barely beneath the surface of what may appear to be a mind wholly conditioned to a white style of thinking on the conscious level. . . .

If my conjecture in this vein is correct, under the proper amount of pressure, the white trappings, the pseudo-caucasian sham of both tribes will be lost and what do you have? The intense soul-filling difference; the *Indian* difference, that exists between the Crow and the Cheyenne.*

The differences between the Crow and the Cheyenne would, indeed, fill a volume. Let us abstract only a few essences which may be applicable to what is happening to them today.

Cheyenne government consisted of a body of chiefs who formed a council analogous to a unicameral legislature. This was a thoroughly democratic body which rarely made a decision other than unanimously. This was, of course, time-consuming and often involved much subtle lobbying, not only among councilmen, but among members of the tribe. Viewed superficially this was a nearly anarchic system. In fact, it was not. Though extraordinarily flexible it was thoroughly *organized*.

The chiefs had terms, usually ten years, though there was ample opportunity for interim change. There was a loose system of primogeniture. There was a complex structure for voting.

The Crow on the other hand, while they had chiefs and a council, had almost no structure to their system. They would elect a chief and follow his adjurations only so long as they chose — which often was not for long. They were, depending upon one's definition of government, very civilized about it. They usually chose to ignore it. The early observers of the Crow were astounded by this, but there was, in fact, a very good reason for the difference between the *internal* and structured Cheyenne system and the *external* and unstructured Crow system.

* Kevin J. O'Neil, "A Brief Sketch Tracing the Crow (Absasoka) and Northern Cheyenne Indians from Their Suggested Historical Origins to the Reservation: 1500–1945," 1974, manuscript in the author's possession.

By 1800 the Cheyenne had almost entirely abandoned exogamy, that is, marriage outside the tribe, village, clan, or "unit." The Crow were always exogamous. Accordingly, there existed no less than thirteen Crow clans within the context of three distinct tribes: the mountain Crow and two separate bands of river Crow. Though they intermarried, they did not agree on much of anything else. The Crow fought among themselves constantly. While one Cheyenne never let the blood of another, the Crows had blood feuds which frequently led to bloodletting. They had a most difficult time organizing themselves for war against a common enemy and suffered greatly for it.

The Crows, quite simply, had more fun than the somber Cheyenne. If the clans feuded, they also had joyous gatherings and interclan athletic competitions. They were as loose as the Cheyenne were tight.

The Cheyenne had rigid rules for courtship and marriage. Chastity was required; indeed, the Cheyenne might have invented the puritan ethic except for the fact that no Cheyenne woman was compelled to marry against her wishes. Being endogamous, the Cheyenne had very strict rules about marriage to a cousin or other relative, however distant. As they were a small tribe this did not always work, but the effort to make it work continued to turn the Cheyenne inward.

While the Crow had a full measure of marital and sexual taboos — one of which was no marriage among relatives — these were observed largely in the breach. Who was sleeping with whom was not a matter of great moment to anyone, and it is a measure of the Crow attitude toward all this that while a good many Crows lost their lives because of interclan feuds or jealousies, almost never were these problems rooted in marital or sexual animosities.

The Crows were, as the brief description of their attitudes thus far implies, a happy people, the least "savage" of the plains tribes, the most naïve, the most skilled thieves (thievery being a matter closely allied to honor), the most gullible, and the most mercurial.

They also were the only plains tribe genuinely friendly to the whites. They had an eighty-year history of never having killed a white man.

That is not to say that the Cheyenne lived unrelievedly grim and somber lives. They had their sports and feasts and relaxations. But they were introspective, taciturn, very methodical, and very hostile to whites.

All these aspects of the two tribes' natures reflected themselves in their respective religions. Again, the details must not detain us here. In general, the Cheyenne were not as superstitious as the Crow. Their religion was intrinsically akin to Judaeo-Christian doctrines; it was inherently monotheistic with an abstract divinity. They had, indeed, sacred objects, visions and dreams, and ceremonies of a "pagan" nature. But they endowed nothing with supernatural powers *except* through the workings of the all-father — the Creator.

The Crows were completely polytheistic, but which spirit of which animal or object was predominant was a subjective matter. As in all other affairs, the Crow had difficulty with consensus. The thing to do was to pick your own spirit, your own power, and let others pick theirs. One Crow brave told Robert Lowie, a careful student of the Crow, "The only thing I ever prayed to was my feather."

The differences between the Crow and the Cheyenne were, in the end, of no moment with respect to their ultimate fate. The Cheyenne fought the white man fiercely. The Crow were the white man's allies. It was Crow scouts for Custer who peered down from the hills along the Little Bighorn onto the great encampment, including the Cheyenne, and told the general that it was probably not a very good idea to attack.

Throughout the entire period of the 1860s and 1870s the Crows were staunch allies of the military; the Cheyenne, the bitterest enemies. It is an irony among myriad ironies that the Crow were treated just like the Cheyenne in the end. Both, by solemnly concluded treaties, were squeezed onto ever-dwindling reservations.

By 1884 the Crow were on theirs, near Hardin, Montana; the Cheyenne were on theirs: they were neighbors — another irony. Throughout the years a few things changed. The government vacillated between the extremes of the General Allotment Act of 1887 (which shrank the reservations further and, in fact, was legislation based inherently on the philosophy of "termination") and the Wheeler-Howard Act of 1934, well intentioned and aimed at land restoration, a revival of tribal government and Indian "self-identification."

After 1934, slowly, the concept of payment for lands lost by broken treaties became law; an Indian Claims Commission was established and payments were made. The Bureau of Indian Affairs kept strict reins on all matters pertaining to Indian welfare — all but statistics concerning Indian poverty, unemployment, sickness, alcoholism, suicide, illiteracy, infant mortality — and general demoralization. This did not reflect much success from new federal policies. In the Eisenhower years there was a return to the philosophy of 1887; bring the Indian "into the mainstream of American life" by "termination," i.e., abolishing the reservations. Pay off the Indians once and for all, buy the reservations, let the Indian be like everybody else.

In the face of growing Indian militancy, a new generation, and a new and intense ethnic consciousness, things began to move and stir in the 1960s. But it was very, very late. There were only 600,000 Indians in all of America. And then came the new element — coal. And lo, there, under the lands of the Northern Cheyenne and the Crow, lay billions of tons of this now precious commodity.

If one were to pick one theme which more than any other has remained a constant in the white attitude toward the Indian it is "removal," removal from where they *are*, meaning land which for one reason or another we want, to some other land which, for one reason or another, we do not want. That is precisely why the

Northern Cheyenne and the Crow came to be (along, of course, with all other reservation Indians) where they are.

The problem with this Jacksonian solution to the "Indian problem" has always been that lands we could not conceivably want at any given time we invariably came to want very badly at a later time. We most assuredly did not want the Black Hills when we gave them in perpetuity to the Indians. But that, of course, was before we discovered that there was gold in those hills. So we sent George Custer to effect a "removal."

Coal we now need much more pressingly than we ever needed gold. And there lies the intriguing question. How do we "remove" the Indians in the light of two drastically altered cirumstances? In the first place, there is nowhere else to which to remove them. In the second place, there has been a revolution in racial attitudes and concepts. True, it began as a black movement, it involved riots in ghettos, great marches and fires, and it was largely urban in nature. But *de jure* and *de facto* there has come about a profound change in American attitudes and it is probably irreversible. We should be extremely naïve not to understand that the Indian is deeply, if differently, involved.

But, of course, there *is* a further aspect to removal. There *is* an alternative. Let power and coal companies simply lease the coal under Indian land, remove it, and leave the Indians richer and happier. Except that the Indians don't quite see it that way. The trouble began with the Northern Cheyenne. We shall examine this trouble in some detail later; it is sufficient for the moment to point out that in the initial stages of leasing, a many-layered federal bureaucracy was naturally involved. The Northern Cheyenne found themselves caught not merely in this giant and complex machine; they were also caught in the high-powered machinations of huge energy companies.

If the Cheyenne and the Crow do act finally "in character," however, it will be in the face of a government policy over the years that can only be described as harrowingly inept and complex. This can hardly benefit either tribe.

Initially, Indians were dealt with by treaties — as if they were, indeed, a sovereign people. This procedure was based on Article I of the United States Constitution, which gives Congress the power to regulate commerce with "foreign nations, and among the several states and with the Indian Tribes." Congress chose the treaty method of dealing with the Indians, thus creating a unique legal status. But the "sovereignty" which this implied was, in fact, vastly eroded over the years.

The General Allotment Act (or Dawes Act) of 1887 not only shrank Indian land from 138,000,000 acres to 86,000,000 acres, it required each Indian to pick 40 acres of irrigable land, 80 acres of agricultural land or 160 acres of grazing land, with the "surplus" land being made available for sale to whites. By God, said the government, you *will* become farmers and that is that!

This created two types of land ownership on the shrunken reservations, because the tribes were allowed to keep some land in commonality, with tribal councils acting as managing trustees. But *allotted* land was real property, individually owned.

In 1934, with the passage of the Wheeler-Howard Act, the government sought to restore "surplus" lands to *tribal* ownership and authorized greater authority for tribal governments. The net result of these acts, plus interim legislation, was that Indian land is now characterized by fractured forms of ownership. There are restricted lands held in trust by the United States for the benefit of the tribe (unallotted); there are allotted lands, but of two kinds: those allotted lands held in trust by the government for the benefit of the allottee, and allotted lands held in fee by the individual Indians. But of the latter, much is so fractionalized, due to successive generations of heirship, that clear title is very difficult if not impossible to ascertain. Nor is all allotted land held by Indians. A number of whites own allotted lands due to a quirk in the law.

While it is widely assumed that the federal government has

jurisdiction over unallotted Indian lands, such is not always the case. The general rule, via sundry court findings, is that the general acts of Congress do not apply to Indians unless so expressed "as to clearly manifest an intention to include them." Indian tribes still retain some inherent sovereignty unless it has been specifically denied them either by treaty or by Congress. Here is the stuff of a half century of litigation, rendered the more likely by the increasing assertion of Indian leaders that *all* acts of the courts and Congress are null and void because the initial relationship between the U.S. government and Indian tribes was by *treaty* "with foreign nations" and that fact necessitates "sovereignty." Doubtless the case is a poor one legally (except in certain instances), but it will not be easy to convince the Indians that legal niceties should prevail over some 370 treaties now filed in the National Archives — all solemnly ratified by the United States Senate.

The problem does not end, however, with complex surface ownership. Some of the myriad treaties and statutes mention subsurface or mineral rights, others do not. In 1938 the Supreme Court held that unless specifically reserved, "Minerals and standing timber are consistent elements of the land itself" and hence belonged to (1) the tribe in commonality or (2) the owner (allottee). Yet in that same year, under the Omnibus Tribal Leasing Act, the government asserted that unallotted Indian land could only be *leased* for mineral exploitation with the approval of the Secretary of the Interior. Was this not a contradiction? Of course, but no one worried about contradictions in Indian affairs including — until recently — the Indians. There were so many contradictions no one could possibly deal with them anyway. Nevertheless, the Omnibus Tribal Leasing Act is today the operative legislation.

Consider now the Crow. The relevant treaties and statutes would fill a bulky appendix. When their huge reservation, which as of 1851 included much of Wyoming, Montana, Colorado, Nebraska and Kansas, had been shrunk to its present 1,558,059 acres, it was revealed that someone had erred. In the last act of reduction, which came in 1920, section 6 of the act reserved all minerals "for the benefit of the members of the tribe in common." This act, however, left untouched the provision of the earlier legislation *that leasing could only be authorized by the Department of the Interior* and it ignored fractured surface rights.

There are about 4,300 Crows on the tribal rolls. But of the some 1,500,000 acres, about 340,000 are unallotted tribal lands; 1,215,000 are allotted lands; and, by virtue of one of the many statutes which Congress passed along the way, 1,400 acres are owned by the federal government for school and "administrative" purposes.

So the questions facing the Crow Indians are hardly simple. Shall we lease mineral rights or shall we not? If we lease, what can we lease — allotted lands? If so, how? Unallotted lands? If allotted lands, what do we do about the fact that such lands are not necessarily owned by Indians?

The Crows did lease 61,123.93 acres of unallotted lands to Shell Oil and Westmoreland Coal Company in 1972. Westmoreland invested $34 million in a rail spur and a dragline, which expenditure was aimed at the extraction of four million tons of coal yearly which was to be shipped to power plants in Minnesota and Illinois. The Crow were given a royalty of 17.5 cents per ton. In addition, Peabody, Gulf Mineral Resources, Northsworthy and Riger, and Amax were issued prospecting permits totaling 178,978.39 acres.

Then the Crows began to think about things. They argued, debated, appointed a minerals committee, and argued some more. The arguments were many-faceted. It was not merely to strip or not to strip, it was a question of royalties.

The Crows announced that they were canceling all leases on the grounds that Westmoreland Coal Company had violated federal regulations in the stripping process. Pemberton Hutchinson, Westmoreland's president, announced that the Indians' actions would have no effect on operations which, he said, "have been developed over the past three years with the Crow tribe's full knowledge and cooperation." Westmoreland, said Hutchinson, had agreed to amendments to the leases which would increase royalty payments. If the Indians could not agree on the amendments, the original leases were nevertheless valid and Westmoreland would proceed. What the Crows and/or the Department of the Interior will do next, no one yet knows.

The Northern Cheyenne, perhaps predictably, have reacted very differently indeed. That difference lies not only in their inherent difference from the Crow but also in different federal legislation pertaining to the tribe. Their reservation, cut off from the Crow's in 1884, totals only 440,233 acres. There are only 2,926 persons enrolled. About 269,000 acres are unallotted, 164,000 allotted; and 6,800 are owned by the United States for school and "administrative" purposes.

The Cheyenne have a slightly less fractured surface pattern and, by the Northern Cheyenne Allotment Act of 1926, mineral rights were reserved for the benefit of the tribe for a fifty-year period — subject, of course, to the omnipresent Department of the Interior. Even so, the surface pattern presents grave problems. Witness the case of *The Northern Cheyenne Tribe* vs. *Hollowbreast* in 1972, in which the district court held that *individual* Indian allottees holding surface rights had no vested rights in the minerals. The court also ruled that individual allottees could not seek damages *or an injunction* (italics mine) to prohibit exploration, drilling and development on surface allotments — an extraordinary decision if one grants that Indians also have common property rights, however limited by the maze of federal regulations and the trusteeship of the Department of the Interior.

It is in all probability contradictory legislation of this kind, plus the fractured land patterns that resulted, which led both the Crow and the Northern Cheyenne into leasing mineral rights in the first place. Between 1966 and 1973 the Cheyenne leased 16,033.05 acres of their land to Peabody Coal. They granted prospecting permits to others, including Northsworthy and Riger, Amax, Consolidation, and Chevron totaling 172,374.32 acres. The acreage constituted over one-half of the entire reservation. For this they received about two and a quarter million dollars, or about 9 dollars per acre. Like the Crow, they were to receive a royalty of 17.5 cents per ton.

Then, in July 1972, the Consolidation Coal Company moved in with a plan for the construction of four coal gasification plants to be fed by 30,000,000 tons of coal extracted from an additional 70,000 acres of Cheyenne land. Consolidation offered a bonus of $35 per acre, a royalty of 25 cents per ton and the construction of a $1.5 million health center. For the Cheyenne this was the breaking point. They went to war — very much in character.

It is imperative to bear in mind that the Cheyenne are a people afflicted with all the concomitants of abiding poverty. It is precisely this poverty that made what happened next remarkable.

The Indians now formed the Northern Cheyenne Landowners' Association and quickly began to lobby within the tribe. On March 5, 1973, the Northern Cheyenne Tribal Council voted 11 to 0 to direct the Bureau of Indian Affairs to "withdraw the Department's approval and terminate and cancel all existing coal permits and leases." Further, the council hired a prestigious Seattle law firm to petition the Secretary of the Interior to acquiesce in the lease cancellation.

On June 8, 1974, *after* the Department of the Interior had indicated that the government would go along at least in part with the cancellation of leases, Northern Cheyenne Councilman Edwin Dahle said, "What it boils down to is a decision over who we sue — the U.S. government or Peabody Coal Company." To Interior Secretary Rogers C. B. Morton's very limited and carefully hedged statement of acquiescence in lease cancellation, Dahle lashed back, "He's directing focus away from the government. They've given us an apple: 'You sue the coal company and we'll give you the money. Just keep the government out of it.'" But, said Dahle, we are ultimately "going to raise hell with the federal government." To Peabody's protest and appeals for negotiation Dahle snapped, "An illegal contract is not negotiable. It cannot be bandaged up. If one corner is illegal, you don't just tear up that corner or patch it up," and he added, "The Cheyenne do not have the land base for sustaining the population as it is. And we do not work toward the goal of eliminating our people and our reservation."

Now the Cheyenne are seeking consensus again. The question the leaders are posing to the people is this: Shall we permit mining at all? We are agreed that we will not do business with these companies. But shall we mine the coal ourselves? They are proceeding in their orderly manner. First they sought and received a $200,000 grant from the government to study the matter. They brought in their own consultants and began their considerations. It seems possible that they themselves will have a run at it by mining some five billion tons on their own. But there is not yet consensus, not quite. Though they may not mine at all, on one thing they are totally agreed. In their initial development study they said, "The Northern Cheyenne intend to change the Indians' historic role of passive subservience to agencies who are charged with the administration of trusted responsibility for the benefit of the Indian tribes, and who in the past have evidenced little more than apathy toward this responsibility."

James F. Canan, area director of the Bureau of Indian Affairs, said that the Morton decision "appears to be a partial victory for the Cheyennes." Dahle disagreed. "It is a tremendous victory for the Cheyennes . . . and it shows that a voice of a minority, no matter how small, can be heard."

But it is not really that simple. Rogers Morton's decision opens a door, but it also contains other doors opening in other directions. Peabody's president, Edwin Phelps, stated, "We thought all along it was a legal lease, approved by both the Tribal Council and the Secretary of the Interior. We're a little confused."

Of the thirty-six violations of lease terms alleged by the tribe,

Morton had, in fact, only conceded three violations. The tribal chairman, Allan Rowland, remained adamant against Morton. He said that the original leases were made by tribal councilmen "ungrounded in fact." And he added that the vital facts were then nearly impossible to get.

Edwin Phelps of Peabody did not help matters when he was asked if his company had taken any steps to minimize the sociological impact of mining on Indians. His reply was, "Do you really think they're any different?" To the Cheyenne, of course, the answer is and always has been a very assertive "Yes." Moreover, Phelps's apparent lack of recognition of Indian poverty, social degradation and economic depression was a palpable shock to anyone remotely knowledgeable about Indians.

The Cheyennes had been angered by the damage done by Peabody's core-drilling rigs, damage to fences and the drawing down of underground water by deep bore holes. They insisted that neither restoration nor compensation had been forthcoming as specified in the leases.

Pemberton Hutchinson of Westmoreland, though dealing with the Crows, demonstrated a similar lack of sensitivity when he remarked, "I think the ultimate confrontation, if there is one, will not come between the coal company and the Indians but between the Indians and the ranchers. The Indian wants to get that coal mined and get his royalties."

Admittedly, some do. Some do not. It is a divisive situation which the coal companies clearly relish — as we shall see.

But the companies would be well advised to study the divisions carefully. A confrontation between ranchers and Indians is highly unlikely. An alliance, even with the Northern Cheyenne, should be given serious consideration. The profound contradictions between the ethics of the coal people and the Indian very closely resemble those between the coal people and the ranchers. It is something for the people in the boardrooms to think about. It is something for the Department of the Interior to think about because it is something for the American people to think about.

What *really* happened to the Northern Cheyenne is shocking. Half of their reservation was leased or exploitation permits were granted thereon, and hence, for all practical purposes, taken out of their control. It was, in effect, gone. That harrowing fact necessitates some closer examination. So does the fact that the Northern Cheyenne, less than three thousand Indians, have so shaken the policies of the Department of the Interior that, whatever the final resolution, those policies will never be the same again. It is a strange commentary, but the Northern Cheyenne Indians are at this moment the most important tribe in America. What has been done to them — and the nature of their response — bids fair to affect not only all Indians but a very large number of whites.

3

The Most Important Tribe in This Country

AT THE VERY ROOT of what happened to the Northern Cheyenne may lie the nature of the United States government's view of "trusteeship." Writing of this trusteeship some years ago, Justice Cardozo of the Supreme Court asserted that it must be treated with "the punctilio of an honor most sensitive." It has never thus been treated.

In an earlier day the responsibility for Indian affairs was split between the War Department and the Department of the Interior. Contrary to popular and current myth, the United States Army was considerably more knowledgeable, understanding, and sympathetic than was the Department of the Interior. Not that the army did not blunder, not that unconscionable events did not occur. But Interior's *entire* policy was deeply corrupt, callous and neglectful.

The Department of the Interior's Indian arm, the Bureau of Indian Affairs, was from its inception a disaster for Indians. Yet it is ironical that its recent (say ten years') "sensitization" backfired on the Indians. The BIA could not exculpate itself from its trusteeship role. What it did, therefore, was to endeavor to mitigate its paternalistic role by hiring Indians, by endeavoring not to throw roadblocks in the way of decisions arrived at by tribal councils, and by lowering its profile. It became an accepted assumption, for instance, that the Commissioner of Indian Affairs (the head of the BIA) would be an Indian, that Indians would largely staff the BIA Washington office, that reservation superintendents would be Indians. Yet the trusteeship which required "the punctilio of an honor most sensitive" could not, in fact, be conducted by an agency now backing away from vital decisions.

For instance, when Interior was slapped with massive documentation from the Northern Cheyenne that the government's role in the Cheyenne leasing process was replete with oversight, undersight, fraud, errors of omission and commission, Rogers C. B. Morton sent out to the area director in Billings, Montana, the text of his decision on the Northern Cheyenne lease cancellation petition. He gave the area director sixty days to render a "full written report summarizing his findings as to each of the separate matters required to be explored by the regulations." The "regulations," as we shall see, were demanding and extensive.

The area director, James Canan, responded with the assertion that his office *had* abided by the "regulations." Canan's dilemma, however, emerged rather clearly in a series of documents covering a period of more than five years. There are revealing sentences in his ten-page report to the secretary. For instance: "It might be mentioned again that both sales [leases] were held at the insistence of the Tribal Council rather than at the urging of any Bureau personnel"; and "It was the hope of the Tribal Council and the Bureau when the coal advertisements were started that it would result in job opportunities for tribal members. Creation of job opportunities always has been an expressed objective of the Northern Cheyenne Council. The coal sale lease forms provide that 'The lessee shall employ Indians, giving priority to lessor and other members of its tribe in all positions for which they are qualified and available. . . .'"

Canan was perfectly aware that as an economic unit, aside from coal, the Northern Cheyenne's 433,000-acre reservation was a small and undiversified base for economic self-sufficiency or solid economic growth. Nor was he unaware that the educational level was the seventh grade and the dropout rate was one-third. He was equally aware that the average annual income was $1,800 and that the unemployment rate ranged from 26 percent to an almost unbelievable 40 percent.

But there, suddenly, was the coal. Between 1966 and 1973 the BIA presided over the granting of permits for the exploration of or actual leases for strip mining involving 214,000 acres, or half the reservation. It is extremely difficult to make a callous villain of the area director, James Canan. But it is equally difficult to avoid the conclusion that somewhere, somehow, something went dreadfully wrong, for if it is true that an Indian tribe can only maintain its identity, culture and self-respect if the essence of it is rooted in its own land and its own use of that land's resources, the Northern Cheyenne were suddenly on the brink of extinction. James Canan did not put them there nor did they put themselves there. Who or what did?

Why, in the first place, did this small, tightly knit people let their land be leased, and why did they let exploration and mining begin without challenging the process long before 1973? Allan Rowland, head of the Tribal Council, put part of one finger on one part of the problem when he said, "We began to ask a lot of questions but we got no answers. We thought the U.S. government wouldn't rip us off so we let it ride until last year."

It would be a fairly safe assertion that of the entire population of Montana less than a hundred people knew of the existence of the *North Central Power Study* of 1971 within the first year after its publication. It would also be fair to assume that of *that* number, no more than half studied it and recognized its tremendous implications as the first bulwark of "Project Independence." There is no indication, documentary or otherwise, that the Northern Cheyenne had ever heard of it — or were told of it. Indeed, those few sharp-eyed Montana environmentalists who had studied it had trouble getting *anyone* to listen to their concerns.

When the coal companies began to apply for exploration permits and leasing, neither federal agencies, state agencies, nor ranchers were aware of the magnitude of what was going on. They were equally unaware of the vast ramifications and interrelationships between strip mining, railroad spurs, mine-mouth generating plants, transmission lines, and so-called reclamation. The oil, coal, and energy companies did *not* inform anyone of what was really involved. Quite the contrary, as we shall see; they were as secretive as CIA operatives.

It is not at all surprising that as of 1966, the period of the first Northern Cheyenne leases, James Canan of the BIA area office saw opportunity for the Northern Cheyenne in the reservation's coal reserves. It is even less surprising that the Northern Cheyenne were eager to proceed. If Montanans were isolated from the facts on a wholesale basis, and if, as was actually the case, the facts were very deliberately kept from them, it is hardly strange that a genuinely remote, small, and inward-looking Indian tribe should have been victimized. What *is* strange is that the tribe discovered it, studied it, understood it, and then took very decisive action.

The genesis of this procedure is obscure. But it would seem to have begun with a fortuitous conversation between Edwin Dahle of the Northern Cheyenne Tribal Council and George Crossland, a young Osage, a graduate of the University of Chicago Law School then practicing in Washington, D.C.

Crossland had become a lawyer precisely because he believed that the ultimate solution to reservation problems lay in highly trained *Indian* lawyers, economists, foresters, and experts of all requisite disciplines. Crossland had worked for the Indian Claims Commission and for various tribes from New York to Alaska, and had become one of the most peripatetic lawyers in the country. He did not have the resources of a large firm behind him. What he did have was a sharp mind, excellent legal training, and a fiery determination to put his training and talents to work for the Indian people.

When Edwin Dahle met Crossland quite by accident at an Indian gathering and expressed grave concern over what he thought
was happening to the Northern Cheyenne, Crossland was intrigued
enough to read the provisions of a few coal leases. He was
shocked. In a very short time he was in the problem up to his
neck. He had the enormous advantage of knowing all the basic
laws plus the almost infinitely complex *regulations* of the Department of the Interior regarding the trusteeship of Indian resources
— including coal. What he spotted almost at once in the leases,
which he cursorily reviewed, was what he believed to be gross
violations of 25 CFR Part 177.

Translated, 25 CFR Part 177 means *Code of Federal Regulations,*
Regulation 25, Part 177. Part 177 was broken down into subparts,
177.1, 177.2, 177.3, 177.4. There were also other "parts." Crossland also concluded that there were a number of other violations
in the leases not merely of regulations but of federal statutes. He
dug deeper.

By the winter of 1973, now acting as a consultant for the tribe,
Crossland had informed the Cheyenne that in his estimation the
law upon which to break the leases was there and that it was solid.
He was not sanguine about administrative remedy. He believed
that the Secretary of the Interior should promptly be petitioned
to cancel the leases, that the petition should go through the administrative channels. However, he informed the tribe, the odds
were against administrative remedy and the situation would then
be ripe for suit. The administrative course, he told the tribe,
"would provoke violent reactions. However, we are not concerned
with what effect such action will have on the profits of the Peabody Coal Company. . . . What we will not abide with is any
attempt by any department official to ignore, without our formal
consent . . . secretarial regulations which are designed to protect
our tribal interests" (". . . *punctilio of an honor most sensitive* . . .").

Having lit the fuse, Crossland suffered from no delusions. He had been through this kind of thing before. Petitions were all well and good — and usually exercises in futility. This should not be merely a petition. It had to serve the purpose of exhausting administrative remedy because, if it did not, the tribe would be turned back by the courts until such remedial procedures had been tried and proved fruitless in their entirety. But even that was not enough; the petition should indeed be labeled a petition, but it should also be a complete brief for court action, replete with the citations of all law, precedents, and massive documentation. This, clearly, was beyond Crossland's resources as a consultant or as a single lawyer. He thus informed the Tribal Council. It was, in effect, advice to "go for broke." That, he told them, would cost money — probably a great deal of money.

It was a most difficult political decision. The tribe itself was not of one mind but time was very short. The council pondered and accepted Crossland's advice. And so there entered into the picture the Seattle law firm of Ziontz, Pirtle, Morrissett and Ernstoff.

While the lawyers began their labors, the Cheyenne were not idle. With the outline of the ultimate petition in hand, they switched to the political route. They had, among other things, discovered that their regular attorney was also an attorney for the Peabody Coal Company. The council sent off a letter on May 24, 1973, a masterly piece of ingenuousness, to Rogers C. B. Morton, asking the secretary if this might not perhaps constitute a conflict of interest and what would he suggest they do about it? There is no answer of record.

They apprised Senate Majority Leader Mike Mansfield of their problems and sent him a copy of their outline petition. Mansfield, and three other powerful senators, immediately wrote Morton a very strong letter.

The Tribal Council wrote to Mr. Nixon's attorney, Leonard Garnnet, providing him with citations on 25 CFR 177, and asked him to intervene in the matter as a presidential adviser.

A series of stories about the Cheyenne's plight began to appear in the *Washington Post* and the *Congressional Record*. Vice-President Gerald Ford was sent a letter inviting his attention to the situation as set forth in the *Congressional Record* and Ford was asked for his personal help.

In all of these communications there was an interesting theme. The petition, said the council, was based with great specificity on violations of 25 CFR 177 and other narrow statutes. But the issue, they said, was a much larger one. It had to do with the very essence of "trusteeship"; it was, they said, therefore a moral and ethical as well as a legal matter. They were afraid that Secretary Morton might not understand this and would deal with the petition merely on the basis of the interpretations of "regulations." In no communication did they mention the Supreme Court of the United States. But it was plain enough.

The great bulk of the leasing on the Cheyenne Reservation took place in four huge sales between 1966 and 1973. In what was now to happen dates become critical. On January 18, *1969*, the Secretary of the Interior promulgated environmental protection regulations governing surface mining on Indian lands. This regulation was 25 CFR. It was the product of two years' study and it was unequivocal and specific. (The *North Central Power Study* was two years in the future.) The heart of the regulation was "the technical examination of *prospective* surface *exploration* and mining operations" (italics mine). No permit or lease was to be issued *prior* to examination and the examination was to concentrate on:

The preservation and protection of other resources, including cultural, recreational, scenic, historic, and ecological values; Control of erosion, flooding, and pollution of water; Isolation of toxic materials; Prevention of air pollution; Reclamation by re-vegetation, a replacement of soil, or by other means, of land affected by the exploration of mining operations; Prevention of slides; Protection of fish and wildlife and their habitat; and Prevention of hazards to public health and safety.

Regulation 25 CFR went even farther. It suggested the specific procedures to be followed in this *prior* "technical examination." Little was left to anyone's imagination, and little latitude was permitted — though that was subsequently to be vehemently denied by the BIA.

Regulation 25 CFR was promulgated on *January 18, 1969*. On *January 1, 1970*, the National Environmental Policy Act of 1969 became effective. In *February 1971* the United States Geological Survey sent out a bulletin in essence setting forth a new royalty basis for coal leases on federal lands from a fixed tonnage rate to a percentage of gross sales. It recommended that 5 percent of gross sales be standard provision. On *November 9, 1936*, under a Charter of Incorporation required by the Indian Reorganization Act (the Wheeler-Howard Act of 1934), the Northern Cheyenne tribe had been restricted from entering into any lease agreement for longer than five years and was prevented from entering into any agreement which would in any way *"operate to injure Tribal grazing lands or other natural resources of the Reservation"* (italics mine).

The significance of these dates resides in the fact that one-half of the Northern Cheyenne Reservation was leased (or permits were granted for exploration thereon) subsequent to the passage or promulgation of these acts and regulations. *All* such permits and leases violated at least one of the acts and most of the permits and leases violated *all* of the acts. The National Environmental Policy Act, for instance, required the preparation of environmental impact statements *prior* to any BIA actions taken in furtherance of the three largest lease (or permit) agreements on the reservation. But no such impact statements were ever made, nor have they been made to this day.

Another critical provision of 25 CFR, contained in Part 171.9, limited the acreage of any one lease to 2,560, except for demonstrable extraordinary circumstances. This provision was violated on a wholesale basis — and was later to prove of vital moment.

Another provision of 25 CFR contained in 171 forbade speculation in mining leases and asserted that all bidders must be bona
fide coal mining companies capable of conducting coal mining
operations themselves. The tribe was to assert that this provision
had been violated repeatedly and that speculators and "dummy"
organizations had been deeply involved in bidding.

While Secretary Morton did not announce his "acquiescence" in
the cancellation of the leases until June 4, 1974, word of troubles
was percolating up and down the hierarchy. In fact, it had been
perking for two years. The reason lay in a most disturbing report
issued by the General Accounting Office on August 10, 1972. The
GAO was very upset because, in spite of 25 CFR, in the close
examination of six large Peabody leases it could find no evidence
that the required "technical examinations" had ever been made.

In view of a palpably dangerous GAO report, the BIA began a
series of what can only be charitably termed lateral arabesques.
Whether Interior knew of these maneuvers is not ascertainable.
The events occurred as follows:

The GAO report was released on August 10, 1972. On November 17, 1972, the Commissioner of Indian Affairs issued a memorandum to: Area Directors, Billings, Navajo, Albuquerque, and
Phoenix Areas, which stated that the GAO was concerned about
25 CFR and that the area directors should remember that back in
the week of April 14–18, *1969* (italics mine), there had been a
meeting in Phoenix, Arizona, attended by "personnel from the
USGS [United States Geological Survey] and Washington and
several area offices of the BIA" at which a "consensus" had been
reached. The memo reminded the area directors that "it was generally agreed by those in attendance at the said meeting that due to
the procedure of offering, in most cases, large blocks of land for
competitive bid it could be both unnecessary and physically very
difficult if not impossible to personally inspect all lands prior to a
sale offering."

At this juncture, November 17, 1972, one witnesses the beginning of the passing of the buck. The memo goes on to state, "The purpose of this memorandum is to reinforce that consensus." So much for "consensus" versus the explicit provisions of the law.

However, since the GAO had brought the matter up, the memo continued, "written evidence of these examinations was not in every instance found in the files." (There is no available clue that it was found in *any* instance.) This being the case, wrote the commissioner, "We wish to re-emphasize [an interesting word since it had never been emphasized or even mentioned] the necessity of documenting the files with a report which *will* indicate that a technical examination, composed of either known data, personal familiarity of field staff officers, physical inspection, or a combination approach *was* made relative to the land in question prior to any advertisement or negotiating actions" (italics mine).

Let us now be charitable and assume that the memo does not say what it says due to inept use of the English language and an inadvertent switching of tenses — from "will" to "was." If we are not charitable, this becomes a blatant atempt, *ex post facto*, to doctor the files.

One way or the other, the memo posed a terrible problem for the area directors. Was it an order to doctor the files or was it to reaffirm a "consensus" in obvious contravention of a very explicit requirement for prior, detailed, written environmental examination? If in doubt, make *some* kind of record and pass the buck.

On December 12, 1972, the office of the Billings area director sent a memorandum to the superintendents of the Crow and Northern Cheyenne agencies which read, in part,

You were informed of the necessity of making these examinations *and the subsequent documenting of the records some time ago* [italics mine]. In view of the memorandum from Mr. Crow [the commissioner's office in Washington] and the circumstances which require it to be written, we request that the necessary technical examinations and reports be made and filed for every permit and lease for coal exploration or mining on lands within your jurisdiction. . . . The need to ex-

pedite the completion of this task is such that it is to be given top
priority to the exclusion of other duties until finished, if that is necessary.

A most extraordinary memorandum. "Some time ago" could not
have been prior to the commissioner's memo of November 17.
The superintendents had thus had less than a month to comply.
The land area involved was nearly two million acres (Crow and
Cheyenne). Actually to have gone *back* to 1966 and make on-the-
site "technical examinations," even *ex post facto*, would have been
a monumental task for which no superintendent was remotely
equipped. To be uncharitable, even a decent "doctoring job"
could hardly have been so swiftly accomplished given the hard
specifics of 25 CFR.

So, quite naturally, nothing at all was done in 1972. The GAO
had revealed a very serious violation of 25 CFR on August 10,
1972; the Commissioner of Indian Affairs had responded with a
memo of "non-compliance consensus" dating back to April 1969
in direct violation of 25 CFR and had then ordered area directors
to comply with 1969's 25 CFR on November 17, 1972; the area
directors had promptly demanded that the reservation superintendents comply with *something* which they had been ordered to do
"some time ago" and were told to give it the "highest priority."
So, while a good deal of violence was done to the King's English
and much paper was used, nothing happened at all.

That may be too harsh a judgment because something did happen, after a fashion, on April 22, 1974, more than two years later.
Naturally, it was another memorandum from the Commissioner of
Indian Affairs to all area directors. It observed that there must be
strict compliance with the specifics of 25 CFR and it also observed
that, after all, it had turned out that Indian reservations were not
excluded from the National Environmental Protection Act as the
BIA had initially assumed. The commissioner observed that with
respect to any misunderstanding that might have arisen in the past

concerning compliance with 25 CFR, this was certainly understandable: *"It is because of the lack of specific data on all mineralized or prospectively valuable lands"* (italics mine). Nevertheless, wrote the commissioner, 25 CFR must be observed.

This was a most interesting memorandum on two grounds. No one who had read the National Environmental Protection Act or the challenge to it by the BIA could have failed to understand that the Tenth Circuit Court of Appeals in *Davis* vs. *Morton* had unequivocally held that Indian lands were subject to the act and that the court had made that finding in 1972, not 1974. As for the lack of specific data on reservation mineralized lands, a quick trip to any moderately equipped library would have revealed that the Northern Cheyenne Reservation had been extensively examined and its mineral resources meticulously set forth in the official publications of the United States Geological Survey in 1923, 1929, 1932, 1936, 1949, 1950, and 1959. Moreover, all of these reports had been made into a compendium and were included in a report to Congress entitled *Mineral Potential in Eastern Montana, A Basis for Future Growth,* U.S. Government Printing Office, *1965!*

The irony is that this document was *the basic report used by and relied upon by the coal company bidders on Northern Cheyenne coal lands,* but that as of April 22, 1974, not only the Commissioner of Indian Affairs but apparently none of the area directors knew that this massive information was available. Let us be charitable again and assume that the reports were obscure. But they were not obscure to the Congress, the coal companies, the leasehounds and the environmentalists.

The matter of Indian royalties is also very puzzling. The first Northern Cheyenne sale occurred in August of 1966. The royalty was set by the Bureau of Indian Affairs at 17.5 cents per ton with a reduction of 2.5 cents per ton for any coal used on the reservation. When the Washington office was notified of the result they expressed pleasure and felt that the price was *"very good in this unproven area"* (italics mine). No one questioned the royalty, though, as we shall see, there was plenty of reason to question it. The Cheyenne were also given a 12-cent-per-acre "bonus" that went along with the royalty.

It is also something of a puzzlement that there was only one bidder at this sale, Peabody Coal, operating through its "subsidiary," Sentry Royalty Company. The field had been extensively mapped and it was very rich.

Perhaps the royalty and bonus went unquestioned because an assistant area director, Ned O. Thompson, had written the Washington office prior to the sale, "There is a lot of activity on state lands in these areas, and both tribes are anxious to get something going. We would like to make the offer as attractive, and with as few obstacles of determents [sic], as possible."

Yet within six months the Washington office was informing the area office that the 12-cent-per-acre bonus was "very nominal" and that in future bids it would be well to keep in mind that in other areas "prices ranging from $16 to $100 have recently been paid for coal or lignite leases." Consider the wild discrepancy and what it meant to the Cheyenne. Twelve cents per acre compared to $100 per acre! "A punctilio most sensitive."

Moreover, if the area office did not know what was happening elsewhere, the Washington office most certainly did, since the office had participated in leases on the Navajo and Hopi reservations, where the royalty was 25 cents per *ton* and where Peabody, the same company involved with the Northern Cheyenne, also agreed to a payment of $6.67 per acre for water pumped from deep wells in the area. Nor does any defense of the unconscionable royalty paid the Cheyenne reside in the quality or quantity of coal per acre in the Cheyenne versus the Black Mesa area. Quite the contrary. The Northern Cheyenne seams are between twelve and eighty-nine feet in thickness; the Black Mesa coal is between four and thirty feet in thickness. Tons per acre on the Cheyenne Reservation range between 17,000 and 95,000 while at Black Mesa the average is 44,000. The Cheyenne sulfur content ranges from 0.3 to

0.7 percent while Black Mesa's averages 0.51 percent.* The thickness of the overburden on Cheyenne land ranges between 60 and 120 feet while at Black Mesa it ranges up to 120 feet. Yet the Cheyenne royalty was 17.5 cents per ton and Black Mesa's was 25 cents per ton!

But the royalty fiasco grows worse, not better. Let us consider the "harmless" stipulation that for coal burning on the reservation there was a royalty reduction of 2.5 cents per ton. Well, no harm done to a few Indians burning coal in their stoves. But though it was subsequently to be denied by the BIA, Peabody and Chevron were very aggressively planning huge mine-mouth generating and coal gasification plants *on the reservation*. In fact, the plans involved the burning of most of the coal at mine-mouth sites. Thus the actual royalty was not 17.5 cents per ton — it was 15 cents per ton. But the Indians did not yet know what the companies were planning, nor did anyone else.

On January 7, 1966, the United States Geological Survey had strongly recommended a royalty of 20 cents on all further leases. This was totally ignored in the second sale in 1969 and in the third sale in 1971. Acreage bonuses, it is quite true, went up in some cases as high as $32. But real money for the tribe had never resided in acreage bonuses, only in royalties per ton. This vital figure did not change.

In July 1972, however, Consolidation Coal Company made an offer that startled the Tribal Council and caused them to review what had happened to them thus far. Consolidation offered a bonus bid of $25 per acre, a royalty of 25 cents per ton or 6 percent of the gross selling price f.o.b. mine, whichever was greater, *no reduction for coal consumed on the reservation*, and the donation of $1,500,000 toward the cost of a new health center.

---

* Low-sulfur coal contains less than 1.4 percent sulfur per ton. As we shall see, the whole question of low-sulfur western coal is fraught with misconceptions. The point here is simply that Cheyenne's coal was lower in sulfur content than Black Mesa's.

It is of vital moment to note that Consolidation did not act through the BIA or any intermediary connected therewith. Its offer was independent and unilateral. It is no wonder that the Northern Cheyenne now began to speculate that the Department of the Interior had not acted in their best interests in their role as trustees. The point need not be belabored. It is starkly self-evident.

If, again, it be asserted that Interior did not have adequate comparative figures with which to deal, or that remote area offices were in the dark in this respect, the assertion will not bear scrutiny. It was widespread *public* knowledge that the State of Montana, prior to 1973, was taxing coal at 38.7 cents per ton and, subsequent to 1973, added 23.8 cents per ton, for a total of 62.5 cents per ton. There is considerable discrepancy between 17.5 cents for the Cheyenne and 62.5 cents for the state.

Contrary to George Crossland's jaundiced view of administrative remedy, the bulky petition which ultimately landed on Rogers C. B. Morton's desk did bring results.

In a document dated June 4, 1974, a document which might well be assigned for a semester's study in semantics, philology, and the techniques of convoluting a language, Morton *did* find wholesale violation of 25 CFR by Peabody Coal Company and by his own department. He asserted that all would be held in abeyance until *Interior* had completed an environmental impact statement, but that due to tribal charges of laxity in his own department, "I have decided that, to the fullest extent possible, outside sources will be used to prepare the environmental impact statement." Morton invalidated Peabody's leases largely on the ground of 25 CFR's limitation of 2,560 acres per lease and directed the company and the tribe to abide by that limitation "or clearly to demonstrate the need to waive this limitation."

On collusive bidding and unlawful assignment, he referred these issues to the Office of Hearings and Appeals "for findings of fact and conclusions of law."

As for "technical examinations," "I am reserving my decision on this question and . . . I am asking the BIA Area Director in Billings to submit to me within 60 days a full written report summarizing his findings as to each of the separate matters required to be explored by the regulations."

If one wades through incredibly bollixed verbiage, it finally becomes clear that Morton stopped everything in its tracks and by sundry devices pulled the underpinnings almost completely from Peabody's leases. Then, suddenly, the prose becomes spare and clear.

The tribe's petition presents extraordinary circumstances. Among other things, the Tribe has expended substantial sums of money in preparing and presenting the petition to me. . . . The tribe and the coal companies may be assured that the terms and conditions upon which mineral development may proceed on the Northern Cheyenne Reservation will require their *joint* agreement and support prior to any further approval by me.

And then, bluntly, "I will defray the expenses subsequently to be borne by the Tribe for attorney's fees. . . ." And Morton made it clear that the tribe was in no way precluded from bringing its own lawsuits against the coal companies. But as Edwin Dahle said, the tribe was as apt to sue Morton as Peabody.

If Peabody was left slowly swinging from the arm of the dragline, the Billings area director can hardly have felt comfortable. He responded on July 24, 1974. His argument was that the section of 25 CFR which required "technical examinations" did not, in his estimation, require that such examination be in writing. And he neatly tossed the ball back to the department by asserting that in the granting of permits, the form devised by the area office stated that 25 CFR must be fully complied with — although, he said, it struck him as somewhat beside the point, since the time to ascertain whether 25 CFR had been complied with was when a "mining plan" had been submitted and not before — and no mining plan had as yet been submitted.

It was a long and complex reply but it was not, on the surface, exculpatory. He could, indeed, have attached a copy of 25 CFR to all permit and lease forms, but (though he did not put it in these words) he presumed that the coal executives *could* read — and *would* read — 25 CFR before they submitted a "mining plan." It was an ingenious answer and not an unimpressive one. But it did not answer the question, Where does the buck stop? Perhaps it did not have to, because the buck should have stopped on the desk of Rogers C. B. Morton. It did not. He passed the action back to the Northern Cheyenne by, in effect, telling them to sue the coal companies and he would pay for it.

The intriguing possibility, if not probability, is that the Northern Cheyenne are, and have been all along, acting in character. If so, they will, indeed, sue Peabody in particular but they will also sue their trustee, the Department of the Interior. If no court will accept a cause of action in this regard, the tribe is most likely to find innumerable ways to harass its trustee.

There are indications, however, that the tribe may go farther than that. At least they are hard at work at the drawing board and they have some strong backing, particularly from Senator Mansfield. They have more than that. Even before Morton rendered his decision, the Northern Cheyenne had called in all manner of experts. They had taken a page from the book of the Shah of Iran. Why *burn* the coal at all? Coal, like oil, can be converted into some 70,000 by-products. The most wasteful use of this fossil fuel is to burn it.

So the Cheyenne, advised by experts from as far away as Australia, began a study of their options. They could renegotiate leases with Peabody and other companies and start all over again. This in no way appealed to them. Their mistrust of the coal companies was profound. They could form their own subsidiary organization and mine and market their own coal. They could form their own petrochemical projects on the reservation and thus not only prolong the life of the resource, but prolong it almost indefinitely, because 5 billion tons of coal could feed a petrochemical industry far into the next century.

This latter plan is most ardently espoused by the imported experts, as well as by Senator Mansfield, who has asserted that it would be the biggest Indian self-help project ever undertaken and certainly one that the federal government should encourage.

To the argument that the undertaking is a monumental task for a remote Indian tribe of less than three thousand people, George Crossland points out that Arab states and emirates are areas consisting of sand, nomads, and oil, yet they are rapidly becoming the richest states on earth. "Ten years ago," he said, "the world's view of the Arabs was that they wandered around the desert on camels and wore sheets for clothing and drank goats' milk. All it took to change that schoolboy stereotype was oil and the energy crisis."

Oil and coal, Crossland pointed out, are merely different forms of the same chemicals. The Cheyenne — and the Crows and the Navajos and the Hopi — are the American *Arabs*. "They now have the power," he said. "The trick is going to be to understand that and to use it. No tribe comes closer to that understanding than the Northern Cheyenne."

Hearteningly, those most deeply involved, Rowland, Dahle, Crossland, and the Tribal Council, are not euphoric. They are too well aware of all the ventures launched with great expectations on a dozen reservations over the past several decades — and all the failures. They attribute this catalogue of sorrows to poor planning and the lack of expertise. They are determined to avoid those pitfalls.

Still, there is the omnipresent Department of the Interior and the "trusteeship." In the Cheyenne view, that is an awesome roadblock. In that view, at least, the Cheyenne do not stand alone. Almost all Indians share it. But, now, so do a swiftly gathering and vocal number of whites.

George Crossland is cautious and he is also wry. In a peculiarly detached way he remarked recently, "This damn world is full of contradictions. I always wanted to be a novelist and I end up a lawyer. I am an Osage but I feel like a Cheyenne. It was the Black Power movement that touched off the Red Power movement — and now it's Black Power again — black coal. It will either save us or be our ruination. The hell of it is, we don't know which way it will go."

4

The Ordeal
of the Cattlemen

IN SPITE OF THE VAST LITERATURE it has produced, the open range cattle industry was a short-lived business. In the form so common to us in novels, motion pictures, and on television it lasted barely more than a decade. Yet the period produced an American myth, a formula for an unending morality play, and a picture of the West that is celebrated in hundreds of ways today — all of which evoke a simple demarcation between the good versus the bad, the free versus the captive, the clean versus the defiled.

Yet, like most myths, it is not all myth. Though it was in fact a giant business backed by enormous capital, it did create a special breed of men and women with special attitudes and, since the period in question involves our very recent past, these attitudes have not vanished. A third- or even fourth-generation rancher on the plains today *has* a heritage of tough independence, a suspicion of his urban cousins, and a philosophy about land, animals, and grass that makes him "different."

Yet in light of what is very much a western pattern, the range cattle industry cannot be excluded from the general picture of exploitation by eastern capital and corporations, and not only eastern but European. As was true with the fur trade, the mining frontier, the transportation frontier, and the homesteaders' era, behind the "romance" (if "romance" it was) of the open range cattle industry lay speculation by bankers and investors far from the land where the profits were to be made — and the losses were to occur.

The cattle which spilled over onto the vast reaches of the Northern Great Plains in the late 1870s and early 1880s came from stock originally raised in the mountains, where, in turn, they reflected the needs of the immigrants along the Oregon Trail. Before the Civil War, trading posts, widely scattered but of vital importance to the immigrant, sprang up along his various routes. It was at these posts that he resupplied himself and here, also, he traded his worn and footsore animals for fresh ones, usually selling very low and buying very high. Since one fresh and fat work steer might be worth two or three depleted animals, it was good business for the trader. Herds developed at these posts. As early as 1856 a Captain Richard Grant, trading out of Fort Hall, Idaho, had a herd of about 600 head. As herds increased in size it became more difficult to graze the animals near a given post and to raise sufficient hay, so the cattlemen drove their animals into the lush valleys of the upper Missouri, into the Beaverhead, the Gallatin, the Deerlodge valleys, and then over west into the Bitterroot.

Several events led to the explosive growth of these herds. The first was the Mormon War of 1857–1858. This led to an evacuation of the gentile ranchers in Utah, many of whom drove their herds northward. The second was the encouragement lent the industry by the increasing demands of the military. The third was the discovery of gold, which, by 1864, had led to the sprouting of gold camps in literally hundreds of gulches, populated by teeming thousands of beef-hungry men. As an indication of the magnitude of this early business, by 1868, in nine counties in western Montana, there were 10,714 oxen and 18,801 cows and calves. Within four years the number of stock cattle had risen to over 75,000.

This market, being essentially local, would have stabilized at some juncture in the late 1870s had it not been for four interlocking factors which, together, caused not merely a further explosion in numbers but an enormously rapid spilling of cattle out of the mountain valleys and onto the Northern Plains and, concomitantly, great drives of cattle from Texas northward onto those plains.

First and foremost, the railroads were building westward. Second, the buffalo herds on the plains were vanishing rapidly and with them the Indian threat diminished. Third, Texas ranges were glutted with cattle; drought in Texas was beginning one of its periodic sieges and the northern ranges were known by cattlemen to bear the finest grasses on the continent. And last, the population of Oregon had stabilized and surplus cattle were thus being driven eastward.

Why did the Texans not simply drive their longhorns to, say, the Missouri Pacific railhead at Sedalia, Missouri? In 1866 they did. But the Texas drives moved farther and farther west for several reasons. This was rough and timbered country to the east — and the longhorns, a peculiarly wild and obstreperous breed, could not be handled in timbered country.

The plains Indians were one thing; they were now corralled and demoralized on their reservations. But in the valleys of the Red, the Arkansas, and the Cimarron, to which the Five Civilized Tribes* had been moved by Andrew Jackson's Indian Removal Policy, the situation was different. These Indians were cattlemen themselves, and by the Indian Act of 1834 they had the right to charge all drovers one dollar a head for passage across their lands. They did so. But by moving westward, the Texas drovers were dealing with the less "civilized" Cheyenne and Arapahoe, who were beleaguered and beset and (unlike the Cherokee) not organized enough to levy fines or tolls.

Moreover, Kansas and Missouri farmers looked askance at the lank longhorns. Not only did they obliterate fences and gardens, they also carried exotic diseases to which the longhorns themselves

---

* The Five Civilized Tribes consisted of the Cherokee, Chickasaw, Choctaw, Creeks, and Seminoles.

were immune. So Kansas and Missouri passed strict quarantine laws that were implacably enforced. For all these reasons, the Texas Trail drives bent farther and farther west — and they also moved farther and farther north as the Colorado and Wyoming ranges filled up.

Information about the vast potential in the open range cattle industry first trickled and then flooded eastward. Eastern papers, often basing their encomiums on tracts published by territorial legislatures or booster groups in the West, carried an ever heavier burden of information about the "beef bonanza." Farm and livestock journals developed special sections on how to invest. In 1883, for instance, the *Breeder's Gazette* reported that "a good sized steer when it is fit for the butcher market will bring from $45 to $60. The same animal at birth was worth but $5.00. He has run on the plains and cropped the grass from the public domain for four or five years, and now, with scarcely any expense to the owner, is worth forty dollars more than when he started on his pilgrimage."* The money began to move in; the cattle on the range multiplied. A Montana rancher, Granville Stewart, who chronicled his experiences in a remarkable book entitled *Forty Years on the Frontier*, expressed the profound change that the boom had wrought in central and eastern Montana:

> In 1880 . . . one could travel for miles without seeing so much as a trapper's bivouac. Thousands of buffalo darkened the rolling plains. There were deer, elk, wolves and coyotes on every hill. . . . In the fall of 1883 there was not a buffalo remaining on the range, and the antelope, elk and deer were indeed scarce . . . but in 1883 there were 600,000 head of cattle on the range. The cowboy . . . had become an institution.

But it was to become more crowded still. More eastern money flowed westward. There was no end to the American appetite for

* Quoted from E. S. Osgood, *The Day of the Cattleman* (Chicago: University of Chicago Press, 1929), p. 86. In spite of its age this remains the classic work on the history of the open range.

beef. There was no end to the number of cattle that could be seen on these endless plains, these rolling hills. What had become of Stephen Long's Great American Desert? After all, was it not true that some 30,000,000 buffalo had once been sustained on this grass — to say nothing of vast herds of elk, deer, and antelope? This seemed no desert but a paradise where a man could make a fortune with a negligible investment; all he had to do was wait. The companies proliferated. In just one year, 1883, twenty companies with a capitalization of over twelve million dollars filed incorporation papers in Wyoming. The money came from New York, Boston, Chicago. But it also came from England, Germany, Scotland, and Holland.

Cattlemen used the public domain. Some, indeed, would file on a good spring or creek on the basis of the old 160-acre Homestead Act. But the cattle were then run on the basis of "accustomed range." This worked nicely until the range became crowded; then, just as the miners before them had done, they set up "claims." These claims were simply announced in a convenient newspaper. This, of course, was unenforceable and it quickly became obvious (as it has again become obvious today) that who controls the water controls the land. The Homestead Act (and its successors) was then used to file on river or stream areas. Running back from those areas the "accustomed range," that is to say, public domain, was fenced. It was, then, the rancher and not the homesteader who brought barbed wire to the Northern Plains. But fencing was not really the answer. Pragmatist that he was, the rancher now set up cattlemen's associations, and sought by creation of "district" roundups and branding to solve his problems. The problems were merely ameliorated.

Though the details of the story are intriguing they have no place in this account. Because the federal land laws which were created by an eastern-oriented Congress to dispose of the public domain to the "yeoman farmer," and thus avoid a landed aristocracy, could not serve the rancher, he (like the lumbermen who followed him in the Far West) resorted to wholesale fraud. As E. S. Osgood, the great chronicler of *The Day of the Cattleman*, put it, "Fraud in the disposal of the public domain is no new thing in the history of our public land policy. It never reached larger proportions, nor developed a greater wealth of ingenuity in the methods employed, than during the last half of the eighties." The problem was ultimately solved when the open range industry collapsed, the size of individual herds was drastically reduced, and the rancher then bought or leased his land.

The industry collapsed because the land had been asked to do what it could not do and be what it could not be.

To the south, good grazing land was becoming scarcer each year. The answer had been to move north. But as early as 1879, in testimony taken before the Public Lands Commission, there was clear indication that the Northern Plains were being dangerously overgrazed.

A remarkably prescient Montanan, R. N. Sutherlin, editor of the *Rocky Mountain Husbandman*, writing in 1883, observed: "The cattle interests in Montana are threatened with imminent danger . . . one is the overcrowding of the ranges . . . a time has at length arrived, when the herd owner can see in the near future mountains of difficulty to combat." These difficulties, said Sutherlin, were drought accompanied by a hard winter.*

The summer of 1886 was a hot and dry one. The range, by fall, had been cropped almost to the roots. The price of cattle in the East had fallen and a number of ranchers had decided to "hold over" shipment until the following year. There were perhaps 800,000 cattle on the range.

In November there were several snowstorms. Then came a warm chinook and then a freeze, forming a vast sheet of ice. On Christmas Eve it started to storm and, as Teddy Blue Abbott ob-

---

* See Osgood, *Cattleman*, p. 91, and Frank Grant, "Robert N. Sutherlin, Prophet for the People," unpublished master's thesis, University of Montana, 1971.

served, "it never let up for sixty days." It got cold and stayed cold. On January 14 it was sixty below zero at Fort Keogh.

In late January came another chinook, followed by another hard freeze, and a terrific blizzard ensued in early February. Let Teddy Blue Abbott give his impressions:

The cattle stood it fairly well for thirty days. When the Chinook started in January I wrote Granville Stewart telling him I thought the loss would not be over 10 percent. In ten days I knew it was 75 percent. The cattle drifted down on all the rivers, and untold thousands went down the air holes. On the Missouri we lost I don't know how many that way. They would walk out on the ice, and the ones behind would push the ones in front in. The cowpunchers worked like slaves to move them back in the hills, but as all outfits cut their forces down every winter, they were shorthanded. No one knows how they worked but themselves. They saved thousands of cattle. Think of riding all day in a blinding snow storm, the temperature fifty and sixty below zero, and no dinner. . . . The horses' feet were cut and bleeding from the heavy crust, and the cattle had the hair and hide wore off their legs to the knees and hocks. It was surely hell to see big four year old steers just able to stagger along. It was the same all over Wyoming, Montana and Colorado, Western Nebraska and Western Kansas. . . .

Spring came at last. The coulees in some places were piled deep with cattle where they had sought shelter and died, and the ones that were left were nothing but skin and bone and so weak they could hardly stand. . . .

Just to show the loss, we had branded by actual count 10,000 DHS calves on the Flatwillow and Maginnis roundup in the spring and fall of '86; this meant as we estimated, 40,000 cattle. On the spring roundup of '87 not 100 yearlings showed up, and on a rough count there were only 7,000 cattle all told. . . . Fully 60 per cent of all cattle in Montana were dead by March 15, 1887; that is why everything on the range dates from that winter.

Assessors' figures on livestock were rarely accurate in those days and we do not know the actual percentage of loss. Nor was Teddy Blue quite accurate in asserting that this terrible winter afflicted all of the plains with equal intensity.

But the larger picture is that even without this extraordinarily severe winter the open range was doomed. It was doomed because the range could not sustain the numbers of cattle (and sheep) pushed upon it. It was doomed, too, because with such enormous numbers of cattle involved, the cattlemen could not devise a system whereby they could use the public domain free in the face of the federal land laws. And it was doomed because the small cattlemen were pressing the larger ones hard. The former *had* filed on the land. They *were* fencing, they *were* buying land. They were putting up hay.

Still, the underlying fact was impaction, overgrazing, an inherent abuse of the land, the destruction of an extraordinarily rich resource.

It took an enormous toll in human and animal suffering to bring about an adaptation. The years between 1887 and 1930 were extraordinarily hard ones for the rancher. Herds were reduced from twenty or thirty thousand to two or three thousand. The cowboy became a fencer, a planter and reaper of hay, a builder of sheds and corrals. And only the tough ones remained to adapt.

But there was more to it than that. A rancher who came to the country in 1880 described the grasses of these benches as "a thick mass of leaves inclined toward the southeast in the fall by the northwest winds . . . and they thought nothing of riding across the country with their feet dragging in the grass. . . . Perhaps none of our range grasses have been exterminated, but on account of the close feeding and trampling of the stock they have been so reduced in quantity as to be almost absent in some places."*

But what, then, of all those buffalo, deer, elk, and antelope remarked upon so consistently in early accounts — according to some estimates, more than 80,000,000 buffalo? Did they not overgraze the plains? In the first place, the accounts also almost always mention myriad wolves and coyotes, natural "thinners" of the

* Quoted in Robert S. Fletcher, "The End of the Open Range in Eastern Montana," *Mississippi Valley Historical Review*, September 1929.

weak and the old. And before man pushed him into the last re-
cesses of the mountains the bear, including the grizzly, was a plains
animal — and a very hardy predator.

In the second place, the herds could drift, backs to the wind,
for vast distances, meeting no obstacles, no fences, no herdsmen
— from thin grass to thick, from wind to calm, from cold to
warmth. In bad years, undoubtedly, many of them died. But the
grass grew again and they flourished again.

The apparent rapid adaptation of the rancher to new conditions
is illusory. The years from the middle eighties into the first three
decades of the twentieth century were enormously difficult for
him. The cornucopia of eastern money ran out precipitously. The
rancher scrambled for deeded land — but now the owners of the
great herds found themselves not only with little cash but also
in hot competition for land with the small rancher and also with
the sheepman.

By the 1890s there were 512,000 cattle back on the Montana
ranges. But there were 1,238,000 sheep. Sheep could graze on depleted land, where cattle could not. By 1900 the number of cattle
had shrunk to 333,000; the number of sheep had increased to
3,047,000. While there was no sustained war between cattlemen
and sheepmen, there were many incidents of violence. There were
also clashes between groups of cattlemen in Montana and between
Montana and Wyoming cattlemen, the latter still seeking to push
northward from their own devastated ranges. Under these circumstances the grasses, if they had ever really had a chance to
grow back, degenerated further.

One of the chroniclers of the end of the open range in Montana,
Robert S. Fletcher, ended his account thus:

Unfortunately, the forage in existence at the end of the open range
era was only the shadow of what it was at the beginning of the cattle
business. The grasses had been cropped too closely, especially by
sheep, in many districts, and died out, giving place to poorer varieties
or to sagebrush and barren ground. Over-stocking had become a cruel

reality in the last years and a hastening agent in the movement toward a new era.

There is a nice ring to those final words "a new era," but Fletcher was writing in 1929 and in fact the "new era," whatever Fletcher was implying, never came. What came were drought, depression, falling cattle prices, and economic collapse.

But what happened to the people involved? In the first place, the industry had never attracted large numbers of people. The easterners, those who had ever actually come west, withdrew. Most of the cowboys, the hired hands, simply drifted off. Most of the ranchers either sold out for a pittance or quit the business. But what concerns us in this study is those who remained.

How *could* they make it? They used little money, if any. They raised their own food or bartered; there were few if any amenities; they scrambled for land; they fenced; they dug wells for gardens; they put land into hay, wheat, barley; they worked unremittingly — and not merely from dawn to dusk. They worked as long as it took them to do what they had to do. But they were still not farmers, they were ranchers.

Why did they stay? One way to get some inkling of an answer is to know their progeny — for it is simply not true that the father passed nothing to the son and the son to the son. It would be misleadingly euphemistic to say that they loved a challenge. No. They were perverse. There was a shame involved in giving up. In the face of an overwhelmingly malevolent environment they shook their fists at God and nature — and they stayed.

Second, having fought long and often viciously to stay, they developed over a period of time a special relationship with the land, a relationship almost impossible for them to articulate and even more impossible for an "outsider" to understand. In a recently published sociological study of the rancher and the strip miner,*

---

* *A Comparative Case Study of the Impact of Coal Development on the Way of Life of People in the Coal Area of Eastern Montana and North*

an apparently naïve interlocutor elicited this comment from a rancher: "The very best that industrialization can offer is some extra money, which is too bad because, for people like me, land guarantees happiness, dollars don't."

Most ranchers are not that simplistic and never have been. They know full well the land does not guarantee happiness; it more often than not guarantees misery. The rancher's relationship with it is love-hate — with a full measure of hate.

Last August I stood in the middle of a withered pasture with a seventy-six-year-old rancher who was muttering and cursing about the dry year. He was cursing the grasshoppers, the dust, the curling grass, the trickle of water in the ditch. He was calling the wrath of God down on cattle buyers, leasehounds, and the Department of Agriculture. Suddenly it started to rain. He looked up at the dark sky and shouted, "And where were you, you son-of-a-bitch, when I needed you last spring!"

There is more than a little of Robert Ardrey's "territorial imperative" in the rancher. Like the wolf he has marked off his turf, and like the wolf nothing so rouses his ire as trespass. He has marked off his turf not merely with sweat and hard work but with vast expenditures of love and hate.

Eastern Wyoming, Institute for Social Science Research, University of Montana, Missoula, Montana, for Northern Great Plains Resources Program, July 1974.

5

Taxes and Communities

FEW IF ANY ECONOMIC HISTORIANS would deny that the costs of mining to the State of Montana have never really been borne by the mining companies. The cost of the *real* impact of their operations has always been shared if not, indeed, largely carried by the general populace. There has been an eighty-five-year battle to change this by changing the lopsided tax structure of the state. Dramatically, three days before the end of the 1975 legislative session the fight was won.

But, in view of a palpably "rigged" tax structure, why did the battle take so long and — directly and indirectly — cost so much to win? The answer is embedded in history. So is any understanding of the magnitude of the final victory and the fact that it is a victory not merely for Montana.

In 1919 a professor of economics at the University of Montana published an apparently innocuous monograph entitled *The Taxation of Mines in Montana*. The professor was promptly fired and the files of the American Association of University Professors, as well as the files of the chancellor of the university, the president of the university, and the Board of Education, literally bulged with information on the case. The details of the story were well

covered also in *The New Republic,* the *New York Times,* and
The Nation. Subsequently, in 1970, the "Case of Louis Levine"
was meticulously reviewed by Arnon Gutfeld in an article in the
Pacific Historical Review as a classic example of the blatant violation of academic freedom by a corporation.

The corporation, of course, was Anaconda, then known as the
Anaconda Copper Mining Company. In light of abundant and
careful research no one today would deny that Anaconda forced
the dismissal of Louis Levine because he published *The Taxation
of Mines in Montana.* Nor, in light of such abundant research,
would anyone deny that Levine's study was accurate to the last
digit.

As of 1919 mines bore a minimal property tax. The operative
tax was called a "net proceeds" tax, and this method of taxation had
been written into the Montana Constitution of 1889. In 1889 it
may have seemed justifiable essentially to exempt mines from taxation, though the wisdom of putting statutory matters into an
organic act was hotly debated even then.

The "net proceeds" tax consisted of a levy as personal property
on the value of mineral wealth after *all* production and operating
costs had been subtracted, and those costs included "extracting,
reducing, refining, improvements, and sales." The tax was remitted
to the county wherein the mining occurred.

These specifics did not appear in the constitution, which
merely asserted that mines should be taxed on "net proceeds," i.e.,
not on any percentage of gross proceeds. The specifics were set
forth by a subservient legislature in 1907 and in still greater detail
in 1921. While those statutes gave the Board of Equalization the
right to examine the books of the corporation, they would have
been fools to try it. The books of one of America's largest corporations (Anaconda was a wholly owned subsidiary of Standard Oil
from 1900 to 1915) were hardly simple, and the board had little or
no staff. Thus, "net proceeds" could be (and on a wholesale basis
were) wildly distorted either by underreporting the gross or over-

reporting the operating costs. How much money in tax revenues the State of Montana lost from 1889 to the 1920s, when certain tax reforms alleviated (but did not prevent) such loss, will never be known. It was immense. One can get but a glimpse of that enormity by figures produced in 1916 when a small group of very momentarily obstreperous Montana legislators produced a tax study. This is what they found:

Gross Proceeds, 1916

Mines	$141,500,000
Farming	81,154,190
Livestock	54,187,960
Railroads	60,199,998

Percentage of Taxes Paid, 1916

Mines	8.79%
Farming	32.14%
Livestock	10.73%
Railroads	17.99%
Others	30.35%

A reform-minded governor (and how he got elected is a fascinating story but quite beside the point) produced figures in 1922 demonstrating that all the mines in Montana in that year produced more than twenty million dollars, but on the basis of the net proceeds tax paid exactly $13,559 to the State of Montana.

Coal mines in Montana in 1919 produced 3,000,000 tons with a gross value of $7,757,103, but paid a net proceeds tax of $682. These mines were owned almost entirely by the Northern Pacific Railroad.

Throughout the years following 1924, the sessions of the Montana legislature were usually characterized by a small "cabal" who slipped through the fine political interstices of the Anaconda Company's net and who pursued tax reform with uncommon persistence and zeal. They had some success because the company yielded a little here and there in the face of growing agricultural discontent. It is important to note that that discontent did not come from the ranchers but rather from the farmers. Its origins lay deep in the fury and activism of the Non-Partisan League. The league, while never as powerful as in North Dakota, where it literally took over state government, nevertheless had seventeen thousand members in Montana in 1917 — and they voted en bloc. Essentially this accounts for the "cabal" and for its persistent pursuit of tax reform.

The danger to the Anaconda Company and the cause of its small retreats was that the infection could too rapidly spread. While it had no doubts of the firmness of its alliance with the larger and wealthy ranchers, it could not be sure that the less affluent rancher-farmer would hold to his innate conservatism on this one vital issue. True, the large and wealthy rancher was represented in the legislature far beyond the proportion of his kind in the state. That had always been true. However, being more numerous, rancher-farmers were a necessary underpinning for the coalition.

Anaconda received a bad shock in 1924, when an initiative was presented to the electorate and passed. It provided for a graduated levy on the production of any mine which produced more than $100,000 gross per year. The levy ranged from .25 of 1 percent to 1 percent. This was essentially a license tax and it produced between $300,000 and $400,000 annually for the next decade. In view of the enormous wealth pouring forth from Montana's mines, principally Anaconda, this was hardly a windfall for the financially beleaguered state. But it was at least something.

Montana's new constitution of 1972 changed all the old rules profoundly. The constitution's tax article was as clean as a new pitchfork's tine. It merely stipulated that the tax structure be determined by the legislature. In view of the company's power, how was a Montana constitutional convention called, and how could a streamlined constitution pass? One answer is that it passed by less than two thousand votes. But the real answer lies in a singular fact perhaps best expressed in figures: in 1969 the Anaconda Company had a market value of $1.4 billion; in late 1971 it had a market value of $260 million. Of this disastrous plunge *Forbes Magazine* remarked, "Less well publicized perhaps than the Penn Central and Lockheed disasters, Anaconda Co.'s downfall nevertheless ranks as one of the great horror stories of corporate history."

While it is true that the loss of its Chilean properties to Allende's nationalization was a rough body blow, Anaconda's fall was by no means attributable to that fact alone. *Forbes* attributed it largely to a nineteenth-century operation in the profoundly changed era of the latter part of the twentieth century and chronicled its complacent but egregious blunders. In the end, said *Forbes,* it was "so busy accumulating for a rainy day that when the rain began to fall, it first couldn't decide which umbrella to open; and when it did, the umbrella proved full of holes."

So in 1972 Anaconda was not worrying about Montana politics. It was desperately trying to avoid bankruptcy. While its giant competitor, Kennecott Copper, was plunging into the western coal business with a vengeance, Anaconda was trying to stave off its creditors. For that, many Montanans were profoundly grateful. Yet it led to some peculiar consequences in the area of taxation, as we shall see.

One of the consequences of the new constitution was that it posed some inevitable problems for the newly constituted legislature, which now met annually rather than biennially. There were innumerable hoary statutes to abolish. There were many more to be passed in implementation of the new document. Two of the leftover statutes were the 1907 and 1921 net proceeds tax, which was now applicable to coal and which was dear to the hearts of the coal companies. And why not? The deficiencies in the tax which Louis Levine pointed out in 1919 were still there in 1972. The state was no more able to examine company books than it had been in 1919; gross production and operating costs were as manipulable in 1972 as they were in 1919; the tax was an administrative nightmare. The push to revise the taxation of coal began in 1969. It carried through the session of 1974 — and failed narrowly. But the 1975 legislature was another matter.

Not only was revenue a matter of concern for a state with a narrow tax base, the whole question of taxation had by now become a matter of *control*. And the 1975 legislature was far more interested in the latter than in the former. Of the 770,000 to 800,000 acres in Montana (or 1,250 square miles) under which the coal lies, subsurface ownership is fractured. The federal government owns some 55 percent, the Northern Cheyenne and the Crow about 30 percent, and state and private interests split the ownership of only about 15 percent. And it is fairly axiomatic that what one does not own one cannot control.

Among the environmentalists, a substantial number of whom work for various state conservation or natural resources agencies, there is an almost pervasive dubiety concerning federal policies. While it is true that the Bureau of Land Management placed a moratorium on the leasing of federal coal in 1971, environmentalists profoundly mistrust the Department of the Interior. Interior, in any event, announced in 1973 that the department could proceed "cautiously on a case by case basis."

The state's case for the ownership and control of water is, in their opinion, not one which can be relied upon. Recent second thoughts by the Bureau of Reclamation do not alter the environmentalists' belief that the ultimate power lies with the federal government, which in the name of the energy crisis is capable of reversing field at any time.

While they believe that the state's new Clean Air Act, the Utility Siting Act, and the Strip Mining and Reclamation Act do indeed give the state some significant powers, the environmentalists do not have faith that these powers can prevent stripping. It is possible, for instance, to prevent mine-mouth electrical generation and the construction of high-voltage transmission lines. Yet there are straws in the wind to indicate that Colstrip's four plants (totaling 2,100 megawatts) cannot be stopped — at least not the first two of 350 megawatts each.

It may be possible to place obstacles in the way of the coal companies (via the three statutes mentioned above) and that the result would be very selective stripping. But no one is sure that the Montana statutes will continually be implemented in such a way as to bring this about.

The federal government, however, does not have the right to institute, alter or prevent the state from *taxing* as it wishes. In this one area the state can act and its act will stick.

Since these environmentalists are politically as well as environmentally sophisticated and knowledgeable, they did not have in mind any tax which would, in fact, be confiscatory. Their "fall back" position did not include the use of taxation for the purposes of preventing strip mining. That would be politically inane. Their interest in a different kind of coal tax lay solely in the proposition that *all* costs to the State of Montana, direct, indirect and hidden, should be covered by coal taxation. Here again, Montanans are much more sensitive to this issue than other states because of the long history of mining tax law that forced state and local government to bear enormous costs that should properly have been borne by the mining industry.

Costly impact does not necessarily diminish as profits diminish. For instance, the Anaconda Company paid *no* net proceeds tax to Silver Bow County (Butte) for the years 1962, 1963, 1967, 1968 and 1971. But community services had to continue, and this meant a startling rise in the mill levy for the average taxpayer. In 1972, thus, Silver Bow County's mill levy (on property) increased 29 percent for the average homeowner. One may sympathize with Anaconda's plight, but there is a difference between sympathy and subsidy. It is precisely this net proceeds subsidy which knowledgeable Montanans sought to alter in the taxation of coal.

Coal companies did pay Montana taxes in addition to the tax on net proceeds. They pay (and paid) a license tax based on the BTU rating of the coal extracted; they paid and pay a new (1973) Resource Indemnity Trust Account Tax, which consists of .5 percent of the gross value of the extracted coal; they pay a Corporation License Tax, as does any other corporation doing business in Montana; and they pay the regular property tax.

Ironically, since the net proceeds tax was remitted to the county where the corporation did business, its abolition was fought by some county commissioners (among others) on the grounds that they would lose vital income. Since the tax was no longer mandated in the constitution, a good many county officials were nervous. Yet environmentalists who have been so critical of the net proceeds tax had never suggested its abolition except with the substitution of a tax which would be greater in amount and more stable in nature, namely, a percentage of *value* severance tax.

Clearly, the counties involved would benefit greatly from such a tax based on mine production and the dollar per ton *value* of the coal, because it would provide a much more consistent and inevitably rising revenue base.

Many of the people from the counties where coal mining is under way, or projected, did not understand the inherent "gimmicks" in the net proceeds tax. One "gimmick" has been operating since 1907, and one might assume that a glance at copper statistics would convince the most ardent skeptic. Net proceeds are whatever the companies say they are — and usually "operating" expenses come very close to gross profits — so there is a much diminished if not entirely absent net proceed.

More than that, the tax was peculiarly regressive. If one glances at the total income from the net proceeds tax in Montana (coal) for the years 1968 to 1974, one observes that there is an inverse relationship between production and net proceeds income. That is, as production increases, net proceeds decrease. Of course, they do, because to increase production one must spend more on machinery, labor, and all other operating and sales costs, *all* of which are deductible from the gross to arrive at the net. This meant that at the very time the social and economic impacts on any given community were rising the most rapidly due to increased production, the alleviatory tax income *decreased*. This was "gimmick" number two.

For instance, Western Energy, the coal subsidiary of the Montana Power Company, produced 521,499 tons of coal in 1969 and paid a net proceeds tax of .82 cents per ton. When production jumped dramatically in ˙1970 to 1,657,737 tons, net proceeds dropped to .71 cents per ton. In the next three years, with a production jump to 5,160,000, 5,500,000, and 4,250,000 tons, the net proceeds in cents per ton were 71, 59, and 38.

One might ask, If production *fell* by more than 1,000,000 tons between 1972 and 1973, why did net proceeds drop from 59 cents to 38 cents? In theory, if production decreases, net proceeds increase. Strangely enough, it never seems to work that way.

The coal companies, of course, insisted that this would level out at that point where production levels out and hence production costs level out. Figures do not indicate that to have been the case, but even if it were, that left "gimmick" number one intact. If history be any gauge at all, eighty-five years of experience should have long since convinced Montanans that there was no way around the "gimmicks" of the net proceeds tax.

The simple, demonstrable, and irrefutable fact was that under Montana's net proceeds taxation system heavy subsidies were being paid to the coal companies by the taxpayers — and the root of the problem was the reliance on the net proceeds tax.

In Wyoming the situation was and is worse. All taxes on coal in Montana for 1971 came to 8.35 percent on the value per ton; Wyoming's percentage was 6.30.

The coal companies attribute the brisker rate of coal development in Wyoming to the higher taxes in Montana. The fact is that

Wyoming's regulations on mining are far less stringent than Montana's and the state administration is friendly to coal development in Wyoming, while hostile in Montana (see Chapter 5). Montana's reclamation law, for instance, is much tougher than Wyoming's. In meeting the standards of Montana's law, the Decker Coal Company estimates its cost of reclamation at $2,380 per acre; Peabody, at $6,500 per acre; Westmoreland, at $2,500 per acre; and Knife River Coal Company, at $1,035 per acre. While the companies announced these figures with the implication that these reclamation costs were a heavy burden indeed, they failed to point out that *all* reclamation costs were deductible as operating costs under the net proceeds tax. Thus, again, the taxpayer heavily subsidized all reclamation costs. Since the Montana Board of Natural Resources estimates actual reclamation costs at $700 per acre, some Montanans quite naturally suspect that coal company figures ranging from $1,000 to $6,500 were simply rigged to take advantage of the net proceeds deductibility clause.

Montanans are proud of their strict reclamation statute — and well they might be. But very few Montanans knew that they and not the coal companies were paying for it. Good environmental impact statements, for instance, are very expensive. The coal and energy companies were usually delighted to make their own impact statements for presentation to the state. While they may, indeed, have hired an "independent" firm to do it, the results were rarely either thorough or accurate. States should clearly make their own studies and impact statements, and the companies involved should pay for them.

The question of coal taxation reform in Montana posed some severe problems for the environmentalists. The Anaconda Company, having no investments in the coal industry, had thus far remained aloof from the political infighting. Diminished though its power may be, that power is still far from negligible. The company has made a remarkable recovery since its young president,

John B. M. Place, took over from the old guard. Nothing could have brought the Anaconda Company into the arena faster than a proposal to alter the net proceeds tax on copper. As a matter of sheer practicality, therefore, the environmentalists sought to confine their reform to coal taxation only. But there was great pressure from the more idealistic and less pragmatic environmentalists to include copper. This would have materially reduced the chances of reform in the 1975 session of the legislature.

The second problem was that of convincing county commissioners in the stripping area, particularly in those counties which have not as yet felt the pressures, that the net proceeds tax was a bad one.

Last, *any* tax reform would be fought by the companies which could and did employ great amounts of money as well as complete unanimity. Their argument was that while taxes, as well as all costs, are passed on to the consumer, buyer resistance has already manifested itself. Indeed, Montana Power's Western Energy chief, Paul Schmekle, asserted that the company could not sell the coal it now has. This argument actually involved the question of whether coal prices would remain stable, increase or decrease. No one, they agreed, knew the answer to that. And, indeed, no one does. But the coal companies could not have it both ways; if the need for western coal is as great and urgent as the companies insist that it is, the buyers of coal will pay a price commensurate with that need. If the need escalates, so will the price. If the need is not destined to escalate, why, then, are some of the country's largest corporations swarming like vultures over the Northern Great Plains?

There are, moreover, various indications that the price of coal is far too low. In April 1974, a meeting was called by Governor Archibald Moore of West Virginia. Of the twenty-six coal-producing states, seventeen sent official representatives. These states produce almost 95 percent of America's coal. It was the consensus of those present that all the coal-mining states seemed unaware of the true value of their energy resources and were not conceiving tax structures commensurate with the inevitable rise in the price of coal.

When the 1975 legislature convened, few prognosticators foresaw much chance for the passage of a tax on the dollar value of the coal mined. This was a gross underestimation of a new, obstreperous, fractious legislature filled with men and women who were not only angry but well informed and young. Not only did they resist massive industrial pressure, they passed a percentage of value tax which shocked the oddsmakers. The new tax provides for a *30 percent levy on the dollar value of all Montana coal sold.* This makes the taxation of coal in Montana today the highest in the United States. To the shocked industry which responded with a barrage of assertions that this tax would drive all the coal companies from the state, Senator Thomas Towe, one of the prime movers of the bill, replied: "If that is the case, so be it. But we do not think that this is the case. The coal is here. You want it badly. If you want it badly enough, however, you are going to have to get used to the idea that you must pay all the costs of your operations, direct and indirect. This is neither a punitive nor confiscatory tax. It is merely realistic. Montanans are through subsidizing the mining industry. Now you must pay your way or you cannot mine."

Moreover, the tax income is split into several categories, including 10 percent for education. Further, this highly environmentally oriented legislature rammed through a bill providing for a referendum to be presented to the people calling for 50 percent of all coal revenues to be placed in an irrevocable trust fund from which only the interest could be spent — and spent in such fashion as future legislatures may determine.

Senator Miles Romney, author of the bill, remarked: "If we're going to be mined, we can't get hooked on this revenue which, this year alone — a year which will later be seen probably as a year of low production — would have produced forty-six million dollars.

We can't get hooked on coal like we did on copper. So we're going to put half the income in a perpetual trust fund and let it build there. If we're mined out in thirty years, we are still going to have something to show for it."

A widely grinning member of the staff of the Board of Natural Resources remarked: "No, the companies won't leave Montana. But with the highest tax in the United States, we've sure as hell slowed them down. They'll be damn selective now and very careful. That's what we wanted and that's what we got. So let's face it. We couldn't count on the Feds. They could undo our tough laws on our environment at any time. But they can't touch our tax law, they just can't touch it."

The environmentalists who had worked for this one bill so hard and knowledgeably were happy but not jubilant. Let Kit Muller, director of the Northern Plains Resource Council, express it: "Let's put it this way. It is progress, real, solid progress. But we have a long way to go. This is no time to relax and we're not relaxing. Yes, the tax helps, and it indicates great strength both in the legislature and among environmental groups. But what does it mean directly to the ranchers out there? Yes, it will *help* the towns and the ranchers. But will it save them?"

The answer is obviously no. It is a battle won, perhaps a crucial one. But the intensity of the war is undiminished.

In point of fact, the people in the towns are not terribly excited about it. One rancher on Sarpy Creek said to me: "What's changed? Not my land, not my water, not the threat to them. Revenue? Okay. But how about my land, my water and my town? It looks about the same to me."

In essence, he is right. And the people in the towns are right not to be jubilant. The towns. What are they and why?

What they have in common is smallness, a tradition which goes back to cattle (or in fewer instances to the Homestead Era) and a common reason for being where they are. They sprang up along the railroad; they were born because that was where the water and fertile soil were; or they were simply the product of topography — they were natural trade centers. They also grew up around early forts — witness the number of western towns whose names are preceded by the word "Fort."

These towns are not very often "pretty"; they are characterized by a large number of bars per capita, by a large number of "farm" equipment dealers, by one motion picture theater, a rodeo and fairgrounds and a community hall (do not read civic center). There are always several churches, which in many places are used in lieu of a community hall. Sometimes this purpose is served by the schoolhouse. There is almost always a cattle auction center.

Depending on his dress, an outlander should be somewhat cautious in any bar, especially late on a Saturday night. Fistfights are common. These fights are usually "recreational," which is difficult for the outlander to understand, especially if he becomes a player in that particular aspect of recreation. These fights are looked upon with considerable indulgence by the local constabulary, who rarely intervene if no property damage is involved.

The small-town bar, however, is an institution widely misunderstood by urban people. In *The Cocktail Hour*, Bernard De Voto analyzed the role of the urban "cocktail lounge" and, in effect, sang its praises. No such chronicler has come along for the small-town bar. The real role of the bar is a rather complex one.

It serves as a center of information for the rancher. A great deal of business is done there. It is a place for social intercourse in a relaxed atmosphere. It is a point of contact between the local equipment dealer and other townspeople, the rancher and the banker. It is a weather forecasting station and a political caucus. It is a center for barter and trading.

While bars are primarily male-oriented, husbands often bring their wives, especially on Saturday afternoons. Language is then watched carefully. Unattended women are frowned upon. "Outsiders" are ignored.

That the ranchers in Forsyth, for instance, have almost entirely ceased going to the bars because of the inundation of coal construction workers is a symptom of social disruption of more than passing moment.

Until very recently, serious crime had a very low incidence in the ranch towns, though that is now changing. Young people, under drinking age, are too often without recreational facilities, especially during the winter months. Libraries, if present at all, offer very limited fare. These towns are hot in the summer and cold in the winter and they are surrounded by a great deal of space. It is, nevertheless, common, especially among young people, to drive to the next town to "see what is going on there" — which is often nothing. A dance or celebration in one town will usually attract people from other towns, often fifty or sixty miles distant. Bad weather is seldom a deterrent. Most families have a four-wheel-drive vehicle.

Whatever their shortcomings — and they have many — these towns have remained remarkably stable in social structure, in interpersonal relationships and in all other respects for a very long time. Some of them were abruptly changed by the coming of the Interstate Highway System, but in many instances merchants simply moved closer to a cloverleaf or interchange and things went on pretty much as before. The population remained relatively stable, though outmigration, especially of young people, has caused some shrinkage of recent years.

The stability of these towns, however, is delicately balanced, economically, politically and socially. When one hundred new people move into Billings, Montana, or Casper, Wyoming, they are absorbed without a ripple. But one hundred new people moving into Hardin, Forsyth, Hysham, Lovell or Busby would constitute a wave of dramatic proportions.

In one of the widely read studies of the impact that large-scale coal development would have on Montana, *Coal Development in Eastern Montana: A Situation Report of the Montana Coal*

Task Force, January, 1973, there appeared this statement: "The total instate population increase resulting from coal development might be 300,000 to 400,000 people. One multiproduct complex would employ more than 3,000 people and might create a city as large as 24,000, which is much larger than any present Montana city east of Billings."

This resulted in screams of anguish from myriad environmental groups and in a veritable barrage of .denials from coal companies and the Montana Power Company. And, in fact, one could only arrive at a figure of that magnitude if one were to assume that *all* of the proposed *North Central Power Study*'s plant proposals for Montana came into being and that *all* of the Bureau of Reclamation's proposed dams, reservoirs, pumping installations, and aqueducts were built.

The debate which these figures launched was (and is) without resolution — except for a highly warrantable skepticism that any such enormous influx can take place. But that debate obscured a point of consummate importance to Montana's, North Dakota's and Wyoming's small ranching communities in the coal areas, a point which the coal and energy companies obdurately refuse to recognize. Absolute figures are meaningless because the problem is completely relative. Small towns are simply not equipped to handle one hundred additional residents without massive disruption of a very old and stable pattern.

Let us examine Gillette, Wyoming, first because it is *not* typical. Its pattern was broken by an oil boom in the 1950s and 1960s. There is substantial evidence that its population will triple in the next few years because of the coal boom. Let us examine it from an outsider's point of view first and from an insider's second.

In 1950 there were 2,191 people in Gillette. It was a typical cattle-farm town — stable, solid, balanced. By 1960 its population had jumped to 3,580 and by 1970 to 7,194 as a result of the oil boom. Within four years Gillette is expecting a second influx of 25,000 new residents; the coal boom. How can Gillette absorb it?

At present, 42 percent of Gillette's residents live in house trailers. Of 68 registered trailer parks within the city limits, only one meets federal standards, the only one with paved streets. There are 700 trailers inside the city limits and more are being hauled in daily.

It was Elden V. Kohrs, who previously worked in Gillette as a clinical psychologist, who coined the phrase the "Gillette syndrome," consisting of, as he put it, about equal parts of "alcoholism, accidents, absenteeism, depression, divorce, and delinquency."

The city planner, William A. Hopkins, asserts that the city simply does not have the money to provide roads, paving, sewers, water, or schools. If it could not do so during the oil boom, what now?

In April 1974, James P. Sterba of the *New York Times* visited Gillette and expressed his shock. "It is a raw jumble of rutted streets and sprawling junkyards, red mud and dust, dirty trucks and crowded bars, faded billboards and sagging utility lines, and block after block of house trailers, squatting in the dirt like a nest of giant grubs. . . . Gillette looks and feels as if the whole town is on the wrong side of the tracks."

John S. Gilmore, senior economist at the Denver Research Institute, told a Senate subcommittee hearing recently, "At worst, mobile home squatters form sprawling colonies often lacking water and sanitation. In some cases, families are forced to live in tents, even into the Wyoming winter."

Stephen Tarver, a fifty-one-year-old accountant and lifelong Gillette resident says, "This is starting to look like a good town to be from — a long way from. We've just started recovering from the oil boom, getting enough water and sewers and schools, and now this thing is coming and we don't seem to be any better prepared for it than the last time." Why not?

Well, says Dr. Gilmore, the economist, "too often companies fail to make available to local government planners and decision-makers their planning output — they may even refuse to discuss the intentions and alternatives they have under consideration."

And that makes things difficult, indeed, because the following companies are involved in Gillette: Amax, Peabody Coal Company, Panhandle Eastern Company, Carter Oil Company (Exxon), Atlantic Richfield, Ker-McGee Company, Sun Oil Company, and Mobil Oil Company. Even if you managed to get two or three cooperating with the city, could you get them all? Not so far, at least.

But according to David Mutch, staff correspondent of the *Christian Science Monitor*, who visited Gillette in January 1974, at the least the mayor isn't worried. He is Clifford Davis, who told Mutch, "I raised cattle for forty years and I didn't think I'd ever sell the ranch. But they offered me a cool million for it." The mayor, who is also Speaker of the Wyoming House, isn't worried. "We just put a new line to the sewer plant, the new water plant is only eighteen months old and we are just contracting for more water, we have doubled our school classroom size in five years and developers from Denver and Houston are coming in to build housing developments. In fact, there are so many people in and out of this office I don't know who or what they are anymore."

The state's planning and development department, however, expects Gillette's population to jump six times by 1985 — to 45,000, and they call that a solid figure. It may, indeed, take more than developers from Denver and Houston to handle the problems if they can be handled at all.

There is in Gillette, however, a very positive split in the view held by the "locals," or old-time residents, and the newcomers. The latter, after all, are mobile blue-collar people. If not transients in the pejorative sense, they do not expect to spend their lives there. Much like the residents of the early gold camps, they are constantly poised to move on. They do not involve themselves in community affairs.

As in most boom towns, prices in Gillette are high and the trailer people often feel that the merchants are bilking them. There is a similar sentiment among ranchers in the Gillette area and many of them, who for years traded in the city, are now going to Casper, Rapid City, or Sheridan. With the new influx, businessmen do not have to "cater" to the ranchers and there is every indication that they do not do so. On the other hand, beleaguered merchants cannot expand because of the impossibly high price of land and construction costs and they greatly fear the advent of highly capitalized supermarkets, chain stores and restaurants—all from the "outside." There is almost universal contempt in Gillette for city administrators and their failure to zone or plan.

Gillette is clearly in trouble. The strains and tensions among the ranchers who trade there, the old-time Gillette residents, and the newcomers are obvious even to the cursory observer. To a remarkable degree specific complaints, accusations, and jealousies lead circuitously to a pervasive sense of uncertainty. What will the coal companies do? How fast will they do it? Will state taxes levied on the companies revert to the county or the city and will the money be substantial enough to help? Rumors are rampant, facts are few, and it is in this atmosphere of uncertainty and confusion that myriad resentments flourish. There is little in prospect that will change all this unless the companies provide hard information and projections. Thus far, they have shown no inclination to do so.

The story at Colstrip, Montana, is much the same in terms of results; it is very different in terms of origin. Colstrip was never a cattle or ranch town. It began as a coal town. Because the pressures of strip mining are the most intense there, at present, Colstrip's origins need a brief review.

The Northern Pacific Railroad was a land-grant line and as such was awarded twenty alternate sections, of twenty square miles each (12,800 acres), along each side of its right-of-way. In Montana, the railroad thus acquired roughly 16 percent of the entire state's land area and it also acquired vast quantities of coal. It is ironical that the railroad's policies were so often determined by its land grants — and not always in a salubrious way for the corporation.

While the Southern California Railroad began burning oil in 1894, the Southern Pacific by 1900, and while the Milwaukee had converted a large portion of its main line to electricity by 1915, the Northern Pacific was having nothing but trouble with its coal. It was deep-mining coal in southwestern Montana at Red Lodge and near Bozeman by the late 1880s. It later opened a mine northwest of Billings. This was all deep mining and it was expensive.

The expense, however, was not the root of the problem. Labor troubles were. Especially at Red Lodge, strikes, violence and shutdowns were the rule rather than the exception. The other mines were in no essential respect more stable.* There was a limit to the stockpiling the railroad could manage and it was obvious by the early 1920s that a prolonged strike would simply shut the railroad down.

The company, therefore, began a search for coal in another area where it could begin under new auspices, union-free and, hence, strike-free. The coal also had to be near the main line. That new area proved to be the Rosebud field (Colstrip today), just west of the Tongue River in southeastern Montana.

But there were problems. This coal, though plentiful, lay very close to the surface. The seam which the railroad geologists recommended averaged 28 feet in thickness but it was "water heavy." That it was low in sulfur content did not concern the company, but that it was lower in BTUs worried them considerably. After all, firemen on the locomotives were a touchy bunch and with this coal there was more work for less steam. Would the firemen go along?

The railroad began a careful and cautious "educational program." The new coal was introduced "slowly and tactfully" and the initial results were "quite gratifying." Colstrip was born and

---

* For a good review of the details see William B. Evans and Robert L. Peterson, "Decision at Colstrip," *Pacific Northwest Quarterly*, July 1970.

strip mining proved to be enormously economical. Whereas coal from Red Lodge had been costing from $2.75 to $3 per ton, the coal from the Rosebud field was costing only 65 cents per ton. The company was saving between $700,000 and $1,000,000 a year. These figures were not lost in the records. A few Appalachian coal companies were watching carefully.

As for labor, the company simply contracted the stripping operation out to a firm called Foley Brothers, nonunion. The union was confused. Underground miners had long been tightly organized. They were a highly specialized work force knit together by common bonds of hatred for the coal companies, the constant dangers of working underground, the tradition of awesome tragedies — explosions, cave-ins, "black lung."

But what manner of operation was this one at Colstrip? Simply a glorified excavation project. A few charges of dynamite to break up the overburden, a bunch of mechanical shovels and an enormous electrically run shovel to scoop out the coal. That's mining? So no union moved in.

Colstrip was not a large operation. The railroad was not in the business of selling coal. It mined what it needed. It is ironical, however, that the commitment to Colstrip delayed the Northern Pacific from converting to diesel fuel for many years and hence it was, in the end, more costly than profitable. Throughout these years the impact on the neighboring community was negligible. Colstrip was a sleepy little town and grew sleepier still when the railroad at last converted to diesel fuel in the late 1950s.

In 1959, the Montana Power Company, through its wholly owned subsidiary, the Western Energy Company, took over Colstrip because it anticipated that its future power needs would require coal-fired steam-generating plants. In 1968 the company began shipping coal to its new 180-megawatt plant at Billings.

In that same year, the Peabody Coal Company contracted to provide a Minnesota utility with coal from a nearby mine, the Big

Sky. The coal boom was on when Montana Power announced that it planned to construct two 350-megawatt and two 700-megawatt mine-mouth generating plants at Colstrip and ship the power northward and westward via transmission lines. Montanans woke up to find a 2,100-megawatt complex in their midst. Colstrip awoke from its sleep abruptly.

On a recent television program, George O'Connor, president of the Montana Power Company, called Colstrip "the ideal planned community." It is entirely company-owned. It lies some thirty-five miles south of Forsyth and most people approach it on state "highway" 315, a narrow pitted and scarred route.

It is difficult to say whether the "tourists" (and they are mostly Montanans curious to see the place they are hearing so much about) should be "briefed" or "debriefed" before they visit the ideal planned community. There should be certain redefinitions involved, especially for the fainthearted, because to those uninitiated in the jargon Colstrip gives all the appearances of a disaster area. One's first view of it is the tall stack of plant number 1, nearing completion, from the top of which strobe lights flash so powerfully as to be blinding at midday. The main street, bounded on either side by trailer houses jammed together like sardines, ends at the foot of a huge ashen pile of obscenely nude "spoils." The "yards" of the trailer houses are barren of grass, and there are no trees and no birds sing. There are traces of paving here and there, but there are no curbs. The side "streets" are narrow and pressing in upon them are the trailer houses, block after block, or section after section, window to window, door to door, wall to wall, nose to nose, eye to eye.

There is an overwhelming sense of transiency as if, indeed, like the Arabs, these jammed dwellers would fold up their flimsy structures in the night and quietly rattle away. Only one building stands with any sort of dignity. It is the old red brick schoolhouse, dating back to the quiet birth of this grim place.

One physician serves Colstrip one evening per week. The sign announcing his schedule concludes "Cash Only." There is no dentist in Colstrip.

There is, at the end of one dusty passageway, a company store. Behind the counter sits a fat girl reading a comic book. You want milk, some eggs and some tomatoes. "There ain't none."

"You usually pretty busy, being the only store in town?"

"Nah, people don't buy here, prices are too high. They shop in Forsyth or Miles City." Forsyth is thirty-five miles away; Miles City, eighty.

Look to the north, behind plant number 1 and its flashing strobes. Great towering, naked-gray spoil banks, ridge after ridge after ashen ridge. On the far edge of "town," sitting starkly alone, are several new apartmentlike structures. Just a couple of them. Drive on, let's get out of here. On the way out you glance at a cardboard sign tacked to a stick, and scrawled unevenly on it is this: "You have just seen the future and it doesn't work."

Commuting to Forsyth is routine. There is a theater there and a bowling alley — and there are bars. But schoolchildren can hardly commute. Colstrip's school population was less than 300 in 1973. Projections from the office of the superintendent of schools places it at 1,800 in the near future. Originally, since it owns the town, Montana Power promised Colstrip residents a new school. Now they promise only "temporary classrooms."

Ranchers and farmers near Colstrip find "trespass" more than annoying. They deeply resent the incursions from the rootless community, teenagers chasing calves with motorcycles, gates left open, strangers wandering around near the houses, cars racing through their meadows. As we have seen, these are serious matters to ranchers, not pranks. The problem has some ominous undertones. Western Energy says that it has plans for Colstrip involving tennis courts, a park, a softball field, a community hall, and much new housing. The cost — $10,000,000; the "citizens" ardently hope that the plans mature rapidly.

Forsyth, Montana, is the county seat of Rosebud County in the heart of the strip-mining country. It grew as a division point for the Northern Pacific Railroad, which came through the area in 1882. It was a typical railroad-ranch-homesteader town. It prospered as the cattlemen prospered, suffered when they suffered, prospered with the homesteaders, and suffered near eclipse when the bad times came. It revived and grew slowly. Throughout the good and bad times it developed that delicate balance typical of the plains town — a stability dependent on the area it served, on the toughness and resiliency of the ranchers and farmers and on the intimate interrelationships of its own residents. Forsyth has yet to feel the real impact of coal development, but the impact is beginning.

The mayor of Forsyth today is not worried. He is Gene Tuma, a former teacher and a former reclamation manager for Peabody Coal. He thinks what is now happening is good for the town.

"We've got a new feed store just started, a new Ford dealer, a new machinery shop, new trailer courts. It is an expanding situation. The economic impact is really great. We could handle the coal mining just fine, if we could just handle the state. They keep passing laws up there that cost us a lot of money."

There are some who agree with the mayor. There are a great many who do not. But while the argument goes on, Forsyth has some severe problems and they are likely to get worse. The mayor, in any event, should take a closer look at the laws they keep passing "up there" because one they did pass was a percentage of profit coal tax, part of which would be remitted to Rosebud County to alleviate the skyrocketing cost of social services and government. It may be the only thing that can save Forsyth.

Yet there is a strange mix of sentiment in the town. The old stability has all but vanished, yet the "Gillette syndrome" is not yet present. Forsyth is under pressure but the pressure is not intense yet — and a considerable measure of it comes from Colstrip. Between the old stability and the "Gillette syndrome" one might characterize the feelings of the citizens as confused and uncertain — with some anxiety thrown in.

Anxiety is not too vivid a word for the "old-timers" who remember the homesteader boom and bust. They remember "the last time" and they are filled with a sense of foreboding. They have never had to lock their doors — now they do. They no longer go out walking at night. The *Comparative Case Study* observes, "They perceive that in most bars they now find themselves subjected to ridicule and the object of provoked fights and some bar owners are beginning to forbid the rougher elements from coming into their establishments."

The people of the ranch towns in southeastern Montana, though uneasy and disturbed by the unwanted influx of people with a "foreign" way of life, tend to believe that it will "all work out" or that it will "level off," and, as one long-time resident put it, "we can get back to the way things were." His wife added, "It's that we don't know what's going to happen that makes it hard. Don't give our names but the truth is I'm frightened about the children. The school [Forsyth] is going to hell. Maybe we can make that up at home with the *World Book Encyclopedia*. But there are gangs now. Sure, there were always fights, but never with knives and these gangs. Don't give our names but we're frightened."

The clerk in one of Forsyth's department stores remarked: "Sure, business is great. This is a good town. We could handle things if we only knew what we were going to have to handle. The goddam city administration is deaf, dumb and blind. So's the county. Something is sure as hell going to happen but those asses can't tell us what. That's the whole trouble here. So we lock our doors and wait. That's a hell of a way to live — and don't use my name."

Southeastern Montana townspeople have no precedents to talk about except bad ones: Gillette and the boom in the old homesteader towns. A few of them remember the dam boom towns,

Hungry Horse and Wheeler, which are now moldering little wide places along the road.

There is, in fact, a precedent of sorts, but the document that sets it forth is not available in many libraries. It is *Community Impact Report, U.S. Army Safeguard System Command, Malmstrom Deployment Area,* U.S. Army Corps of Engineers, 1970. It is a lengthy, detailed study of the anticipated impact on ten north-central Montana towns which the construction of the Safeguard antiballistic missile facilities was to produce. In the construction phase, the project involved the employment of "several thousand persons." In the "operative" phase, it was to involve very few persons. But the army was clearly concerned about the impact on the small cattle towns in the area. And, wrote the commanding general of the Safeguard system, "It is the purpose of this report to inform Government Officials and community leaders at all levels, of the anticipated community impacts which may result from the Safeguard program, and to provide them with potential sources of assistance and courses of action for alleviating these impacts."

The report is a model study of depth and detail. In each of the communities involved a study was made of schools, sanitation facilities, medical facilities, roads, churches, public utilities, recreational facilities, law enforcement capabilities, housing, and dozens of other considerations. From the beginning local public officials and civic groups were kept posted on all facets of the program.

It was, in effect, not only a massive inventory, it was a plan which included a listing of all federal agencies to which applications for financial aid should be addressed, with instructions as to how these agencies were involved, under what title, and what local factors constituted eligibility.

While, for instance, the report found existing hospital facilities "capable of supporting the total peak projected population increases," it also found "a severe and critical shortage of physicians and outpatient facilities" and made specific recommendations as to what was needed and where and through what federal agencies aid could be obtained. It averaged out increased enrollment costs for schools, as an example, at a total of $3,640,000 annually for the period 1970 to 1976, and set forth in detail what departments of HEW were involved, how to apply for aid, when to apply, and what statistics to include.

Nothing so characterized this plan as constant, candid and specific information provided to all levels of state and local government and, probably more important, constant liaison with business, church and social groups.

The ABM boom never developed due to a tradeoff in the SALT talks with the Russians — which is doubtless one of the reasons the existence of this study is little known. Still, before it was known that the impact would not occur, the towns and communities involved were quietly gearing up; there was no disruption, people were well informed and calm — and the vast majority were pleased. They knew exactly what was going to happen, how and when. They also knew what to do about it. There was a singular lack of tension or discontent. The study was probably less costly than the some dozen groping studies made by the State of Montana subsequently on the issue of strip-mining impact.

The difference lies in the fact that all plans and projections were provided in the case of the ABM and literally *none* have been provided by the coal companies. To say that coal companies do not have plans and projections which are at least as specific as the army's is absurd. To say that they have not provided even basic information to state and local governments and civic groups — or, worse, that they have provided false, partial and misleading information — is a commentary on extraordinary arrogance and callousness.

There was, indeed, conflict in Montana as to whether ABM sites should be located in the state. But that is beside the point here. That was a separate argument — and once the determination had been made, the people were in no sense misinformed or ill-informed. That made all the difference. It is also important to remember that this ABM impact involved only 3,000 people coming into an area with facilities in a fifty-mile radius. The impact of coal strip mining and related activities is obviously vastly greater.

The coal and energy companies have an excuse — or rather two answers — for their reticence. The first is that they cannot give out facts and figures because they are involved in highly competitive enterprises and cannot give their competitors an advantage. The second is that environmentalists have delayed or prevented the construction of energy-producing facilities to a dangerous extent for the welfare of America and in the interests of the health of the American economy they are not going to provide these "eagle freaks" with information that will then be distorted and used against themselves and to the detriment of the country.

Let us consider the second argument first. Utilities *are* behind schedule — as, for instance, were oil refinery facilities when the Arabs shut off the oil and the refining industry was forced by the government to provide it with hard figures. But the reasons for dwindling refining capacity in the United States had little to do with environmentalists. It had to do with the fact that limited refining kept the price of gasoline up and, moreover, refineries were much cheaper to build and operate outside the United States.

As for utilities, government surveys covering the period between 1966 and 1968 and involving fifty-five plants which were behind schedule only demonstrated that *four* delays could be attributed to the resistance of environmentalists. While a more recent study covering the period 1966 to 1970 indicated that 7 percent of the delays involved resistance of environmentalists, this is still minuscule. Then why are the utility companies behind schedule? The head of the Federal Power Commission in 1971 asserted that it was due to technological inadequacy.

Since the demand for power began skyrocketing (and because the demand was great, so was the profit), utilities have used antiquated equipment which has been "scaled up" with quickly designed "innovations" to make quick profit from the demand. Their research and testing have been inadequate, resulting in breakdowns and delays. Technological errors have been numerous and this compounds the delays. The environmentalists are usually merely convenient scapegoats.

As for giving one's "competitors" an advantage if plans are released, one might assert that competition and hence free enterprise are ill-served if the result of secrecy is damage to the public welfare. Government may ultimately have no choice but to demand full revelation. Utilities and energy companies might bear in mind that if such full revelation were required by federal law, considerable danger exists that wholesale violations of federal antitrust acts would emerge as a consequence. Fewer and fewer Americans are convinced that the oil, coal, and energy companies are in any real sense competitive and less and less frequently are they misled by contrived arguments to the contrary. It may be a long way from Gillette and Forsyth to Washington and Congress. Still, it is a shrinking world. Maybe the distance will ultimately prove shorter than the great companies think. It might be wiser to cooperate with the people in the "boondocks" than to deal with the antitrust division of the Department of Justice.

Perhaps only the fact that Montana, Wyoming and North Dakota are such huge states can explain why Montanans hear and know so little about a town in southern Wyoming, Rock Springs. But if the residents of Forsyth, Hardin, Decker, Birney, and Ashland have heard of the "Gillette syndrome," it would be well if they had also heard of the "Rock Springs disaster area." Rock Springs is only a few miles from the Utah border. It is a town probably gone beyond restoration.

While it was a prime source of coal for the Union Pacific Railroad, it was, like Colstrip, essentially a sleepy little town with an old, stable balance. That ended swiftly. In 1971 Rock Springs had a population of about 11,000; today its population is 26,000. In 1970 the Bechtel Power Corporation started construction of the Jim Bridger power plant some thirty miles away — a gigantic 2,000-megawatt, coal-fired plant. As at Colstrip, Pacific Power and Light and others were involved. Three thousand workers poured in. As a preliminary comment, the worker turnover as of today is 60 to 80 percent per year. The wages are very high. But Rock Springs is hell to live in or near. It is barren, windswept, hot, dusty, and in winter bitterly cold.

The problem is not confined to Rock Springs itself. Sweetwater County had a population of 18,391 in 1970. In four years that jumped to 45,000. Not only was there coal in Sweetwater County, there was also soda ash and oil and oil shale. The county has the third highest per capita suicide rate in the United States.

Rock Springs has only six primary-care physicians and there is only one hospital in the county, built in 1893. Sixteen thousand patients passed through its emergency room last year. If trailers are ubiquitous, so are tents, because trailer space, if it can be obtained, costs $90 a month, at least if the worker wants a water line, electricity, or a sewer connection. Roughly half of the entire county population lives in trailers. Those who live in tents have worse problems. In 1973 on January 2, the temperature stood at 32 degrees below zero and it stayed at 20 degrees below for the next three weeks.

Because so much of the surrounding area has been scraped away for trailer camps and roads as a consequence of stripping, Rock Springs, which is on a windy plateau at 6,000 feet, endures almost daily dust storms — and the dust permeates not only trailers, tents, and buildings, it granulates food and turns the limited water supply a dirty brown.

Jack Jones is a seventy-year-old state legislator and manager of the town's Chamber of Commerce. He said, "You look around and you think, why the hell, there's land in every direction." The problem, he said, is that the price put on the usable land by the

Union Pacific and the Bureau of Land Management is so absurdly
high, no one can buy any land to build on and "people are predict-
ing we're going to double our population again in four years. You
can't keep up with it."

One of the six beleaguered doctors, Dr. Donald J. Rohrssen, remarked, "We're overwhelmed, and most of the physicians are no
longer accepting patients." He added, "When suicide is attempted
here, it is a very real thing. It is usually a high-caliber gun in the
mouth. The attention-getting Hollywood variety of suicide is very
uncommon here."

While a *New York Times* reporter, James P. Sterba, did a fine
short piece on Rock Springs on July 7, 1974, one has to go there
to believe it. It is so infinitely ugly, brown, barren, jumbled and
dirty that one can only wonder that worker turnover is only between 60 and 80 percent. And again, there is *no* indication that the
industries creating this hellhole, while busily ripping up as much
land as fast as they can, have any concerns or interests in the human beings they employ. But it will get worse, much worse, because the gigantic Jim Bridger plant has yet to spew its poisons
across the land. That lies in Rock Springs' near future — and in the
future of the land and people for miles and miles around. It is not
merely that one's sense of esthetics is shocked; it is that such places
are as dehumanizing as the worst ghetto in any city.

To the nervously waiting people in all the towns and country-
sides where the impact is just beginning and where, as in Forsyth,
a kind of illusory optimism of the "we can handle it" type is
frequently expressed, one can only hope that for their own peace
of mind these people do not visit Gillette or Rock Springs — places
for which it is very likely too late to change the direction of
things.

The ranchers and the towns were once essentially inseparable.
The process of separation is now well under way. So what of the
rancher?

Bill Gillan is a rancher from the Forsyth area. He is a member of the Northern Plains Resource Council, a ranchers' environmental group, and had been asked to attend a hearing in Billings by the subcommittee on Fossil Fuels Taxation on July 19, 1974. He got in his car and headed for Billings in the 100-degree heat.

When he got to the meeting room on the campus of Eastern Montana College he found himself in strange company. About the only friendly faces he could see in the room were those of Mrs. Boyd Charter, a rancher's wife from the Bull Mountain area, and Kit Muller, both representatives of the Northern Plains Resource Council. When he ran his eye down over the list of testifiers he felt uncomfortable.

Robert Corette — Montana Power; Western Energy Company
C. Eugene Phillips — Pacific Power and Light and Decker Coal Company
Patrick Hooks — Montana Coal Council and Westmoreland Coal Company
Tom Gwynn — Knife River Coal Company
Dale Slotten — Montana-Dakota Utilities
Jack Rehberg — Montana Petroleum Association

And with these gentlemen there were a battery of attorneys and experts. The subcommittee, with a staff of two young assistants, sat down in front, and Bill Gillan could tell nothing from that set of inscrutable faces.

He felt a little relieved when the relaxed and obviously informed lieutenant governor, Bill Christiansen, started the meeting off with a half-hour presentation boldly but courteously telling the companies that the "net proceeds" tax, one of the basic taxes under which Montana was then operating, was a bad tax, manipulatable, almost impossible to administer, and in any and all events insufficient. What Christiansen wanted (and the lieutenant governor is Montana's "energy tsar" and head of the Montana Energy Advisory Council) was a "percentage of retail value" tax.

"We all know," he said, "and you gentlemen know it as well as I do, that a net proceeds tax simply means that you subtract *all* of your operating costs from your gross proceeds and you give us that figure and that's what we tax you on. And we'd have to have a hundred auditors to find out if the figures were reliable."

Christiansen ran through various complex alternatives but obviously supported a tax on the *value* of the coal rather than on the unit of production (a flat rate per ton). And he said that obviously the cost of coal was going to rise — it was a seller's market — and that, in any event, such a tax would quite properly be passed on to the consumer as a cost of doing business.

Then, one after the other, the coal spokesmen rose and, referring to complex charts and graphs, asserted that they were, in fact, paying exorbitantly now, that the price of coal was not going to rise, that they could not sell the coal they already had, that inflation was devastating to them, and so on far into the afternoon.

Bill Gillan's hand kept shooting up but it was two o'clock before anyone recognized him. He came down to the lectern looking uncomfortable and out of place. He did not know, he said, about all those words like ad valorem, severance, net proceeds. But he did know his taxes last year went up almost $600 because the county was being impacted with new people because of coal. He said the roads were so bad you couldn't keep an axle on a car for more than six months. Big trucks were doing the damage, coal equipment. Then he said, "I have no charts or even any notes. What I really want to tell you about is my daughter. Over our way we put a lot of stock in education. Well, our school is producing illiterates. In the fourth grade my daughter had eight teachers last year. They never even learned her name. One of her friends has a real talent for Spanish. Well, she got four months of Spanish before that teacher left and then they switched her into English and the teacher didn't know as much about English as that Spanish teacher knew about Spanish."

Gillan turned to face the subcommittee. "You fellas keep talking about the future. What you got to understand is that it's already here. No, it isn't in Billings yet. But it's in our small towns in the coal areas; it's on our ranches. And you can't pull it back. The damage done to my daughter is being done *now*, not tomorrow. Our county can't pay these bills no matter what mill levy they put on us."

He paused and rubbed his hand across short, iron-gray hair. His face was a study in frustration. He waved his arm, encompassing the battery of lawyers and tax experts, and then turned back to the committee.

"I listened to these fellas about how hard they have it. I listened but I don't believe it. Maybe where we live and where they live we got a different definition of what's hard. What's hard is this: we're turning out kids in 1974 that can't read or write or figure and don't know there's even a world beyond the road home and what they call the road to what they call the school. You've got to understand that it's happening now — and you can never pull it back. It's gone forever. We got to have help and fast, and it seems like these coal companies ought to pitch in with some taxes." And he looked hard at the audience and climbed back up to the rear of the auditorium.

Mrs. Boyd Charter, one of the founders of the Bull Mountain Landowners' Association, a group of ranchers north of Billings fighting the coal companies, never did get to testify that day. All she really got for her trip was to lean over to Bill Gillan and say, "All you got to understand is that they are deaf and blind. The pity of it is they aren't also dumb. Just deaf and blind."

Kit Muller of the Northern Plains Resource Council, pervasively informed, urbane and articulate, made no impassioned plea. He just talked about the fierce impact on the coal counties, the skyrocketing costs, the rising crime rate, the breakdown in social comity. And he said he thought the coal and power companies ought to face up to minimum social obligations. Muller had testified too often on too many coal-related impact issues to believe that there would be any conversions in that room that day. He did slip a few copies of a memorandum around. It concerned the government's "Project Independence" and it was from Frederick B. Dent, Secretary of Commerce, to the secretaries of Defense, Interior, Transportation, Labor, State, and the Attorney General.

In the memo Secretary Dent suggested that the federal government reduce private sector entry risk by guaranteeing a market for a specified volume of production for the synthetic fuels industry. He proposed a subsidy of $98.112 billion over the fourteen-year life of the project. This, of course, is the conversion of raw coal and oil shale into fuels. The program, the memorandum says, "presents formidable ecological problems as to shale and coal but they appear solvable." Mr. Gillan shook his head. He wondered, he said, if any of that $98.112 billion would ever get to his daughter's school. He didn't guess it would.

Mr. Gillan did not understand the coal people. They did not understand him. Neither "side" will ever understand the other. The *Comparative Study** makes this generalized statement:

> The majority of ranchers in southeastern Montana interviewed to date are against all-out coal and energy development and would really like to see the coal people go away forever. As a group, these are mostly younger men who have inherited and are upholding a family tradition of cattle raising. They are traditionalists. Although many of these informants run very large and profitable ranching operations, others have smaller spreads and are doing less well economically. While limiting development to strip mining [as opposed to the construction of mine-mouth generating plants] might be tolerable, they and their hired hands, think the whole business is wrong.

There is no quantification in the *Comparative Study*, but one would be hard put to argue against it. Indeed, the exceptions are

* *A Comparative Case Study of the Impact of Coal Development on the Way of Life of People in the Coal Areas of Eastern Montana and North Eastern Wyoming*, Institute of Social Science Research, University of Montana, prepared for Northern Great Plains Resources Program, June 30, 1974.

so few and far between as to be difficult to locate for testimony.

One of them is Burton C. Brewster, owner of the Quarter Circle U Ranch Company near Birney. Brewster says that the average native rangeland in southeastern Montana requires three acres to run one cow for one month, "so it takes 36 acres to run one cow for a year." But, says Brewster, "An acre-foot of coal weighs 1,750 pounds. A 20-foot seam of coal under one acre weighs 35,000 pounds. The 36 acres to run a cow will produce 1,260,000 tons of coal."

Brewster points out that at a 20-cent-a-ton royalty this will produce $252,000. Brewster's argument does not stop there, however. "I will be surprised if 10 percent of our land is mined; that will leave 90 percent for the cattle. With the money generated by this 10 percent of mined land, I am sure my grandchildren can make a better ranch of this than I have known. . . ." Nor is Brewster a newcomer. His father located there in 1882 and Brewster has lived there for seventy-one years.

There is nothing wrong with Brewster's figures, and he has obvious faith that strip mining can be "controlled." He parts company with the vast majority of ranchers, however, over the word "controlled" and his analogy is one they will not buy. They have watched the huge machines at work and they know how quickly they can chew up 36 acres. One of his neighbors snorted, "What Brewster wants is to eat his cake twice and keep it, too. He'll end up with all the money he could spend in a thousand years but he won't end up with no ranch and he won't end up with no cows. As for his grandchildren, that pile of money will do one thing, it'll wreck their lives."

Others, but only a few, take Brewster's side but put their faith in reclamation. The same neighbor snorts again, "They know better. It's just money. You can't have lived on this land for more than ten years without knowing that reclamation is a pipe dream."

Brewster's view is also attacked by the anticoal majority for what one nearby rancher called "the shallow-well thoughts behind it." He remarked, "Them rich grandchildren can go to a New York school. They'll have to, because there won't be a school worth goin' to here, nor a town a feller'd want to buy his goods in. You can't mix an industrial town and a ranch town and come up with nothin' but the end of the ranch town."

In fact, the general conflict between the pro- and antidevelopers goes deeper than that. Over the long years the rancher has evolved an ethic, a modus operandi entirely foreign to coal company officials. There are taboos involved which may seem anachronistic and may, indeed, be so. But they have origins deep in the history of the cattle industry.

The three initial "don'ts" are almost universally honored. Don't ask a man how many acres he owns or leases; don't ask a man how many cattle he runs; don't ask a man how much he sold his cattle for. Information of this kind, of course, is readily available at the courthouse, or at any number of other places, including a few visits to the auction. But the questions are never asked and the information never proffered.

This ritual, however, is merely the manifestation of a whole complex of rituals, all rooted in history and *not*, as some academics would have it, in myth. In the frontier West one asked an absolute minimum number of questions of anyone. The reason was simple. A healthy percentage of the people who came west had rather cogent reasons for doing so. One of the very basic ones was a serious need for anonymity.

In fairly recent years, the social structure in ranch country has begun to break down. But the remnants are still there and in some respects rather powerfully so. Neighbors were often separated by great distances, but, since the problems they faced were common, blizzards, droughts, rustlers, etc., they went to extraordinary lengths to help each other and stand together. This was, of course, simple pragmatism in the earlier period. It became traditional. To whatever extent the fast automobile, Interstate highways, television, and mobility have weakened and sometimes fractured this tradition, it is a gross mistake to assume that it is gone – and one of the most dangerous approaches to anyone in ranch country is to place oneself between neighbor and neighbor. Nothing more characterizes the approach of the coal and power companies to ranch and rural landowners than precisely that posture. East and now west (because of transmission lines), the ubiquity of this angry complaint testifies to the near universality of industry's blunders in this critical procedure.

For instance, almost without exception the ploy used by power company officials in negotiating for rights-of-way for transmission lines has been to inform A that his neighbor B has already signed the agreement and accepted the offer. The identical technique has been used in endeavoring to negotiate leases in ranch country. What the "leasehounds" and company officials cannot seem to understand is that that is a gross violation of a very old ranch and rural tradition. You do nothing to break the intricate web of what holds remote peoples together. Historically, that web has meant the difference between life and death. That may, indeed, no longer be literally true. It is, clearly, a weakened tradition, but it is speedily reviving. Groups of citizens have spontaneously formed all over the state and nothing so characterizes their meetings as the recounting of how each was approached and lied to or abused.

In the *Comparative Case Study* this is borne out again and again, though the "informants" are never named: "Mining companies make fools of us. They always lie about what they're intending to do and how much of it they intend to do. They are sneaky, deceptive and so on. They get you to sign easements through lying and then it's too late to get a fair deal."

The *Comparative Case Study* goes on to chronicle the use of bluff, coercion, and intimidation. This is salt in the wound because deception of this kind not only threatens the web of tradition, it violates still another old verity. This one, too, had utterly pragmatic roots and has suffered much diminution in recent years. But it is still there.

Because it was short of many things, the West was short of law enforcement people and facilities and shorter still of judicial structures based on precedential legal procedures. It therefore developed its own systems which, while often summary, were imperative.

Contracts were rare and "fine print" nonexistent. There was no time for that, nor was there any viable body of law which required it. Accordingly, trust was the essence of all agreements. It was not that the rancher was more inherently honest or dishonest than anybody else. It was simply that the whole structure of doing business would collapse if a word was not as good as a bond. The man who lacked credibility lacked the one basic ingredient without which the system could not operate. He was, therefore, ostracized. This was not a moral matter, it was a matter of simple necessity. You did what you said you would do and did not do what you said you would not do because otherwise you could not operate. It is quite true that this concept has also undergone fierce attrition in recent years. But no one who knows the rancher and his business today could be naïve enough to assert that it is gone.

However, corporations do *not* operate that way. They are contract and fine-print institutions. They are subtle and skilled negotiators who will leave no word in a document that has a nuance. They have layered fall-back-and-advance position papers. All this is utterly foreign to the tradition of the rancher.

There is yet another ritual the rancher observes and it, like all the others, has deep and pragmatic roots. Before changes in federal law marked the demise of the open range concept of "customary usage" on the public domain, ranchers had, again, to devise their own system or suffer irreparable loss. Mutually, therefore, they agreed upon whose range was where. They could not afford "range wars," though a few occurred. Such conflict was very much the exception and not the rule.

When the law and circumstance forced them into "deeded land" marked off by fences, they carried with them a very strong concept of "trespass." Well into the twentieth century, this concept was sharpened by rampant cattle rustling. This was a problem rarely understood by urban Americans, who had difficulty in comprehending why a man who drove off a few cattle from another man's herd was hanged forthwith. The sense of "trespass" is still very much a part of the rancher's view of things, especially when one is dealing with thousands of cattle and forty or fifty thousand acres.

Yet, again, almost ubiquitously, the companies will send a survey crew onto a rancher's land without asking for permission. The theory is simply that if they get caught, they will leave. But the chances are fair enough that they will first get a lot of work done or, indeed, that they will not get caught at all. It is for them, in any event, no big thing.

But it *is* a big thing, as a survey crew recently discovered on the Redding ranch on Sarpy Creek. They encountered John Redding, Jr. (age thirty-eight), and a 30.30 rifle. The survey crew chief decided to bluff it out. John, a large but rather placid-looking man, fired. "I'm a fair enough shot," he said, "so I fired about four inches in front of his toes. It kicked up a little dirt. They left."

"What would you have done if they had not?"

A rather long pause. "Well, they were trespassing, you see."

"Did they file any kind of legal action?"

A look of mild surprise. "Why, no. They just quit their jobs."

Just a short distance and time away a pilot of a helicopter working for Amax was setting out large white crosses in preparation for an aerial mapping run. He was flying low up the creek bottom when he saw a group of gun-carrying ranchers. He was motioned to the ground. The pilot, Harold Skaar, said, "The man told me, 'Better check your helicopter for bulletholes — I've been shooting at you.'" Skaar sought to explain his mission. The answer was simple enough. "You're trespassing." Skaar replied that firing at an aircraft was a federal offense. "I told them I would contact the FBI." In due course the FBI arrived but another neighbor had al-

ready filed a trespass complaint against the Amax helicopter crew.
A news story the following day merely reported that the incident
took place in the vicinity of the John Redding ranch.

Bud Redding, Sr. (age seventy-one), is not much disturbed by
bulletholes. There is a big one in the roof of his pickup cab.

"Well, it was August. No hunting season. I was coming up from
a section I lease. There was this sort of 'whang.' I knew right off
what it was. It came from the north or northwest, fairly close by,
I'd say. Damn poor shooting."

"Any idea of who — coal company people?"

"I wouldn't think so. They're dumb about us but not that dumb.
I just don't know who."

"Why don't you go armed?"

"Oh, no need. I got an equalizer." The "equalizer" is a short
length of chain with an iron ring on one end. He grinned. "That's
sufficient, I expect."

A few miles away lives Mrs. Redding's sister, alone on her own
place surrounded by chickens, ducks, and her own iron will. Pemberton Hutchinson of Westmoreland may have forgotten her
when he remarked of the Sarpy Creek area, "We've gotten enough
people to agree that, at least for the time being, we don't have to
go the condemnation route.* We needed to settle with eight land
owners, and we settled with six — that's enough." But it will be
hard to ignore Mrs. Redding's sister. She is big, handsome, raw-
boned and directly profane. A Westmoreland "scalper" told her,
"You'll be down on your knees begging to sell."

She snorts and then laughs. "Hell, I told that SOB to get the hell
off my property and never show his pasty face here again. And he
scuttled off and, by God, he's never been back. It's a damned insult
sending a pipsqueak like that. I told him, send your big guns,

* Eminent domain was denied the coal companies after 1973, but between
1961 and 1973 they had the power to condemn land — and that power more
than any other backed the rancher against the wall.

sonny, but the day they see me on my knees, that's the day hell will freeze over."

Then there is Mrs. Montana Garvish, a sixty-seven-year-old widow with fourteen grandchildren and eight great-grandchildren. She has been on her 4,000-acre ranch since 1912. The Burlington Northern ran into Mrs. Garvish — or maybe it was the other way around. They planned to run a spur through some of her meadowland and served the usual condemnation papers. She was adamant. The railroad hauled her into U.S. District Court but she did not haul easily. When the court found in Burlington Northern's favor, Mrs. Garvish announced that she would appeal — and if it had to go to the U.S. Supreme Court that suited her fine. The Burlington people had visions of an interminable delay and they could not afford that, nor did they like the gathering hostile publicity. They rerouted their line around her meadow.

Then there is Bruce Cady, who ranches north of the Reddings. Cady is a quiet, iron-gray-haired man and his ranch sits astride some rich coal veins which Westmoreland would dearly love to follow. Cady's approach seems to be silence. His eyes are very blue and very direct. He simply stares at "scalpers" and that is that.

Kenneth Johns lives south and east of the Reddings. He has not budged. And a glance at the map shows that these ranchers are so strategically located that they split Westmoreland's surface rights and, in effect, have them boxed into a rather small area to their west. Sooner or later Pemberton Hutchinson has to face them all again. If he wins, it will be a fight he will be a long time forgetting.

It is no different up north in the Bull Mountains. The chief spokesman for the Rosebud Protective Association is the "Marlboro Man" (of television commercial fame), Wally McRae. He detests the appellation but he is stuck with it.

"I don't do what I do for money. . . . We derive a psychic wage from ranching; we sacrifice income for life-style. . . . It's free out here. . . . Why in the hell should I electrify your toothbrush in Minneapolis?" With McRae it is Peabody Coal not West-moreland. The issue is the same.

Or, on the Tongue River near Birney, the fifth-generation owner of the Bónes Brothers ranch, a very pretty, articulate Carolyn Alderson, puts it this way: "To those of you who would exploit us, do not underestimate the people of this area. Do not make the mistake of lumping us and the land all together as 'over-burden' and dispense with us as nuisances. Land is historically the central issue in any war. We are the descendants, spiritually, if not actually, of those who fought for this land once, and we are pre-pared to do it again. We intend to win."

Boyd Charter (age sixty-six), who runs six hundred cows on fifteen sections of rangeland in the Bull Mountain area north of Billings, has a face that looks like the land he lives on. It is deeply lined and creased, the nose is large and a little bent, two lower teeth are missing, and the startlingly direct eyes are slightly hooded. Charter is clearly a man to be approached with some caution, though, like John Redding, he is a gentle man and a gentleman.

One of the vice-presidents of Consolidation Coal Company did not approach him with caution. Charter recalls, "I told that son-of-a-bitch with a briefcase that I knew he represented one of the biggest coal companies and that he was backed by one of the richest industries in the world, but no matter how much money they came up with, they would always be $4.60 short of the price of my ranch." The coal people are something of a puzzlement to Charter. They more than anger him, they deeply surprise him.

"Some people cannot understand that money is not everything. . . . He must have decided that I was stupid, because he offered me a contract for one dollar entitling him to explore for coal. I had to tell him the door swings out just the way it swings in." The eyebrows arch with incredulity.

Charter is succinct in describing what the range cattle industry is all about. Every rancher knows that cattle fed on lush, green, irrigated pastureland or hay "shrink" when trucked to the railroad.

They "shrink," or lose weight, when herded and corralled. This "shrink" is a matter of great moment to ranchers because, depending on the length of the haul, it can run up to 8 or 10 percent.

The tourist driving across the Northern Great Plains sees vast, undulating miles of brown and rather sparse-looking grass. To him, thinking of his watered lawn at home, it is dead. To the range rancher it is gold. No other feed will put tighter weight on beef. Let Boyd Charter say it:

> You hear that this area is no good. But when you come right down to it, it is the cream of the western cow range. There isn't another country that lays out of doors where you can run a cow and put any weight on her for less money. One good man with ambition could care for 1000 head of cattle in eastern Montana where it would take five men to a 1000 head of cattle where you have to feed hay six months out of the year.
> You take this grass. It's not washy; it puts a lot of weight on cattle. It's hard and has a lot of strength to it and protein. Montana beef is choice beef because of the grass which makes it harder and gives the beef a harder finish.
> To make it in two or three words, you can raise a calf here for ten cents on the dollar compared to any country where you have to put up a lot of hay and own a lot of machinery and have the expense of hiring men.*

As with John Redding, Wally McRae, Bruce Cady, or any of this breed of men and women, there is in what they say that not so faint echo of the 1880s. Montana's range grasses were then the plains' finest. And those who knew that and lived (and live) there and adapted to become as indigenous as the grass are singularly independent and hardy. They may not march entirely to the beat of a different drummer, but in the background there is another rhythm. The old voices whisper there. It will not do to ignore them.

---

* In an interview in the *Plains Truth*, a publication of the Northern Plains Resource Council, Billings, Montana, June 1974.

The feelings about trespass, deceit, division, are stones in a complex matrix of tradition rooted in an earlier necessity — and are reviving in a present reality. Like an old kerosene lamp, these customs may dim or flicker, or even seem to go out. But those old lamps had a way of flaring up — a gust of wind, a pocket of oxygen and they would flash up. Hands could get burned that way. Or houses. With Chicago, it only took Mrs. O'Leary's cow.*

As we shall see later, a new and powerful political coalition had formed in Montana by about 1970. Let it suffice now to give merely an intimation of its nature. At a public hearing on a bill providing for a moratorium on rural subdivision, which was presented to the 1974 session of the legislature, the House chamber was overflowing. The mix was a strange one. The ranchers were everywhere; so were the "environmentalists," mostly young, many from the University of Montana, mostly long of hair. They sat intermingled, checking each other's notes, nodding at favorable testimony, scowling at "the developers." That night, again intermingled, they filled Helena's bars. It was not riotous. But anyone with eyes and ears open could see, hear, and feel something new.

The bill passed the House but was killed in the Senate. After its demise, one lank rancher tipped his hat back on his head and put his arm around a very long-haired young man. "It's all right, son, we'll get 'em next session," and they walked off down the corridor together.

Many surprised Montanans regard this as a temporary and quixotic alliance. There is sound reason for believing that it is not. The Montana Stockgrowers' Association is a powerful organization and, as has been pointed out, its alliance with the Anaconda Company–Montana Power Company complex is an old one. Yet at its 1974 convention it came out flatfootedly against the building of

---

* Since this writing Bud Redding has sold his ranch to Westmoreland Coal Company. He calculated that his ground water was gone anyway. I have not spoken with him since. But I know how desperately sad a day it was for him and his family.

Montana Power's two 700-megawatt power plants (plants numbers 3 and 4) at Colstrip. Their principal concern, they said, was "the impact which such a major project would have on increased social services and the resultant effect on the tax structure." They were, indeed, being true to their old conservatism with respect to taxes. But this was nonetheless a major breach in a hitherto solid front. And it goes much farther than that as we shall see. It will take time to ascertain if these new alignments are permanent. The cynics may be right when they assert that it is but a momentary common cause. But it would be dangerous for industry to bet on it. The problems of water, reclamation, land and taxes are abidingly basic; and once people begin to know and understand each other, it is difficult to rupture their relationship, especially if they have discovered that all along they have really loved the same things.

II

THE FRAGILE LAND

6

When the People
Flooded In

IT WAS INEVITABLE that someone, the desert concept notwithstanding, would take a close look at the map of the Great Plains and see the potential in the great rivers that emerged from the Rocky Mountains to course unused across those arid lands. It was inevitable that someone would think of the Nile, and thinking thus, would see that properly diverted and used, this huge amount of water would convert the desert into a vast, green belt of a million farms.

It is ironical that the man who most encouraged these assertions and carried high the banner of a growing host of converts was the same man who quickly repudiated the whole idea and became the enemy of the reclamationists.

It was John Wesley Powell's misfortune — or his good fortune, depending on one's point of view — that his dreams, and he was a dreamer, were always ultimately subservient to the scientist in him, and he *was* a scientist.

In the middle 1880s Powell was convinced that the plains rivers could be diverted to provide farms with their own reservoirs. Indeed, he even predicted that a fish culture would replace cattle on the plains, for every pond could be stocked with fish. Powell did

not then understand the plains, but he was to come to an understanding of them rather quickly. Others did not, including the
Congress of the United States.

In spite of Powell's early assertions, he knew from the beginning
that the wholesale reclamation of the Great Plains was an impossibility. Powell was misunderstood by zealots. He did believe in
the efficiency of reclamation and his principal concern was the
financing of topographical surveys and stream-flow studies which
were already being done under the aegis of the U.S. Geological
Survey. And he was sometimes carried away, probably to keep
U.S. Geological Survey budgets growing.

He told the delegates to the Montana Constitutional Convention
in 1889, for instance, that he had a workable plan for irrigating
more than a third of Montana's total area and that "no drop of
water falling within the area of the state shall flow beyond the
boundaries of the state."

The story of the zealots who appropriated Powell and his final
repudiation of them in 1893 is a fascinating one, but it does not
apply to our concerns.* What matters here is that only Powell and
a few other scientists actually measured the stream-flow involved
and considered the topography and nature of the land through
which the rivers flowed. Having done so, they asserted with
abundant documentation that irrigation on the Great Plains was a
chimera except in very limited areas for limited purposes. But
what matters more is that, in spite of Powell's expertise and his
prominence, no one listened. The government launched a massive
reclamation program. But the point is not that reclamation in the
entire West was without its successes. It was not. The point is that,
once again, as with the federal land laws and with the cattlemen,
action was taken based on ignorance of the land to be acted upon

---

* See Stanley Davison, "Hopes and Fancies of the Early Reclamationists,"
in *Historical Essays on Montana and the Northwest,* ed. by T. W. Smurr
and K. Ross Toole (Helena: Western Press, 1957).

and the results, while not in this case tragic, were nil and very expensive.

The public excitement engendered by the prospect of Eden in Middle America, the propaganda and pressure groups formed to further the concept, the pseudo-scientific assertions made by promoters with various covert purposes, the speculators in land, all led to a policy rooted in myth. No historian of the plains today, especially hearing over and over again the word "reclamation" as used by the coal and power companies, can escape a sense of *déjà vu*. The words are the same, the pseudo-scientific jargon is the same, the pressures are the same. But so are the plains. As we shall see, they will be no more amenable to man's ignorance of their nature in the future than they have been in the past.

If the dreams of the reclamationists resulted merely in disillusionment and expense, standing behind that set of dreamers and schemers was another. But this time the consequences were to be awesome, both in the terrible toll of human suffering and, again, to the plains.

With a kind of random awfulness, a great migration of people flooded into western North and South Dakota and all of eastern Montana. Quite simply, the circumstances were as follows: land prices, particularly in the Middle West, had been rising steadily since the 1890s and it was becoming increasingly difficult for farmers to expand; the railroads, most particularly the Great Northern, hated seeing empty boxcars headed from west to east and believed that farm development on the plains would benefit them greatly; the Northern Great Plains entered one of its periodic "wet periods" about at the turn of the century. During such periods wheat, in particular, could be grown with great success. And it was excellent, high-protein wheat. These were the basic factors that fell into juxtaposition with a dreadful kind of simultaneity.

In the context of this setting a congeries of collateral developments took place — or perhaps it is more fitting to say that these

factors acted as a magnet for men with disparate ideas and purposes. It was a powerful magnet indeed. Its attraction, once again,
lay in Eden, the making of a garden from a desert.

Now, however, the solution was not water; it was "scientific
dry-land farming." This was backed up by a kind of massive land
hunger, made sharper by the fact that by 1900 Americans had become convinced that all the good free land on their continent had
been taken up. "Scientific dry-land farming," however, a new and
startling concept, changed that view very precipitously. For if it
would work, if its ardent and intense proponents were right, in
1905 there were still more than 56,000,000 acres of the public
domain unreserved and unoccupied in the Northern Plains region.
Some 41,043,000 acres were in Montana east of the Rockies.

If it would work. That was the question the "scientists," the
speculators, the railroads, the promoters, western chambers of
commerce, and "locators" went to work on. *Of course* it would
work. There was proof of it. The problem was to spread the
word. The word was "spread."

It would at least be a clear-cut circumstance if one could say
that all this was done by beady-eyed cynics and con men. Though
very much in evidence (in retrospect), such cynics were clearly in
the minority. As with reclamation, zealots were myriad. But the
most effective promoters were those who sincerely believed that
an agricultural, technical breakthrough had indeed occurred.

The fact is that dry-land farming, or dry farming, was not a
mysterious practice. It had been routine in western Kansas and
Nebraska since the 1880s; it had been practiced in Utah by the
Mormons since 1855; and it is being practiced all over the West
today. What happened on the Northern Great Plains, therefore,
needs some explanation. It was well put in the midst of the greatest
enthusiasm (1911) by E. C. Chilcott of the Bureau of Plant Industry in an article entitled "Some Misconceptions Concerning
Dry Farming" in the *Yearbook of the Department of Agriculture.*
The most serious misconceptions, wrote Chilcott, were:

(1) That any definite "system" of dry-farming has been or is likely to be established that will be of *general applicability to all or any part of the Great Plains area* [italics mine]; (2) that any hard and fast rules can be adopted to govern the methods of tillage or of time or depth of plowing; (3) that deep tillage invariably and necessarily increases the water-holding capacity of the soil or facilitates root development; (4) that alternate cropping or summer tillage can be relied upon as a safe basis for a permanent agriculture or that *it will invariably overcome the effects of severe and long continued droughts* [italics mine]; and (5) that the farmer can be taught by given rules how to operate a dry-land farm.

Like John Wesley Powell before him, Chilcott was anathema to the new school. Chilcott, in any event, was not as prestigious as Powell.

There were others who issued warnings. R. N. Sutherlin, editor of the *Rocky Mountain Husbandman* since 1875 and still aggressively involved in hardheaded prophecy up into the 1920s, was as deeply skeptical of dry farming as he had been of the open range cattle industry. Though the "boosters'" efforts did not get well under way until 1907–1910, Sutherlin was alert to impending problems as early as 1890. When James J. Hill built the Great Northern into Montana's Milk River region in that year, and both the railroad and the local press began asserting that excellent crops could be grown there year after year without irrigation, Sutherlin asserted, "There is no district in Montana of any considerable size where crops can be grown safely and successfully one year after the other without artificial watering."

As Sutherlin continued his articulate warnings about the hazards of dry farming, the Great Northern boycotted his newspaper, as, later, did the merchants of the city of Great Falls, where the *Husbandman* was printed. Throughout all of the boom period, Sutherlin's warnings were consistent and almost ruthless — but to no avail.

In response to the enormous pressures of the railroads and of a new, largely railroad-financed organization, the Dry-Farming

Congress, and in further response to intense political pressures from western politicians and chambers of commerce, Congress passed the Enlarged Homestead Act of 1909. The act passed in spite of a plea from the National Conservation Commission to await classification of the land of the Northern Plains which "would ultimately fix with certainty, according to the productive value of the surface, a reasonable home-making area for each class of agricultural land, and thus solve the problem without mistake or friction." It was not until the 1930s that this was, in effect, done and it was ascertained that, in general, 160 acres of humid-area land was roughly equivalent in productivity to 2,560 acres of semi-arid land.

The Enlarged Homestead Act of 1909 should have struck the average plainsman as a laughable piece of legislation because all it did, in essence, was to increase the acreage obtainable under the old Homestead Act of 1862 from 160 to 320.

Indeed, many Montanans did laugh, but farmers on the deep loam of Minnesota, Indiana, Ohio, and Kentucky did not. Neither did clerks, barbers, miners, tradesmen, and workers anywhere in the East. Here was land, a lot of it, free for the taking — and it was almost free to get there. A one-way settler's fare was only $22.50 from St. Paul to Billings on the Northern Pacific. Or the homesteader could rent an entire boxcar for $50 in which he could carry friends, animals, household goods, fence posts, or lumber. In short order, all the other railroads were offering similar bargains.

The Enlarged Homestead Act of 1909 lit a very short fuse and the explosion occurred promptly. Even before historians had revealed that the original act of 1862 had been a whopping failure, an early land historian, writing in 1924, observed, "The first real breakdown of the Homestead Act was its attempt to cross the plains. For this task it was ill adapted. . . . On the plains the Homestead Act was a failure from the stand point of both individual and nation."

How many people came? We do not know because the census

of 1910 was taken before the influx was well under way and the census of 1920 occurred when the outmigration had already become a flood. But by sampling county records and land office filings in key areas, it is probably conservative to estimate that between 1909 and 1917, 80,000 homesteaders inundated eastern Montana. Of the western Dakotas we know little, but it is probable that the figures are similar.

The greatest prophet of "scientific dry-land farming" was Hardy Webster Campbell. Though born in Vermont, Campbell had come west at the age of sixteen and, after some experience with farming in Nebraska, had settled in Brown County, Dakota Territory, in 1879. Campbell was an observant man and a good farmer and over the years he developed what came to be called the "Campbell System" for dry-land farming. This system, also to become known as "the scientific dry-farming method," was, in fact, not without some roots in actual soil science.

The purpose of the dry-land farmer is to capture and hold precipitation and to prevent evaporation. For this purpose the hard crust of earth is broken up by deep plowing. There are two reasons for this: one is simply to prevent runoff and to let the water percolate into the soil; the other is that the hard-crusted surface has in it pores, or myriad small chimneys, so that such water as does manage to percolate into these minuscule holes also evaporates out from them when the intense heat of the day beats down on the hardpan surface. If this crust is broken, pulverized, and if it is then compacted again (with a subsurface packer which leaves an inch or two of a kind of dust mulch on the surface), two things occur. The deep plowing encourages the rise of subsurface water toward the surface by capillary action. The finer the soil particles the greater the capillarity; the compaction discourages evaporation. The myriad chimneys in the hard crust are plugged.

But does this very compaction itself not prevent the percolation of precipitation down into the subsurface? It does. Therefore, the process of plowing and compacting is geared to the precipitation.

The farmer must move with great rapidity after any rainfall. A single hot day or two without cultivation will result in catastrophe.

But whether this system works or not is very dependent on the type of soil, which must be a sandy loam. Sandy loam soils vary greatly in relative composition, but there are extensive areas in the Northern Plains where the soil is in no way suited to this system.

Moreover, the system depends on precipitation. If the soil is proper and the precipitation is at least 15 inches annually and *if* that precipitation comes at the right time, dry farming will produce good crops. It was precisely these "ifs" that Campbell and a burgeoning number of disciples ignored.

By 1895 Campbell was operating fine farms for the Northern Pacific in North Dakota. In that year, too, subsidized by the railroad, he started espousing his views in his own magazine, *The Western Soil Culture.* He became increasingly messianic. It was the system of cultivation that mattered, it was the mechanics of what you did to the soil that held the secret. In due course, Campbell came to assert that rain, in truth, meant nothing. In fact, it leached the fertility from the soil. That was why soil in the semi-arid regions was so much more fertile than in the humid regions. And, he said, "a farmer in semi-arid country can grow better average crops than they are growing in Illinois today, because we can secure the ideal condition, and control it, and they cannot do it in Illinois because they have too much rain."

By 1910, the Dry-Farming Congress had more than ten thousand members, all devotees of Campbell's System. Campbell himself was the object of adulatory articles in dozens of national periodicals. The railroads sent out hundreds of thousands of glowing brochures, they instituted a "colonization program" and even had representatives scouring Europe for "colonizers." They ran demonstration trains showing what magnificent crops could be produced on the Northern Plains — and among the exhibits were great shocks of golden wheat "at 70 bushels to the acre."

The *Great Falls Tribune* asserted, "Hardy Webster Campbell, the father of dry-land farming, has brought a miracle to the plains states. Now half of their area can be reclaimed without irrigation and they will be the last and best garden of the world." The *Havre Plaindealer* trumpeted, "Campbell's soil culture methods provide the farmers with enough security to laugh at the severest drouth ever known to them." A grim R. N. Sutherlin replied, "Dry farming is a misleading misnomer and it misrepresents our conditions here to the easterner or would be settler."

But they came, oh, how they came. And for that brief time conditions were ideal. The wet cycle was on; the war in Europe sent the price of wheat skyrocketing; towns sprouted like dandelions, twenty-three new counties were formed; in every new town a new bank, in all the old towns more new banks. In 1900 there were 7,000 farms in eastern Montana; by 1920 there were 46,000. In 1909 there were only 250,000 acres in eastern Montana planted in wheat; by 1919 this had risen to 35,000,000. And it grew! In 1909 Montana produced only 3,560,000 bushels of wheat; by 1924 (a very bad year) it produced 40,852,000 bushels. Land prices were out of sight — and all the free land was gone.

And then swiftly, implacably, remorselessly, and inevitably the great flat, rolling land retaliated. Drought is a much misunderstood phenomenon. Like cancer, it starts small and metastasizes. It started far in the north in 1917. In 1918 it appeared in central Montana in hotly glowing spots. By 1919 it had spread all across Montana and into the Dakotas and a great burning finger probed down into Wyoming. Again, like cancer, there were brief periods of remission — in some places. But it burned on, sometimes with an intensity so great that men, mice and even the insects were desiccated. They fled or perished.

Eleven thousand Montana farms blew away eastward on the edge of the blast furnace winds of the 1920s. In places the humidity hovered at 4 percent, skin cracked, boards warped, sand-blasted buildings in the new towns looked a century old in a year's time.

East, north, south, west, some sixty thousand Montana homesteaders fled. They had come in boxcars, they left on the rods of
freight cars. They left in tilting Model T Fords, their goods tied
and piled on handmade roof racks. They left in buggies and wagons. The lucky ones left on trains. Behind them they left dead
and dying towns.

Drought is a complicated phenomenon. From somewhere, from
nowhere, the grasshoppers came. They came, obscenely gushing,
clacking, roaring, a sky-darkening blanket that settled over all the
land. They ate the tarpaper on the homesteader's shack, they ate
the shingles and the clotheslines. The darkened wheat stubble
vanished under their billion bodies. They sickened, gorged, and
those humans still left to fight whatever there was to fight shov-
eled them into great haystacklike mounds and burned them; the
gray smoke rose and stank and the pile crackled like old kindling.

Drought is one awesome aspect to the face of nature. Like a
giant explosion or a tornado, it does inexplicable things. It leaves
large islands in the holocaust untouched, green and productive. Its
heat and winds carve marvelously beautiful table rocks on hill-
tops. It converts rivers into checkered tile roads; it makes gullies
out of flats; it kills rattlesnakes. But there is one thing it does not
kill; it does not kill the seeds of native grass. Those seeds lie dor-
mant, hard as tiny pebbles, just beneath the surface of the cracked
earth. They are patient. They will not sprout until the rains come
again. They may not sprout for a very long time.

But exotic seeds, or domestic seeds, are dumb seeds. They
can be coaxed to sprout by the most ephemeral hint of time or
moisture and they emerge to be seared, never to sprout again.
Moreover, drought is most assuredly not a visitor at all. This
man seems not to understand about it. It is an integral part of the
long rhythm of the ancient Great Plains. It lives there, latently,
always. It is merely that it sometimes sleeps and sometimes wakes.
Its cycles, as we shall see, are nearly as predictable as the cycles of
a hibernating bear.

Further, drought is an economic thing. As a consequence of this particular recrudescence 214 banks failed — more banks than exist in Montana today. The average value of *all* farmland in Montana was cut in half by 1925. Farm mortgage indebtedness reached $175,000,000. County land ownership increased nearly 5,000 percent and the actual drop in valuation of farmland was $320,000,000. The cost of county administration jumped 149 percent; overall county expenditures rose 587 percent. Taxes per farm acre rose 140 percent in three years.

But what of those who stayed? What of the cattlemen who only a few years before had suffered their own catastrophe? Once again, what of those who stayed? How did they eat? What did they use for money? *Why* did they stay?

As with the cattlemen, the pragmatic questions are more easily answered. The *why* is obscure and more difficult. In the first place, the homesteaders and the cattlemen suffered this together. The cattlemen had already retrenched to survive. Because the price of beef was very low when the homesteader flooded in, the rancher sold him land because the price of land was high, which meant, in effect, that he was retrenching further. But he harbored his money — unless, of course, it was deposited in one of the many failing banks. Even so, the drought took an awful toll of cattlemen as well as homesteaders. Many of the ranchers survived because they drove or shipped their herds into the valleys of the mountains to the west — and waited. Others survived, as did the homesteaders, because they lived in those areas where the drought was least intense — and once more they pulled in their belts, hunkered down, ate beans, and hated the land — but there was that perversity.

Only roughly half of the homesteaders had had previous farming experience, and the vast majority raised only wheat. That was the cash crop. That was where the money was. But the wheat was the most subject to drought. It was the first to go. It was the next year's crop for which they borrowed the money. It was to harvest the wheat that they bought tractors and threshers and combines — on credit. It was the wheat the towns were built for. They were granary towns. It was the price of wheat that was shooting upward, so it was for wheat that they borrowed more money to buy more land upon which to raise more wheat.

The survival rate of the experienced farmers was much higher. Why? The answer was diversification. They had dug incredibly deep wells. They had gardens, chickens, milk cows, goats, a few head of meat cattle. They raised alfalfa, beans, potatoes.

Listen for a moment to seventy-one-year-old Bud Redding. His father homesteaded in southeastern Montana in 1916. "Well, I sure remember those years. Of course this particular part of the country was not so hard hit. We got good subsurface water here, but no irrigating water. Sure it was dry farming.

"Well, first off, you got to have some respect for thistles. The last thing to go in a drought is a thistle. We fed the cows thistles. You think a cow won't eat a thistle? Hell, a hungry cow will eat shingles. We fed 'em 'thistle hay.' Sure, we had a good well, damn good well. So we had beans. My dad, first he tried cooking up a bean mash for them cows. They didn't much like it. So he just took to soakin' the beans in water. They ate that. I never heard of cows eating soaked beans before or since but it worked. We all ate beans. I liked them then and I like them now.

"You ever ate porcupine? Well, a porcupine will live through damn near anything. I've ate more porcupines than I can count. If they've been eatin' the bark of pine trees they taste like turpentine but if they've been rootin' around in old dry corn they taste fine.

"And we had hogs. A hog will eat anything and then you eat the hog.

"The neighbors were pullin' out fast. My dad went around and I did too sayin' 'Why you pullin' out? This is good country. You better stay. Hunker down.' But they left. Not all of 'em, but a lot of 'em. Nobody ever said this was easy country. The first winter we spent here was in a tent. If you didn't ride a horse thirty miles to a dance you wasn't warmed up yet when you got there. That's nothin' for a good horse and nothin' for a good man."

Bud sold his 6,400 acres, as mentioned earlier, in 1975. But he is still an excellent example of the "merging" of homesteader and rancher, for essentially that is what happened: with land going for taxes, the homesteader slowly expanded. He had been something of a rancher anyway; he had run cattle. In the intervening years the Reddings ran cattle, grew wheat, corn, barley, alfalfa, potatoes, watermelons, and they ran hogs. The Reddings adapted. They adapted to everything except the power of the coal company.

Just two rolling hills from John Redding's former house is a giant pit and at the bottom of it a huge machine, a Marion 8200 "stripper." It has a boom 215 feet long. It rises 365 feet into the clear air. It has a bucket that scoops up 75 cubic yards of earth per minute. It is owned by Westmoreland Resources. John Redding's ranch stood astride the richest veins of coal — and he would not sell. The innumerable coal representatives who approached, harassed, threatened, and cajoled the Reddings did not understand why they would not sell. Didn't they realize the enormous power of the companies? As it turned out, they did. Didn't they realize that energy-hungry America *will* have this coal? Didn't they know power when they saw it? Finally, and in exhaustion and sorrow, they did.

Bud Redding was in a final fight — for his land and for his way of life. What the great and powerful outsiders did not understand was that he had been fighting a far more awesome power for fifty-eight of his seventy-one long years. So had his family. John Redding, Jr., thirty-eight, was no different. You could hear it with great clarity in almost everything they said, in the way they talked about horses, water, range, grass, flies, heat, cold.

Bud Redding, Sr., won't wear a seat belt. He explains, "I rode too damn many buckin' horses when I was younger. You don't put no rope acrost your legs and tie yourself to no ornery horse. A truck's for workin' but so's a horse. I just can't belt myself down in no pickup. It's instinct, I guess."

Or, "I dunno, the real workin' horse is pretty much gone. Course we do all our work by tractor and that's okay. Still, those horses were somethin'. Thirty miles there and thirty miles back and he ain't footsore and I ain't saddle sore. They sure did fit the country and they sure did fit men."

Or, "Them 'scalpers' [coal company leasehounds] come to me and they offer me $137 per acre. And they says that's a real good offer 'cause the lawyer's appraiser says that's 75 to 100 percent above the actual value of this land. Well, I says, 'I ain't an unreasonable man but my appraisal's a little different. I'll sell for $1,000,000 per section. That's 640 acres.' And they says, 'How do you come up with a silly figure like that?' I says, 'Well, ask them what my wife's life and my kids' lives are worth — and tell them that's the way you appraise land out here — which means I'm sellin' out dirt cheap at a million dollars a section.' " I don't know what Bud Redding finally sold for. I hope it was a million dollars a section.

The Reddings were beaten. Some of his neighbors have been; many Montana ranchers have been. But there was never a time in Redding's life when the difference between defeat and victory was a wide one. And there are many, many holdouts remaining.

Redding is a slight man, about five feet, eight inches, and maybe 150 pounds. He is a gentle man and you would never call him perverse. But he is. The coal companies at least know that. But they still do not know why. It is worth a moment's reflection.

When the open range cattle industry collapsed before the turn of the century and when the hard winter of 1886–1887 was over, the cattle that were left were skin and bone. But they were incredibly tough. Call it "natural selection" or what you will, but when the survivors were crossed with the survivors an enormously hardy breed resulted.

It was no different, really, with the people who survived, except that the toughness was not merely dependent on genes but on tradition as well. It will not do to write off this view of the rancher as "romantic." It is too palpably evident to anyone who knew them or knows them. There are few Americans as "traditionalist" as the rancher. There are few so intimately and irrevocably tied to the land.

When, the second time around, the homesteader-rancher was again struck with catastrophe and survived, it was not so much a new turn of events as another twist of the old turn. Bud Redding did not come to Montana until 1916 — but the whole heritage of men and land was already there. He absorbed it.

No, the coal company people don't understand Bud Redding; they don't understand Wally McRae; they don't understand Boyd Charter; they don't understand Carolyn Alderson, and all the others still holding out. They never, never will.

Nor do they understand another vital fact. Whatever the final revenue Montana may gain from the mining of coal, the process is ephemeral. Agriculture is self-renewing. Far and away it is Montana's leading industry. It is a billion-dollar-per-year industry — and unless we destroy it, it will not be gone in thirty years.

7

Reclamation:
Lipstick on a Corpse

DUKE MCRAE RANCHES in southeastern Montana. He is the owner of the Greenfield Cattle Company, which consists of some 34,000 acres south of Colstrip. Early on, when the leasehounds far out-numbered the ranchers in the area, he sold five or six sections (640 acres per section) to the Peabody Coal Company and the land has been leased back to him. He used the money from the sale to buy twelve sections nearby.

But McRae doesn't like it. He says, "Some of my property has been reclaimed three times and it still doesn't look good." He has been offered up to $12 million dollars for his property and turned it down.

Wallace McRae is Evan's cousin. Over the last four years Wally has become the most articulate of the antistrippers. He is much in demand wherever and whenever there is a panel or pro-gram on the subject. He has been on CBS and has testified before the House Interior and Insular Affairs Committee. He owns the Rocker Six Cattle Company — 30,000 acres. He is the principal spokesman for the Rosebud Protective Association, of which some fifty or sixty ranchers are members.

Referring to Montana Power's demonstration reclamation plot at Colstrip, McRae remarked, ". . . if photography could kill grass it would have been a desert long ago. But that's not reclamation. No lawn in the state gets beter care. Reclamation is restoring land when it's treated like our range grass. . . . Western Energy's [Montana Power's] ten-acre reclamation showcase is a mecca for everyone who's out to prove that it works. . . ."

McRae has yet to say that it will never work. But he believes that it will take at least fifty years, not four, to find out. There are old-time ranchers aplenty, however, who assert that in this semiarid land it will never work at all. There is not as much conflict between this negativism and McRae's long-term reservations as may seem to be the case. They all bitterly resent the stripper. Testifying before the House Interior and Insular Affairs Committee McRae said:

> My grandfather was running a few sheep in southeastern Montana during the terrible winter of 1886. A friend of his rode one horse and led another to bring my grandfather back to frontier civilization, but grandfather refused to leave the sheep to die. When his friend told him that the sheep would surely die from hunger and cold, and that my grandfather would probably perish as well, he was told that "when the last sheep dies, I'll be there to skin it."
> This is my heritage, and my land and livestock are no less important to me than they were to John McRae my grandfather. I can assure you that I and others like me will not allow our land to be destroyed merely because it is convenient for the coal company to tear it up.

But there is a gigantic hooker here. Wally McRae and a substantial number of the ranchers involved do not own the coal beneath their own land — the federal government or the Burlington Northern Railroad does. They own it by a series of very complex and interlocking land laws dating back to 1869. So, however tough, however determined, however strongly they feel, the ranchers must keep a wary eye not merely on the coal companies and state government, but also on the (to them) amorphous and faraway federal bureaus.

There is another harrowing problem for the ranchers, one

which is the key to the threats and harassment which so constantly beleaguered them between 1961 and 1973. It is the Montana law of eminent domain. All states have eminent domain statutes which provide for the condemnation of private property for "public use." The laws in most states were conceived so that highways could be built where they ought to be built, so that public utilities could run their lines where they had to, and so that railroads would not have to make right-angle turns around some rancher's section lines. Manifestly reasonable and necessary.

In the 1950s it became apparent to the Anaconda Company that deep mining for copper was rapidly becoming unprofitable. The great hill at Butte was shot through with many hundreds of miles of tunnels, shafts, and drifts. They were mining almost a mile beneath the earth. Moreover, whereas they had once been extracting ore running about 35 percent copper, the copper content was now extremely low. The only answer was open-pit mining, by which they could recover vast quantities of copper untouched by the old method.

The pit, however, would become huge. The deeper the pit the larger the surface area required. If the pit moved westward it would swallow up the downtown section of Butte. If it moved eastward and northward, it would involve land which the company also did not own. Accordingly, in 1961 Anaconda, which was still exceedingly powerful in the legislature, pushed through legislation by virtue of which the eminent domain statute was amended to include mining in the "public use" category. No one was yet aware of the problems this would cause with respect to coal.

When the coal rush began, however, the myriad companies found themselves armed with a power of awesome magnitude. They could and did say to the ranchers: either sell or lease to us or we can and will condemn. Under the amended statute, the rancher could not win in court. He could only use the courts to challenge the amount of money which the companies were offering. He could not prevent condemnation. While the coal companies lost this power by legislative action in 1973, the threat of its return is ever present.

Transmission lines were another matter. By virtue of the Utility Siting Act of 1973, the state Board of Natural Resources was given substantial power over where such lines might be built, or, indeed, whether they could be built at all. This power did not supersede the eminent domain statute; it profoundly mitigated it. It did not, in any event, pertain to the average rancher with federally owned coal under his land — with no assurance that either federal or state action might not return to the companies the power they had from 1961 to 1973.

The confusion in the law and the split between the ownership of surface and subsurface mineral rights opened the door to speculators and lease brokers. These people added their threats and harassments to those of the actual company agents in the field, except that they were less restrained. Often the rancher thought he was dealing with a company agent when, in fact, he was simply dealing with a lease broker after a fast buck.

The ranchers have a very imperfect picture of what the federal Environmental Protection Agency — and a dozen other agencies — is up to and they wonder what is running through the mind of Russell Train, chairman of the Council on Environmental Quality, who seems to say one thing one day and another the next. And then they wonder about Congress. Here they seem in large part bleakly pessimistic. After all, it is the populous states that have the political clout. They want their air conditioners and electric toothbrushes. Who gives a damn about the Northern Great Plains. We've had "national sacrifice areas" before. Look at Appalachia. So they were not surprised, in any event, when an AP dispatch originating in Washington on April 18, 1974, produced the headline: COAL STRIPPERS TO GET MORE RECLAMATION FLEXIBILITY. The story begins, "Following complaints from the coal industry, the Interior Department plans to issue new strip mining regulations

which will give strippers greater flexibility in restoring disturbed
land" — and then trails off with various statements by the EPA
and the Council on Environmental Quality.

Let two antagonistic views of reclamation stand cheek by jowl
to represent the extreme polarization. The place, Montana Power's
demonstration plot at Colstrip. Mike Grende, the power company's reclamation manager, stands knee-deep in waving grass.
Initially, twenty-seven varieties of grass were planted (though less
than half the varieties sprouted), which is today thick and lush. It
has, however, been very heavily irrigated and fertilized:

"This shows that reclamation can be done," says Grende. He
asserts that it will sustain cattle within five years. R. L. Hodder, a
research associate for the agricultural experiment station at Montana State University at Bozeman, is equally optimistic. Hodder
admits that fertilizer has been used but asserts that this practice
will cease once sufficient organic matter has been built up to
"force" the plants to grow. Hodder says that irrigation was employed only the first year for one-to-three-hour periods. Nothing
had been irrigated since. "We should be producing what is needed
here — not necessarily what was here previously. . . . Some people absolutely can't see what they're looking at — and some refuse
to," and Grende adds, "You can't be an expert on reclamation if
you see just one side."

A number of ranchers say that that is precisely Grende's problem. One of them is Carolyn Alderson of Birney, Montana, whom
we have already met.

"We're suffering from a disease that can be terminal if it isn't
controlled — its called lackadata. . . . We're not comforted by
assurances of reclamation when in fact there is not one acre of
reclaimed land in the Northern Great Plains which has been returned to agricultural production much less grazing."

Wally McRae is saltier. "They [the coal companies] don't
know and they don't give a rat's rear end. They aren't going to
do a damn thing until they've caused a problem."

Ed Dobson, young, lank, and somber, dropped into John Redding's ranch to show some slides on a June evening last year. The
room was full of ranchers from the Colstrip area. He flashed a
slide of the demonstration plot, tall grass waving, thick and
beautiful.

"Well, now that's pretty. But they don't say they hauled in 6
inches of topsoil, used 100 pounds of nitrogen per acre and 60
pounds of phosphorus and seeded with 160 pounds of seed per
acre."

A voice came from the back of the room. "Jesus, you give me
all that and I'll grow tomatoes on the main street of Forsyth."

Dobson clicked on another slide. It was a close-up.

"Let's take a peek at what's coming up under all that thick
wavy grass. Thistles, good old home grown thistles. A nice mat of
thorny thistles."

He clicked on another slide. "Now here's another demonstration
plot. This one is the showcase of a mine twenty miles north of Bismarck." There on the screen was a small, deep blue "fishing" lake
surrounded by trees and magnificent grass. Then, "click," and
the next slide was an aerial view of the same "lake" taken at about
two thousand feet. The "lake" was a small pond surrounded by
one thin row of trees and a fringe of grass; beyond that, concentric, ever-widening spoil-bank rows, gray, raw, and infinitely ugly.

A voice from the darkness: "What kind of fish you reckon they
got in that there lake?" A rejoinder: "They call 'em Knife River
Shark. They eat acid."

Ed Dobson folded up his screen and moved on. Someone asked
him, "Where you bound, Ed?"

"To wherever I can get ten people in a room."

Undoubtedly, though Dobson has made the circuit before, he
will do a replay for the Bull Mountain people — ranchers in the
area just north of Billings. Here live, among others, the Boyd
Charters on 30,000 acres. The Charters were instrumental in the
formation of the Bull Mountain Landowners' Association. There

the "enemy" is the Consolidation Coal Company. As we have seen, the Charters are tough people. No one knows that better, now, than the survey crews for Consolidation. There is that strange, straight-eyed perversity. The Charters go back to the beginning. Reclamation strikes them as laughable.

Is the *real* problem concerning reclamation Carolyn Alderson's "lackadata"? Is it true that ranchers will see the truth before their very eyes and, as R. L. Hodder says, "can't see what they're looking at"?

In both cases the answer is no. We *do* have data. Not, indeed, utterly irrefutable, but very frightening in their implications, data strongly indicating that reclamation on any appreciable portion *of the Northern Plains is an impossibility.* As for Mr. Hodder, that he believes what he says is doubtless true. The problem is that if he knows grasses, he does not know the land in its large aspects, and knowledge of one without the other leads nowhere — or to catastrophe.

Let us begin with a statement that appears in a lengthy report produced by the National Academy of Sciences. The National Academy is an *independent* organization of scientists. It has for years been the most prestigious such body in America. Projects are undertaken with great care. Each proposed project must run a gamut of criteria. If accepted and launched, the finished product must undergo an extraordinarily severe review. The research (which draws in authorities from any and all fields required) is monitored throughout. Only when the review process has been completed and endorsed can the report be disseminated.

The academy's report on strip mining asserts on page 1, "*Surface mining destroys the existing natural communities completely and dramatically. Indeed, restoration of a landscape disturbed by surface mining, in the sense of recreating the former conditions is not possible*" [italics mine]. The report confines itself to reclamation and does not go beyond that.

It does *not* say that nothing can be made to grow on strip-mined land. It *does* say that rehabilitation requires more than achieving a stable growth of plants. Whatever the technology, the absence of a climatic "safety factor" means that even supplying all of the very complex and delicately balanced requirements "will not guarantee success."

There is, however, a distinction of some importance here, because in some areas the academy, though in a very reserved way, anticipates that "rehabilitation" is possible, i.e., the land can be returned to a "form and productivity in conformity with a prior land use plan including a stable ecologic state that does not contribute substantially to environmental deterioration and is consistent with surrounding aesthetic values."

But, obviously "rehabilitation" is not "restoration," and it is not "reclamation."

By "restoration" the academy is referring to the return to "the conditions of the site at the time of the disturbance" in full measure. This, says the academy, is simply "impossible." Is this mere semantics? Not at all, because the coal and energy companies mean precisely that when they speak of reclamation. Moreover, they very often go beyond that and speak of "higher use" for the restored or reclaimed land — it will graze *more* cattle, it will produce *more* wheat, *better* crops, etc.

One phrase in the report is very significant, climatic "safety factor." Over and over again, for example, the Montana Power Company, on statewide television, shows the viewer beautiful scenes of the tall grass waving in its demonstration plot. Always the mellow-voiced narrator speaks of "average" rainfall — in this case fifteen inches. But the very essence of the Great Plains is that it is an area of violent extremities. One can, indeed, average out extremities. The problem is that grass and water cannot. The point being (new topsoil, irrigation, and fertilizer quite aside from the point) if, as is inevitable, the area involved has a long run of years with six inches, four inches, nine inches of precipitation, what happens to ground cover suitable only for a minimum of fifteen inches of precipitation? What happens is that it dies, does not reseed, and, with nothing to hold the earth, it blows away.

There has been abundant experimentation with the mortality of viable seeds, especially in the foothill sections of the middle intermountain area. In the first place, in the desert Southwest one must speak of hundreds of years for "natural revegetation" to occur. In areas of "high" rainfall the rate of "natural revegetation" will take place more swiftly, perhaps in forty to sixty years. But the coal companies, who in Montana cannot by law wait for natural revegetation, must plant seeds. Yet often less than 10 percent of the viable seeds emerge and, if left to themselves, less than 50 percent survive the second growing season. So one is constantly seeding — unless one can constantly irrigate and fertilize. But water for irrigation of any large portion of the plains is simply not available.

One of the reasons for confusion is, again, a misunderstanding of the plains. Indeed, where good soil, relatively level land, and *adequate precipitation* are present, reclamation is not only feasible but rather simple. In point of fact, such land can not only be reclaimed, but restored to a higher use. One need only drive through Illinois to see old strip-mining areas glowing with health. Near Morris, Illinois, for instance, a large recreational site with magnificent grass, ponds, lakes, and canals exists precisely because the land was strip-mined and restored some years ago. In many areas of Appalachia the problem is not moisture, it is the precipitous nature of the hills. They are simply too steep to reclaim.

Some coal industry people whose operations have always been in humid areas are doubtless completely sincere in their belief that reclamation is possible — indeed, a matter of course. The problem lies in their misconception of the plains. And it is a very old misconception.

The second generation of plainsmen had already begun to notice the cyclical nature of drought. But weather records were not kept until very recently so that this "pattern" was not obvious. It was a lurking memory. Then the archeologists got busy, and first with tree-ring studies and then with more sophisticated methods, the picture of cyclical drought on the Great Plains began to emerge. Then, because the meteorologists were most anxious to improve long-range weather forecasting, they began to examine the past. One of these men concentrated on the Great Plains area, where, for eight years, he was the director of the National Center for Atmospheric Research near Boulder, Colorado. Dr. Walter Orr Roberts says, "There have been something like eight successive serious dry periods spaced approximately twenty to twenty-three years apart. We don't know why this has happened. But when I see a repetition that has carried on for that many cycles, I always suspect there must be some fundamental cause for it."

In any event, meteorologists and archeologists are by now thoroughly cognizant of the fact that serious droughts are cyclical in the very nature of the Great Plains and, judging from the land itself, have been for thousands of years.

The Great Plains was in the last spasms of the dust bowl era when the late Charles Greeley Abbot predicted that there would be another deadly visitation "beginning about 1975." Abbot was an astrophysicist, then secretary of the Smithsonian Institution, and the date of his prediction was 1938. So it is not quite accurate to say that cyclical drought patterns on the plains had attracted no scientific attention until the 1950s and 1960s.

The point is that Walter Orr Roberts is no exception. There may, indeed, be argument among the astrophysicists and meteorologists on the precise length of the cycles. Roberts places them on a 20-to-23-year basis. Meteorologist Harry Geise of Sacramento agrees. Like Roberts, Geise relates the cycles to sun spots, and since detailed records of sun spots have been kept since the mid-1700s, this helps the tie-in with tree-ring studies and archeological evidence. But not all scientists buy the sun spot correlation.

Abbot had believed that the cycle was a longer one, 46 years, and that drought in the prairie states was somehow connected with the rise and fall of the waters of the Great Lakes.

J. Murray Mitchell, Jr., a climatologist with the government's Environmental Data Service, agrees with neither theory. He believes the cycles are created by "interaction between the atmosphere and the oceans." He asserts that the sun spot theory breaks down on the lack of coincidence with the cycle as irrefutably indicated by tree-ring studies. Yet he agrees, in substance, that the cycle has a 25-to-27-year swing.

Donald L. Gilman, chief of the National Weather Service's long-range prediction group, is, understandably, a cautious man. He will not predict a drought for any given year. Yet, he says, "the High Plains have had it pretty easy the last fifteen years. We know from past records that more extremes are possible — wet and dry, warm and cold. People making plans on the basis of the [weather] experience over the last decade or two could be in for a real shock."

It took thousands of years for the grasses of the area to adapt to these great extremes. These were a mixture of grasses, shrubs and gorse which we now simply identify as "native grass."

But of what did adaptation consist? First of all, on an almost infinitely complex series of relationships between a thin topsoil, seeds, wind velocities, rates of humidity, the *seasonality* of moisture, temperature, evaporation, insects, rodents, and mammals.

The soil scientists are well trained and remarkably dedicated. Like so many of us, however, the demands of their specialty bind them into narrow confines. They cannot also be historians, archeologists, astrophysicists, and geologists. They can, indeed, produce magnificent hybrid strains of grains. They can ascertain the precise chemical components of soil. They understand plant diseases. But as is the case with "reclamation" on the Great Plains, the ultimate answer as to whether it can indeed be brought

about lies in the melding of the instincts and penetrating observations of the old-time rancher, as well as in the intensive application
of chemistry, hydrology, geography, meteorology, botany, astro-
physics, history, ecological economics, and other disciplines. The
soil scientists should above all exhibit extreme caution, especially
in the realm of prophecy. Will cattle be contentedly grazing on
Montana Power's demonstration plot within five years, as Mr.
Hodder asserts? That very much depends on factors far beyond
his capacity to predict.

After suspenseful waiting by environmentalists for over a year,
a thick and vastly detailed environmental impact statement was
delivered to the Department of Natural Resources and Conservation on January 1, 1975. It was a massive report made by contract
between the department and scientists of almost every discipline
concerned with the stripping of coal and all related environmental
matters.

Concerning Montana Power's planned construction of 1,400-
megawatt (in total) plants numbers 3 and 4, the report is unequivocal on damage to plant life — and, indeed, on human health.
The culprit, of course, is SO_2, oxides of sulfur. The report predicted
damage to crops and range grasses over a *500-square-mile region*. It
warned area ranchers and farmers that they could expect to see
SO_2 damage in several forms. It predicted that they could expect
that the damage would increase during periods of drought because vegetation under "water stress" is less resistant to pollution.
It asserted that "acute damage" would be done in the first few
years when the power plants "come on the line," and that sensitive
species such as alfalfa may be completely defoliated in a single
growing season. Moreover, said the report, the *total* seed production of annual species would, in all probability, be destroyed.

After several years the damage would be chronic. Production
would probably be reduced 20 percent with no visible symptoms.
Moreover, *all* plant life would be weakened and much more sub-

ject to insect infestations and diseases. Indeed, the scientists felt that this type of "secondary agent" pollution might, in the long run, be the most damaging of all.

SO_2, said the scientists, would also cause damage in the form of "acid rain," especially during the growing season. Again, there would be few visible symptoms, but very significant production losses would occur. These two new plants *alone* would create very significantly damaging acid rains over a *7,500-square-mile area*. This, the report pointed out, would include the city of Billings, where various chemical pollutants from oil refineries had already placed all manner of vegetation under considerable stress.

But, one may ask, are these not really imponderables? Does it all not depend on the actual and theoretical efficiency of stack scrubbers? Do we know the velocity of high-altitude winds, the percentage of actual boiler capacity to be used, the temperature of the air, the humidity — and other complex factors? The answer is yes. All have been calculated and often at minimal levels. The assumption on scrubbers, for instance, is placed at the level of the removal of 98.8 percent of particulate matter. The fact is that even at this very high level of efficiency no scrubbing system extant *in the world* removes the deadly submicron-sized material.

It may be germane to remind the soil scientists employed by the power company — soil men only — that a few years ago they had devised a system to beat drought. They created drought- and rust-resistant wheat and they pounded into the farmers' heads year after year "summer fallow, summer fallow, summer fallow, strip farm" — and the farmers did.

It took from the 1920s to the mid-1960s for the real results to show. The summer-fallowed lands let the precipitation soak in and downward. As a consequence, the water table rose closer and closer and then finally *to* the surface. It brought with it salt and alkali that had previously nestled down close to the aquifer. Today in Montana alone 280,000 acres have been rendered cropless by "saline seep," and some 16 *million* additional acres have been identified as dangerous potential "saline seep" areas. We have as yet no "cure." It is a significant fact that the French government, by edict in 1800, stopped all summer fallowing because of saline seep. They substituted crop rotation.

There is a lesson in that. As Willard Gaylord wrote, "The cure to one problem usually comes packed with the cause of another." Probably there is a larger lesson still and one we had better learn quickly. The rugged face of the Great Plains belies a critical part of its nature. It is almost infinitely complex and terribly fragile. There is something almost obscenely arrogant about man's ignorance of the land he is now ripping apart. But not, thank God, all men. Just those who put profit, profligacy, and conceit above the harmony of life.

But *all* scientists, physical, natural, and social, are caught, perforce, in the shrinking nature of their specialities — which is the direct consequence of the "information explosion" of the past thirty years. It has simply become impossible to be a generalist. Except for a few areas in the humanities, the holistic view of anything is a rare view indeed.

Yet it is precisely that holistic view that we must develop if we are to plan for and deal with the impending coal crunch on the Great Plains. In theory, at least, we could do that simply by gathering together everything we have known and now know about the plains, collating and indexing it, finding a prestigious generalist (a person who can assemble, ponder, and write), and saying to that person, "Have at it." But that is in theory. The fact is the task would be too monumental for the time available. There is too little time even to give our generalist some very crucial facts. They have not been gathered yet.

The answer, of course, is obvious. We need more time. Not an acre of coal should be stripped until we have all the facts and our generalist has put them all together. That, however, is simply not going to happen.

There is one rather inadequate alternative. It is to stall and delay

while we search out more facts and, in the meantime, to be obdurately skeptical of the proposed easy solutions. It is to say to
Mr. Grende and Mr. Hodder standing knee-deep in their waving
grass, "That is very pretty but given myriad other factors it has
little bearing on what worries us."

Even the Bureau of Land Management is beginning to have second thoughts. Those thoughts began as their files thickened with
requests from the coal companies for permits to mine federally
owned coal. In 1971 the bureau declared a two-year moratorium
on permits on the grounds that enough allocations had already
been made to keep the coal companies busy. It was a strange moratorium, probably actuated by the fact that the bureau simply
could not keep up with the paperwork. But that may be too harsh
a judgment, for the bureau itself had previously launched an in-
depth study which was beginning to reveal a shocking "lackadata"
in its own calculations.

The ranchers, in any event, were grateful for small favors.

8

Water, Water, Nowhere?

PART OF THE TROUBLE may have begun with the maps. After all, a printer has just so much latitude, and a river is a river. True, he used a larger line for a larger river and a smaller line for a smaller one. But one cannot indicate the volume of flow and, indeed, one may often have a quite impressive line when, in fact, the river bed is dry.

If one looks at a map of the plains today it is threaded with large and small rivers, like the veins in the face of an old man. And often, observing these rivers (sometimes only at full flow), it seemed self-evident to the observer that an enormous amount of water coursed unused from the Rockies down across this barren land. That this water *could* be used on that land was a concept so persistent that it is a study in the enormous tenacity of ideas — both bad and good. It remains incredible, however, that in so many instances there is no correlation between the mortality of a bad idea and the weight of the mass of the evidence against it.

We have seen that John Wesley Powell had sufficient figures to explode the Eden idea at a very early date. But it would not explode. It still has not.

In a hearing before the Senate Appropriations Committee in

July 1890, Powell was severely pummeled about his views of water and the West. What Powell was after was a moratorium on settlement (under the Desert Land Act) until his topographical work could precisely delineate which lands could be irrigated and which could not. He ran into a veritable buzzsaw of opposition. Senator Hale of Maine:

"Do you conceive that there is any risk or doubt in the government's assuming that relation and undertaking to deal with the flow and use of water in the great streams? Do you think it is better than to leave it to nature and the common incidents of human life?"

Said Powell, "You ask me the question, and I will answer. I think it would be almost a criminal act to go on as we are doing now, and allow thousands and hundreds of thousands of people to establish homes where they cannot maintain themselves." Remember the date, 1890.

Powell, of course, lost. So, as we have seen, did the National Conservation Commission when it asked for a similar moratorium prior to the passage of the Enlarged Homestead Act of 1909. It merely wanted a land classification study made so that settlers would have some idea of what was arable, irrigable and livable. It lost its case.

These are merely two examples of a very persistent western theme. No one does *anything* until some kind of intense pressure, be it population pressure or economic pressure, forces action. The action that takes place then is sudden, random, and uncontrolled — at least by the government and on the public domain.

Nevertheless, nature has its way, and the violation of the integrity of the land simply results in human suffering — which ought, of course, to result in a lesson learned. It usually does not.

Coal cannot be mined without water. The actual process of stripping coal takes very little water. In all likelihood the process will have dramatic, traumatic and enormously deleterious effects upon subsurface water (and hence upon the land for miles around and beyond any given mine), but the fact remains that strip mining per se requires little water.

When, however, one begins talking of mine-mouth generating plants and coal gasification plants, one is talking about vast quantities of water.

It is vital to bear in mind that this water is not merely used and returned to the river. It is converted to steam, the essence of the generating process. It is not merely a coolant — though, indeed, it is used as such. Nor is the steam reconverted to water. Nor can it be. It passes off into the atmosphere. Even if reconversion could take place, a very slight increase in the temperature of the water would wreak havoc with the river for miles below discharge point. Not only is the steam itself dirty and thus a pollutant, but in the "gasification" process (as opposed to the "generating" process), water is employed in atomized form under intense pressure to convert the "cooked coal" (which is cooked by the burning of other coal) into gas. This water is not even let loose into the atmosphere in the form of steam. It literally becomes part of the gas. Accordingly, gasification plants require even more water than generating plants — though both use such huge quantities of water that the distinction is actually minuscule.

In the late 1960s, when the talk turned to stripping on the plains, environmentalists were deeply disturbed. But, of course, no one in his right mind would suggest mine-mouth generation, since the water simply was not there. That was before the publication of the *North Central Power Study* of 1971. Then, there it was boldly, bluntly, and with all its gargantuan implications: forty-two mine-mouth generating power plants in Montana, Wyoming, North Dakota, South Dakota and Colorado; twenty-one located in Montana, two of Brobdingnagian proportions — 10,000 megawatts; seven of 5,000 megawatts; one of 3,000 megawatts, and the remainder of 1,000 megawatts each. Had these crazy industry people forgotten water?

No, they had not. The *North Central Power Study* was followed by the *Montana-Wyoming Aqueduct Study*, which delineated potential reservoirs, major water conveyance conduits, minor water conveyance conduits, potential hydropeaking statistics, river flows at high and low water in acre-feet, pumping station locations, and the unit cost of water delivered to a given area.

A funny thing happened to these studies on their way through the hands of the coal companies, power companies, state boards of natural resources, legislatures, *and* environmental groups. They became obsolete, inoperative, "just a plan that cannot ever be put into effect." When an expert on population impact was asked if he had figures on the influx of people based on the size and location of the plants proposed in the *NCPS*, he raised his eyebrows in surprise. "Oh, we don't use *that* report for input. It's not a *current* plan. The companies aren't taking it seriously. No one is anymore."

An environmentally oriented legislator in Montana's last session was asked what he thought of the *NCPS*. "Oh, hell, it was just a trial balloon. It's out the window." When asked the same question, three separate coal companies' officials asserted that it was just one more study. Studies, they said, are all over the place. "We have an energy crisis. They're making studies of solar power and all that. It doesn't mean anything."

Maybe. But, as already indicated, the *NCPS* took a solid year of hardheaded calculation and hard work by management representatives from nineteen investor-owned utilities, six corporations, two public power districts, and one federal and eight municipal representatives. It represented a vast lot of work on the part of Assistant Secretary of the Interior James R. Smith, and it is *there*, reduced in scope, no doubt, and with alterations and mitigations, but it is still there.

One of the moving forces in an organization called the Environmental Information Center (Montana) put it this way: "Well, they say nobody's paying any attention to it, but it's odd.

If you add little bits and pieces together, I'd say the plan is very much alive." He pointed at a report on his desk. "For instance, here is another report, dated April 1972. It is done by the Bureau of Reclamation. It is titled *Appraisal Report on Montana-Wyoming Aqueducts.* Read it and see how it fits." It fits. So do a number of other reports. But this one gets down to the nub of the matter. Water.

Surface water sources for the entire Fort Union Coal Area consist of the Missouri, Yellowstone, Powder, Tongue, Bighorn, and Little Bighorn rivers. Let us concentrate on what is happening in one of the great river basins, the Yellowstone.

The Yellowstone has an *average* annual discharge of 8.8 million acre-feet per year. An acre-foot of water is the amount it would take to cover one acre of land with one foot of water. In dry years, such as the Northern Plains witnessed in the early 1960s, the Yellowstone's discharge was only slightly over 4 million acre-feet. The *Montana-Wyoming Aqueduct Study* states:

Under plans now being evaluated [precisely what plans it does not make clear], coal could be used for the generation of electric power and, if competitive processes are demonstrated, could be converted into synthetic pipeline gas or liquid fuels. Projected water requirements show that about 2.6 million acre feet may be required annually to meet a development level that may be attained in less than 30 years. The study of water resources shows that water requirements of this magnitude could be supplied by full development from existing and potential storage reservoirs and by construction of aqueducts to transfer water to points of use.

From the Yellowstone drainage this volume represents 29.7 percent of the river's *average* annual flow. It could very well represent 50 percent of that flow in dry years.

But that is *proposed.* What has already happened, how and why? Here, in a series of proposals and reports, one detects panic. *Coal Development in Eastern Montana: A Situation Report of the Montana Coal Task Force*, January 1973. Under "Water Resources," merely a prediction of "massive new water uses," and, "Little is known about what actual levels of water consumption will be reached." The best the task force could do was this: "The Department of Natural Resources and Conservation has a record of nearly 8,000 filed surface and ground water rights in the Fort Union Region of the Yellowstone Basin. Because all rights are not filed, the actual number of rights might be as high as 12,000."

So one turns to a document prepared in December 1973, by the Montana Energy Advisory Council for submission to the Old West Regional Commission. It is bulky! Unhappily, it turns out to be "A proposed series of projects to evaluate the potential physical, biological and water use impacts of water withdrawals and water development on the middle and lower portions of the Yellowstone River drainage." It is a request for a grant to study the basic matters involved. It is a discussion of methodology and hoped-for results. It is, quite simply, a cry for help.

So, we turn to January 1974 and a report submitted jointly by the Montana Energy Advisory Council and the Montana Department of Natural Resources and Conservation. Again, it is bulky — and it has a good title, *A Study of Filed and Use-Appropriated Water Rights in Portions of the Yellowstone Basin in Montana.*

It starts off well and gives background information on Montana's water rights situation. Simply enough: it was chaotic. One moves on to "Existing Water Rights Situation in Montana." Well, the 43rd legislative assembly of 1973 passed the Montana Water Use Act. This act, says the report, has resulted in "an enormous undertaking" because of the former chaotic situation. One reads on with growing sympathy and also with growing alarm. "New, large water filings are being made on the Yellowstone River, existing water rights have been purchased for conversion to energy-related uses, and options on stored water have been taken by dozens of energy companies, with applications filed for any future stored water that may become available for industrial purposes."

Who is steering this ship? How *much* have we lost? How much has been stolen?

Well, a few facts emerge: application by Utah International, Inc., received November 1973, to appropriate one hundred cubic feet per second from the Powder River; application by the Montana Water Storage Company, received December 1973, to appropriate 730 cubic feet per second of the Tongue River to be diverted to a 130,000 acre-foot storage area; application by Water Reserve Company of Montana, January 1974, to appropriate 550 cubic feet per second from the Tongue River to be diverted to a proposed 91,000 acre-foot storage reservoir. Application by the Montana Power Company, December 1970, for 250 cubic feet per second from the Yellowstone River.

But the rest of the report? It is a proposal for a study of the basic issues involved with a cost summary, grand total, $353,000.

One's mind flashes back to the "inoperative" *North Central Power Study*. On page 18 (sprawling across southeastern Montana and northeastern Wyoming) is a crystal-clear map of "Water Conveyance in the Gillette-Colstrip Area." One huge aqueduct extends from Miles City on the Yellowstone to Casper, Wyoming, on the Platte; another from Hardin to Gillette; a dozen others, large and small.

And while Montanans sweat about the law, the brand-new Water Use Act, the *North Central Power Study* asserts: "The Committee knows of no overriding obstacles (legal) to development of large generating complexes and a transmission system in the North Central Region."

The Bureau of Reclamation in its aqueduct study exhibits splendid pictures not only of existent reservoirs and dams but of "potential" reservoirs: Moorhead reservoir, astride the Wyoming-Montana line, would impound 100,000 acre-feet; Hole-in-the-Wall reservoir would impound 20,000 acre-feet; Box Elder reservoir would impound 30,000 acre-feet; the Little Bighorn reservoir would impound 40,000 acre-feet. Then, the *big* one, Allenspur

Dam on the Yellowstone River, would impound 1,500,000 acre-feet. The dam, to be built just south of Livingston, would completely block the most beautiful entrance to Yellowstone Park, Paradise Valley. It would put that lovely valley under 380 feet of water and create a reservoir twenty-five miles long and five miles wide.

What of the federal government's role in all this? Well, its contribution did not end with the *Aqueduct Study*. The Bureau of Reclamation has, as of now, allocated industrial options of almost 700,000 acre-feet of stored water from the Boyson and Yellowtail reservoirs.

Montana's reaction to the enormous raids on its water, raids from many sources and in an incredibly short period of time, was, as we have seen, one of near panic and a proliferation of proposed studies. Why, one may ask, had such a vital matter not been studied in depth years ago? Why was Montana's Environmental Quality Council caught so short? Why was the Department of Natural Resources so laggard in response with specific data?

In point of fact, Montana's response has been astonishingly positive and swift — and it is only in relationship to the enormity of the coal-stripping invasion that confronts state government that the response can be considered otherwise.

As for water, the historic logic behind who got how much was based on the "Prior Appropriation Doctrine." This simply meant that a right was obtained by taking the water and putting it to a beneficial use. Only so long as it was beneficially used was the right valid. As for competing appropriators from the same source, priority in time was determinative. This is the way it was and the new Montana Water Use Act of 1973 did not alter that basic concept.

But, over the years what matters in the water right picture is who *really* appropriated how much and when. Indeed, from the 1860s, when the water right was used for the purpose of placer mining, up to the present time, few things have been as volatile as water rights.

Sometimes pushed into the picture by violent water feuds and small wars, the courts (state district courts) began to "adjudicate" rivers and streams. They would call in all the contentious water users on a given stream, take testimony, review the "filings" in the county courthouse, determine whether there had been continuous beneficial use, and then apportion the water by "decree." The rancher or farmer then had a presumably inviolate "decreed right" to the water of that given stream.

But the legal casebooks literally bulge with charges, counter-charges, and sometimes with changes in the original adjudication. In Montana these "decrees" were never filed with the state but only in the county courthouse. Not until 1973 and the new Water Use Act did the law specify that "first in use, first in right" was only valid if the decree were registered with the state. However, there are fifty-six counties in Montana. The keeping of the files has often been offhand. Worse, the failure to file a notice of a claim in the courthouse did not necessarily invalidate the right. There was, and are, accordingly, a number of water users whose right to the water consists solely of some document buried in an old desk or, sometimes, simply buried in an old memory.

Worse still, in adjudication cases the district judges were hardly experts in water flow, and as a consequence they often appropriated far more water than flowed in the stream or river in question. The result, of course, is that no department of the State of Montana *ever* knew how much water belonged to whom and where and since when.

If this be the case, why did the state not act long ago? Why wait until 1973 when the thirsty giants had already descended upon us? First of all, it is the rule and not the exception for state legislatures to let sleeping dogs lie — even if the sleep is intermittently interrupted with snarling. Second, Montana is a rural state, and for government to involve itself in any way with water matters is politically explosive. Only the clear and present danger of the loss of vast quantities of water to the coal companies could convince a rurally oriented legislature to pass the Montana Water Use Act of 1973. But "to administer, control, and regulate water rights, establish a system of centralized water rights" is obviously a monumental task for a grossly understaffed Department of Natural Resources to undertake. As we shall see, once it had crossed the Rubicon, the legislature was willing to go much farther.

But even all that leaves severe problems of another nature. The State of Montana has "river compacts" with other states, such as the Yellowstone River Compact with North Dakota and Wyoming. By virtue of these compacts the states have long since agreed to apportion water among themselves "in the interests of interstate comity." These compacts are binding and extremely complex. And the ultimate question remains: How much water is really available for interstate appropriation?

Moreover, Indian water rights are an entirely separate matter. Their rights reside fundamentally in treaties. Yet a battery of court decisions have converted the Indian water right situation into a nightmare of legal complexities. If, indeed, it takes a lawyer with special training in international law as well as water law to make minimal sense of the Indian water rights, what is the position of the tribe when dealing with coal companies? One view is set forth in a Ralph Nader Study Group publication: *Damming the West: Indians Sold Down the River.* It is not a pretty story.

Chaotic as it is, it gets worse — because none of these hindrances and problems involves ground water, only surface water. Yet in many respects, if not most, ground and surface water are inseparable. What affects one affects the other. Adequate and pure ground water is a critical aspect of any agricultural use of the land. What does strip mining do to ground water?

The answer is that we know startlingly little about it but

what little we do know is all bad. Ground water and the 25-to-70-foot-thick layers of coal that underlie the enormous Fort Union coal area are intimately associated and have been for eons. Coal is an aquifer and in many instances a kind of double aquifer in that one seam of coal lies beneath another with an intervening seam of clay or other material between. Ground water not only follows along the surface of the coal layers but permeates those layers and is, in turn, filtered by them.

As the National Academy of Sciences pointed out, "In most of the western coal fields the coal beds that lie close to the surface are also aquifers. Many of the wells that have moderate yields used for domestic purposes and livestock obtain their water from coal beds at depths of less than 500 feet. . . . Removal of the coal by a surface mining operation would intersect the aquifer that is the source of water for several hundred wells in the area."

Though, again, data are terribly inadequate, what little we know is frightening. Wayne Van Voast of the Montana State Bureau of Mines made a study of subsurface water in the Decker area, near the Tongue River, where a strip mine is, in effect, just getting under way. His research started before the stripping. In 1970 the State Bureau of Mines drilled twelve observation wells around the mine site. Very early in the stripping process, the water level had dropped 10 to 50 feet — and this more than a mile and a half away from the mine site. Van Voast estimates that ultimately the drop may be between 40 and 90 feet, affecting not merely wells but the entire land surface, since water moves surfaceward via capillary action.

Moreover, Van Voast found that the water that flowed into the pit from which the coal had been removed contained over 300 times as much sodium as water in the nearby Tongue River; 9 times as much carbonate, sulfate, and dissolved solids; and 30 times as much nitrate. He also found trace metals which had not been there before — copper, lead, zinc, and nickel.

After the mining has taken place and the pits are filled with the "spoils," will the water table rise again and will the new "aquifer" work? We do not know. But the chances seem to be that *if* the water table rose, without the coal as "filter," that water would be highly alkali, a phenomenon already demonstrated in the "saline seep" areas — though from a different cause.

One of the frightening things is that while the total area, for instance, to be mined at Decker is three square miles, the Bureau of Mines study indicates that the ground water levels and the quality of that water will be affected over approximately *twenty* square miles. Were this to hold true elsewhere, one would have to multiply the actual area stripped by six if one were to assess damage.*

One also encounters a constellation of problems which do not appear on the surface with the construction of reservoirs, pipelines and aqueducts. Reservoirs are not always quite what they seem. They take up land, and usually the best bottom land where the rivers have enriched the soils. The four reservoirs proposed in the *Montana-Wyoming Aqueduct Study* alone would involve 70,000 acres. Moreover, dams and reservoirs often create serious downstream siltage problems, drastic channel changes and serious erosion, to say nothing of fish kills. Moreover, reservoirs cause enormous evaporation and, depending on weather conditions, a tremendous amount of water is thus lost. Several of the proposed dams in the *Montana-Wyoming Aqueduct Study* (particularly the largest, Allenspur) lie directly over earthquake-prone zones. In 1959 a quake that registered 7 on the Richter scale caused the collapse of a "mountain," burying nineteen campers, damming the Madison River, and creating a new lake — Quake Lake. This was only a few miles from the proposed Allenspur dam. Geologists have long known that the entire area is "faulted" and earthquake-prone.

In only one report is mention made of the matter of demographic changes — and that is the report of the National Academy

* See *Hydrological Effects of Strip Coal Mining Near Decker, Montana,* Montana Bureau of Mines, June 1974.

of Sciences. There is no reference to the problem elsewhere and absolutely no data exist. Yet, as the location of the railroads drastically altered population patterns on the plains as they probed westward, so, too, says the academy report, would any drastic change in the present flow-system of water. A major transbasin transfer of water would be "a major factor in directing future development." The availability of water along the routes of conveyance, even in rather minor amounts, would result in new towns, alter the economic activities of existing towns, and result in a swiftly changing population pattern. And the report adds: "At this time there is little evidence that adequate mechanisms for planning exist at any governmental level, particularly on a scale commensurate with the potential impact of redistributing water over large scale areas. . . ."

As was the case with the railroads, one might anticipate massive land speculation and its attendant scandals and wild promotions. One might also anticipate a heightening of the already tense situation which exists between the ranchers and *any* "invader." If they are hostile to the coal companies, they would be no less so to speculators and "developers" (whom they already detest).*

Having passed the Water Use Act in 1973, it quickly became apparent to the Montana legislators that it was too little and too late. That legislature had been a remarkable one. It was the first legislature to convene under Montana's new constitution. Any old-time legislature-watcher could hardly have been other than astonished at this new assemblage. It was filled with new faces, the age level had plummeted, all of its hearings were open to the public, environmentalists were buzzing around like bees — and a good many of them, mostly young, had very sharp stingers. There were *women* in this session! Moreover, most of them were young,

---

* It is a side issue, but a kind of war already exists between ranchers and farmers and large-scale land "developers." This is more a western and central Montana phenomenon at present, though it has been moving eastward. Not only are most of the developers not Montanans, a few are Japanese or European, which goads some ranchers into sustained fury.

good-looking and well educated. The place was chaotic. It was, indeed, enough to sicken the heart of the old-timers who had so long performed so well for the Anaconda Company and the Montana Power Company. One "eight-termer" remarked, "It's that goddam new constitution! The state is wrecked beyond repair."

So it would seem, because that first session rammed through some fiercely radical (for Montana) legislation, and the second, in 1975, was more radical still. In point of fact, it may prove that the legislation is radical for *any* state. It passed the Montana Strip Mining and Reclamation Act, the Coal Conservation Act, the Montana Utility Siting Act, the Montana Water Use Act, and the Montana Severance Coal Tax.

Not only did these pieces of legislation have teeth, the teeth were sharklike, double-rowed, and exceedingly sharp.

The problem, of course, was that the sessions adjourned leaving newly created boards and commissions to implement the legislation, a monumental job. The deeper problems lay in the fact that in *all* of the environmental areas involved basic data were simply nonexistent. Not only were the boards and commissions short of money and staff, they were short of the most critical commodity of all — time. The forces moving into Montana were moving swiftly, they were huge, they *had* data, and they had all the expertise that money could buy. The story of the initial struggle between a very small but very dedicated group of men and women and the giants will come along in due course. We are concerned here only with the Montana Water Use Act.

The legislative session reconvened in January 1974. It was as fractious as ever, except for a last-stand group of senators who did manage to kill some excellent legislation.

On January 28, 1974, Governor Thomas Judge sent a letter to the president of the Senate and the Speaker of the House. Behind this letter lay a great deal of work and a great deal of thought — and not merely on the governor's part. Lieutenant Governor William Christiansen and the small group of technicians, lawyers and experts around him had much to do with what happened.

The letter was about water. The governor wrote, "The value of our coal and water has not gone unnoticed by powerful private and public interests beyond our borders. Increasingly, the granting of rights to use these two resources is taking the decision-making authority for our future out of our hands and placing it in the hands of interests located in the financial centers of our nation, far removed from the concerns and controls of Montanans." Primarily, said the governor, he wanted to talk about water. He reviewed the extent of the water already committed, the pending requests and the whole chaotic story. He called the potential results "staggering." He said of the rush for Montana's water, "This is unacceptable." And then he called for legislation declaring a three-year moratorium on all further water appropriated from the entire Yellowstone River basin. The only exception was for those who had already been cleared under the terms of the Utility Siting Act and had thus been issued a Certificate of Environmental Compatibility and those who could meet those standards within three years but whose requests were for 20 cubic feet per second or less. In effect, the governor was asking for a lockup of the entire drainage. Moreover, legislation thus introduced required a two-thirds vote in each house — a majority which had not been achieved in the history of the legislature on any significant piece of legislation.

He got the vote and he got it fast, and the great drainage was locked up. How many moratoria had been proposed for the usage of land or water on the Great Plains over a period of the preceding seventy-five years is anybody's guess. Various individuals (like Powell) or commissions must have petitioned Congress or individual states many dozens of times. No moratorium had ever been granted, except for the leasing pause by the Bureau of Land Management. Now there *was* one, and one that involved a huge area.

Though the stated objective of the moratorium was to grant time to the state for the scientific assessment of water resources, the moratorium meant much more. A reminder: one cannot build mine-mouth power plants without huge quantities of water. If there is no water, there are no aqueducts or dams or reservoirs. Without water, and hence huge generating plants, there is no massive air pollution that so characterizes these monstrous complexes.

So, in effect, Montana, to the palpable surprise of the great coal and energy companies, demonstrated not only that it had power but that it was willing to use it. It proved it again more powerfully in the 1975 session. Yet no knowledgeable Montanan was euphoric. Power is what power does. They had stalled them, but that is all. The companies are infinitely patient and very skilled. There is no assurance that, in fact, Montana has any federal allies at all. There is a good deal of evidence to the contrary.

On July 13, 1974, however, Montanans got another boost — and from a very unsuspected source. The Bureau of Reclamation had finished a four-year study. It had been widely assumed that the study would simply affirm the bureau's a priori stance that the national energy crisis necessitated the stripping of western coal on a crash basis. That was, in effect, the stated policy of the White House in "Project Independence." It had clearly been the bureau's view as set forth in many documents, most notably, the *Montana-Wyoming Aqueduct Study*.

But now the bureau had *some* of its data and its report reflected very serious doubts about the whole project. The reason? Water. Even with interbasin and interstate transfer, said the report, there was not enough water. (One can only hope that somewhere John Wesley Powell was listening.)

Moreover, for the first time the bureau concerned itself with ground water and with its loss and contamination. It suggested a major acceleration of rain-making, particularly in the upper Colorado and Rio Grande river basins, but it quickly backed off from the process as a panacea. The bureau was worried about rap-idly increasing salinity caused by irrigation runoffs and municipal and industrial wastes. In addition, said the bureau, the western states were being severely afflicted with erosion. All told, the re-port stated, there was serious erosion of 155,000 square miles, or almost 15 percent of the entire area of the western states, and there was more moderate erosion on 330,000 square miles.

The report made rather eerie reading because it sounded like the bureau of old, in the days when its name and its function were reflective of each other. It is, after all, the Bureau of *Reclamation*. But since the 1930s, along with the Army Corps of Engineers, it had been a great builder of dams, conduits, and reservoirs, the primary function of which had been the *production of power*. The bureau increasingly allied itself with industry, and as it did so it increasingly alienated its real and intended constituency, the farmer and the rancher. As early as the 1950s it began to become one of the several ogres of the environmentalists. Among other things, its projects had led to large-scale wildlife losses and massive fish kills; its projects had drastically altered wetland patterns and changed the migratory habits of innumerable bird species.

But here, as of old, was the bureau talking about irrigation and the need to cultivate semiarid land to produce food for worldwide needs. Here, *mirabile dictu*, was the bureau saying that water was the key to raising the economic status of the Indians and pointing out the nature of Indian impoverishment. Here was the bureau stating that by the year 2000 energy production would consume 3.2 million acre-feet of water annually — with about 2.5 million acre-feet for power plant cooling, 600,000 acre-feet for coal gasi-fication and mining, and 150,000 acre-feet for oil shale processing. And, said the bureau, the only way to get that water would be in a massive shift from agricultural to industrial use.

The report pointed out that about 25 percent of the West's 6,500 towns had either insufficient water already or poor and brackish water — or both. And, shockingly, the report asserted,

"open space does not have to be green to be useful and attractive."
That, *indeed*, did not sound like the bureau!

The peroration of the report was at once an assertion and a
plea. The most critical problem, it said, was "the lack of basic
biological information." And it recommended seventy-two areas
for in-depth studies over a five-year period. These studies would
involve eighteen federal agencies at a cost of $138 million.

Montanans' responses to the bureau's report were guarded. Did
this really represent an about-face by the bureau? Would *they*
stand up under intense industrial and governmental pressures? One
of the organizers of the Northern Plains Resource Council put it
aptly: "It depends on so damn many unknowns, doesn't it? What
if the Arabs turn the spigot off again? What if we get a couple of
very cold winters and the people in New York City are wearing
blankets to the office? What if the President stonewalls it and cuts
off a bunch of heads? What if, and what if? We will have to
wait and see, that's all."

And that, indeed, we will.

9

How to Get a Shock out of Farming: Transmission Lines

THE WESTERN QUARTER of Montana, that portion lying west of the Continental Divide, is mountainous and heavily forested. It is a tumultuous kind of land; its great heaving mountains are interspersed with valleys, verdant meadows, and streams, lakes, and riverⁿ. It is lumbering country, mining country, farming and ranching country. The mountains have conditioned people, as the plains did, but in different ways. Montana should not be one schizophrenic state, as it is; its boundaries should never have been drawn as they were. But we are stuck with them.

Western Montana is pulled westward. Eastern Montana is pulled eastward. This is an economic fact which has translated itself not only into politics but into attitudes and states of mind. In a way, the mountain Montanan has always been introverted. There has been a physical separation of groups, one valley settlement separated from another by massive ramparts. But more than that, the mountain Montanan has looked inward for another reason. What he wanted, or did not want, was more often attainable from the state legislature than from Congress. The West was born in the gold rushes, and when in due course its vast mineral riches came to be controlled first by several huge mining concerns and then by only one, the Anaconda Company, that power flowed into the legislature. Since in Montana the miners were also the lumbermen (and the railroad men), there was no real distinction in the nature of the power — and it was very great. Again, it expressed itself in the legislature and in the *state* executive and judicial branches.

Eastern Montanans were rarely concerned with these matters. What they wanted, or did not want, was attainable from Congress. There they fought their battles, and their petitions were sent to Washington rather than Helena. Company policies were deeply but pragmatically conservative. The eastern ranchers were philosophical conservatives. The coalition solidified and much of the political history of Montana was conditioned by that coalition. But the deeper consideration was that one section simply had no real stake and hence no real interest in what was going on in the other.

Colstrip, Savage, Forsyth, and Hardin were as remote from Butte, Helena, and Missoula as Los Angeles is from Pittsburgh. That is as true today as it was in 1890, with several startling and very recent exceptions. They are exceptions of significance. Let us examine the irony involved by a momentary scrutiny of one small western Montana town, Hamilton, located in the Bitterroot Valley about fifty miles south of Missoula.

Hamilton has a population of about 4,000. It is a town dependent upon farms, small ranches, and the lumber industry. It is a clean, neat, and very orderly community. It is very conservative. Its magnificent setting has attracted out-of-state people, but most of them are retirees from southern California or middle western urban areas — and most of them are also conservative. The population is growing slowly.

In the fall of 1972, a public hearing was called so that the populace could be informed that a new power line was to be constructed by the Montana Power Company from Missoula to Hamilton. An environmental impact statement had been drawn up for the power company by Wirth and Associates, an "independent" environmental consulting firm in Billings. Several copies of this statement had gotten loose in the valley several weeks before the hearing. Word spread with great rapidity. As a consequence, when representatives of Wirth and Associates and the power company showed up at the high school auditorium for what they obviously thought would be a pro forma performance, the auditorium was jammed with utterly hostile people, not only from Hamilton but from the entire valley. They came prepared to make statements and they made them. Wirth and Associates, however, came first with maps and explanations. Several times during the presentation there was loud laughter from the audience and on other occasions hisses and boos. When the Wirth representatives sat down, looking washed out and nonplussed, person after person marched to the stage to express either total incredulity or fury.

Hamilton found out that evening that it was suffering from a critical power shortage. It had been unaware of that fact. It was imperative, the people were told, that a 161-kilovolt (161,000-volt) power line be constructed at once or dire things would happen.

The Bitterroot Valley is bounded on the west by the sharp and jagged Bitterroot Mountains. The Bitterroot-Selway Wilderness Area, the nation's largest, starts on the valley side of the steep slopes of those mountains. The valley is bordered on the east by the Sapphire range, less jagged than the Bitterroots but very beautiful. Behind the Sapphires lies the Pintlar Wilderness Area. The foothills of the Sapphires are great, swelling, rolling range and farmland. The power company's plan was to slash its 161-kilovolt line directly across these foothills, which are very visible from the curving highway along the valley's bottom. Along that highway there are already two power lines of 69 kilovolts each.

Why a third corridor? Could not the voltage be increased on the two existent lines? It could, replied the power company, but only by about 20 percent, and that was not enough. Why, then, could these lines not be removed and the new line installed in the old corridor? Too expensive, replied the power company. None of the valleys' residents was unaware of the fact that the power company had the right of eminent domain and hence the right to condemn any property it saw fit.

Within a week after the power company's presentation a group had formed called the Hold-the-Line Committee and money was being solicited for a suit. The money was not hard to raise. But what were the grounds for a suit?

Along with its twin, the Anaconda Company, the Montana Power Company had long had a reputation for almost paranoid secrecy in its plans and operations, a penchant for secrecy mixed with a kind of blatant arrogance. The company had had its own way in Montana for more than sixty years, and it had always proceeded without let or hindrance.

The basis for the suit was, essentially, that any game with odds about the same as craps was worth the stakes. Only in court could one subpoena records and cross-examine experts. That was not much to go on, but these were very angry people.

Moreover, something stank. A critical power shortage in Hamilton? So, eyes turned to the east. Most residents of the valley had to get out their maps to find the town of Colstrip. And when they found it, they had to scramble for information as to what was going on there. When they were briefed on that subject, it all began to fall into place.

Unbeknownst to the vast majority of *western* Montanans, the Montana Power Company, of course, had vastly expanded the operation at Colstrip and it had gotten a splendid start before the Utility Siting Act had been passed in 1973. By the time the Hold-the-Line Committee had hired a lawyer and begun to probe into affairs at Colstrip, the company had almost completed generating plant number 1 of a projected four. Plants numbers 1 and 2, each of 350 megawatts, had been authorized before the Utility Siting Act. Plants numbers 3 and 4, huge 700-megawatt plants, had not yet been authorized. Moreover, not only was the company proceeding apace with plants numbers 1 and 2, it had obtained a water allocation from the Yellowstone River on December 18, 1970, amounting to 250 cubic feet per second. Moreover, and most significantly, it now transpired that the Montana Power Company had a contract with Puget Sound Power and Light Company in Seattle, a company which was sharing the cost of construction at and would receive power from Colstrip, about a thousand miles away.

But how does one get power from Colstrip to the Pacific Coast? Quite simply — by building *twin* 500-kilovolt lines across some of the most wild and beautiful parts of western Montana to connect with the Bonneville Power Authority's facilities.

Also, a 161-kilovolt line was proposed to run from Colstrip to Anaconda, then due west over the Sapphire Mountains, skirting the Pintlar Wilderness Area to Hamilton, and then continuing westward across the Bitterroot Mountains, again just skirting the Bitterroot-Selway Wilderness Area, proceeding then across southern Idaho to connect with Puget Sound Power and Light.

A 161-kilovolt line is not really large enough for the efficient exportation of substantial quantities of power. But once permission for right-of-way is granted, environmentalists are convinced that the 161-kilovolt lines would quickly be converted to 500 kilovolts.

These lines, it must be emphasized, would run through some of America's most pristine, wild and beautiful country. They would provide power to Washington but leave in Montana all the wreckage that massive pollution implies — air, land and water.

Had the power company cleared all this with the Forest Service? Well, not exactly, but they had had a series of meetings. The request was in. The lines had been meticulously mapped. At another very small and unpublicized meeting in Hamilton, the Bitterroot line was discussed between company officials and the Forest Service, and a news story came out the following day stating that Orville Daniels, supervisor of the Bitterroot National

Forest, "closed the meeting by complimenting the MPC [Montana Power Company] for coming to the public early in the planning stages of the Anaconda to Hamilton line." And Daniels said, "Let's keep the cooperation flowing." The Hold-the-Line Committee did not miss the irony. It had taken a massive public outcry and preparations for a lawsuit to bring the company out of whispering sessions in the back room of the offices at Butte.

To no one's real surprise, the Bitterrooters lost their case in court. They *had* presented expert testimony by hiring Donald Teske, a consulting electrical engineer from California. But Teske had to rely on company figures. After Teske drew his conclusions on the witness stand in court, the power company found that it had made certain errors in the information provided to Teske, particularly in the projections concerning population growth in the valley. The power company had used an 8 percent growth figure, basic to Teske's conclusions. The error, said George O'Connor, president of the power company, was Teske's, not the company's. "We never had more than a 5 percent growth rate," he said. But, in fact, the 8 percent figure *provided by the company* had been the figure given the valley residents as justification for the line.

After Teske's testimony, again based on company power-load figures, the company discovered that they had made an error due to faulty meters. Again, Teske's findings were thus invalidated. It was too late. The money had run out. The case was lost. The cause, however, was not.

The case attracted wide attention and received full coverage in the newspapers of western Montana. Western Montanans began to look eastward again. And well they might have — for the Colstrip-Anaconda-Hamilton-Idaho-Washington line was, in fact, small potatoes. It began to dawn on western Montanans that what happened at Colstrip or Savage, indeed, what happened anywhere in the coalfields of eastern Montana was of great moment to western Montanans. The massive lines would move not only northward, but westward, through the wild forest and lake lands. Suddenly the wildlife people, the fisheries people, the caterers to tourists, the Indians on the Flathead Reservation, were alert to a danger of great substance.

Moreover, it now became public knowledge, largely due to the probing of a newly sensitized press, that it was not merely a plan involving the Puget Sound Power and Light Company, but also the Bonneville Power Authority, the Portland General Electric Company, the Washington Water Power Company, and the Pacific Power and Light Company.

The Confederated Flathead Kootenai tribes reacted swiftly and positively. They voted at once to close a 20,000-acre "sacred" section of reservation land "to all industrial development." They had the power to do it — and they did it. Still, all alternative routes would pass through the reservation. The resident Bureau of Indian Affairs officer, Bud Mehle, told the Tribal Council that the Bureau of Land Management would be responsible for drafting an assessment on behalf of all federal agencies of the environmental impact of the transmission project. But Bearhead Swaney, an influential member of the council, was not impressed. He said, "We are unalterably opposed to the construction of these lines through the South Fork of the Jocko." Swaney is no negligible antagonist. He is a barrel-chested, well-educated, articulate, and impressive man and he means what he says.

The real power involved is not the BIA nor even the BLM. It is the Forest Service. And while a small portion of the reservation, called the Jocko Valley, might well be interpreted as "sacred ground" to the Flatheads, there exists no statute or regulation which would enable the tribe to close the entire reservation or other portions thereof to power lines. The power company *has* the power of condemnation — and there is little, indeed, that Bearhead Swaney can do about it.

In the meantime, the Department of Natural Resources called for a series of public meetings in communities along the proposed twin 430-mile corridor. Ten to fifteen such meetings were planned, as well as a statewide public opinion survey.

The power company had hardly been idle. It issued a pamphlet entitled "Answers to Your Questions About Montana Power's 500KV Colstrip–Hot Springs Transmission Line." The pamphlet begins with a homey letter from President George O'Connor. It is addressed, "Dear Landowner: The two 500KV transmission lines Montana Power plans to build from Colstrip to Hot Springs have been routed across your property . . ." and O'Connor, after a short introduction, turned the matter over to his staff, who used a question-and-answer format. Here are a few examples:

Q. Will construction or Montana Power personnel carry guns?
A. No. No one on the job will be permitted to carry firearms.
Q. Will the transmission lines adversely affect people?
A. Years of experience with 500KV lines have produced no evidence of ill effects on humans or animals. Linemen constantly work next to live transmission lines as a matter of routine. It is possible for a person to experience a static electricity shock by touching the metal of equipment insulated from the ground by rubber tires (such as a tractor) and parked under a line. The shock, similar to that experienced by shuffling across a living room carpet, is completely harmless. All permanent ungrounded structures, such as barbed wire fences, will be grounded when the lines are built to prevent such nuisance shocks.
Q. Can I sprinkler irrigate under the lines?
A. Yes. Sprinkler irrigation is a common practice under 500KV lines. . . . There are no limitations on irrigation.

There are many such succinct questions and answers. The problem is that many of the answers are simply not accurate. It is difficult to believe that this is due to ignorance.

For instance, the answer on sprinkler irrigation. On July 3, 1974, Kanv R. Shah, an electrical engineer from Jackson, Michigan, a consultant for public utilities all over the country (and not a "professional" environmental consultant), testified before a group of state and federal officials concerned about Montana Power's proposed twin 500-kilovolt lines. He was very critical. He said, among other things, that such lines are particularly dangerous around irrigation systems because if water spray touches the wires (which at their low point are only 37 feet above the ground), anyone touching any part of the system could be electrocuted. Shah, of course, is only one electrical engineer, and one might say that all that is involved here is a technical disagreement.

The fact is, however, that as transmission lines have grown larger, longer and more numerous in recent years, electrical engineers have become increasingly concerned. This is especially true of the monstrous voltages now involved. We are swiftly moving from what used to be the huge 500,000-volt lines to lines carrying 1,200,000 volts. Are these huge lines dangerous to men, animals and plant life? Yes, under some circumstances.

Electrochemical pollution is a very complex matter. We do not fully understand it. But we can at least partially assess its effects.*

Transmission lines are not insulated like lamp cord wires. They depend on air as the insulator. Air is a good one, or at least it is a good insulator if not pushed beyond its capacity to insulate. Electricity passes in and along transmission wires at enormous velocity. If too much voltage is jammed into a given wire, however, electrons shoot from the line into the atmosphere. This "jumping" is called *corona discharge*. It is a complex phenomenon and it produces very complex results. We can get at both, however, via analogy.

Let us consider electricity as consisting of electrons traveling at unbelievable speed along the wire, mostly along its surface. This is why such lines cannot be "insulated" in the lay sense of the

---

* A good explanation in lay terms may be found in Louise B. Young, *Power over People* (New York: Oxford University Press, 1973). Though Ms. Young, a physicist, bases her conclusions on studies of a 765-kilovolt line in Ohio, her book is very valuable and the only nontechnical treatment of this subject available. I have relied heavily on her study.

term. The larger the wire, the more electrons can be packed into and onto it without their bumping into each other, end to end, and hence "jumping" off the "track." Or, the wider the highway, the more racing cars one can put on it without crashes and spin-offs into the infield or over the wall. Conversely, the smaller or narrower the highway, the more closely packed the cars, the greater the loss of cars.

In theory, one could pack unlimited electrons onto a wire simply by enlarging the wire. There are hard and practical limits to that, however, and even if there were not, any roughness on the surface would cause "jumping." And to an electron no wire is very smooth since microscopic indentations become massive pits, Corrosion greatly increases the chance of jumping. So do raindrops, snowflakes, particles of pollen, or, indeed, any object at all, however tiny.

But the compelling factor here is cost. Larger wires require larger insulators which require larger towers which require more workers and more maintenance. Power companies have long since recognized that it is cheaper to build smaller lines and take the loss of "jumping," or corona discharge. Lord Kelvin first enunciated the principle, namely, the economical size for a conductor is precisely that for which additional charges on the investment equal the cost of the energy lost.

Unhappily, corona discharge is not merely wasteful. It is at the very least annoying and in diverse ways. To confine a discussion of its environmental effects merely to "shocks" is greatly to underestimate the complexity of what takes place.

As the electrons shoot off into the atmosphere they collide with enormous impact with complex molecular structures and shatter them. These collisions change the actual chemistry of the air. The oxygen, nitrogen, and other gases are kicked out of stable balance and new, unstable molecular combinations are created. Though something of an oversimplification, it is accurate enough to say that any and all of the new molecular structures have a higher energy content than the former structures. They are, in short, excited. The consequence is that the former stable chemical and electrical structure of the atmosphere has now been rendered unstable and unpredictable — and, in proper combination, disruptive of the lives of people who live near them.

One of the new structure by-products is called ozone. Some ozone is always around, usually very high in the atmosphere where the sun's ultraviolet rays first encounter oxygen. Though it would be untrue to imply that 500-kilovolt transmission lines exude ozone in toxic quantity (since there are no known cases of ozone poisoning therefrom), it is equally untrue that we should have no cause for concern as extra-high-voltage lines of 1,200 and even 1,500 kilovolts proliferate across the country. Quite demonstrably, *large* doses of ozone are very dangerous indeed. Laboratory rats exposed to ozone in 6 parts per million (6 ppm) for four hours either die or suffer from massive hemorrhage. In the same laboratory animals, smaller concentrations of .1 ppm repeated daily for an extended period result in lung tissue damage, emphysema and fibrosis. If one charges the concentration to .15 ppm and exposes laboratory animals for only three hours to that dosage, there is a pronounced reduction in the resistance to infections of all kinds.

It must be borne in mind that these are very high dosages of ozone and there is no evidence that 500-kilovolt lines produce such concentrations. What concentrations *do* they produce? We do not know because of the myriad variables. What we should be concerned to find out, however, is the ozone production of 1,200- and 1,500-kilovolt lines. We do not know anything about the ratio of increase of ozone production to increased voltage, decreased wire size, conductor size (and location) and atmospheric conditions.

Ozone has various commercial uses. It is a germicide; it is effective in the prevention of the growth of fungi; it is effective in the purification of sewerage. Until quite recently these attributes of ozone led to its use in air conditioning and ventilating systems and most especially in the use of ultraviolet bulbs in public and hotel and motel bathrooms.

It was not until very recently that the U.S. Department of Health, Education and Welfare issued a warning that ozone thus employed as a bactericide (unless it was used in concentrations which were toxic to *human beings*) was not effective as a germicidal agent. It set that toxic level at about .04 ppm. The additional problem revealed by HEW's researchers was that high relative humidity rendered ozone much more lethal.

Electrostatic precipitators, which are so widely used in industry, including coal-burning generating plants, to remove polluting dust and particulate matter, accomplish this by means of high-voltage electric discharge. It is a kind of scrubbing system. This process is, in all respects, the same as that which occurs in corona discharge.

By 1969, based on research done only as of that date, the ozone production level was set by government standards at .1 ppm since it had been determined that exposure to levels above .1 ppm was "biologically damaging."

Power companies assert very positively that extra-high-voltage lines produce ozone only in minute and rapidly dissipated quantities. What they fail to add is that ozone levels may already be very high in a given atmosphere — say Los Angeles — due to an extended inversion, high relative humidity, the proximity of other industrially produced ozone. At what point may the danger level be reached? Power companies cannot and have not answered that question. The "dissipation" to which they refer may be very insignificant indeed if complex atmospheric conditions are extant. In the end, it does not matter what finally "triggers" the level of toxicity. At least it does not matter to those who have been poisoned.

We cannot even answer questions based on radical conditions. If we assume that we live five hundred yards from a 765-kilovolt line, that it is peak load time — 6 P.M. — on a wet and thundering evening, we know that corona discharge will occur. We know that we can smell the pungent, almost sweetish odor of ozone. We know that the hair will rise on the back of our necks and on our arms, we know that the line will crackle and sway and be surrounded with a blue aura, we know that our radio and television sets will blank out. But that is all we know. How far will the ozone extend, in what concentration, and for how long? We have no idea. At five hundred yards' distance would it be safe to step outside? We don't know, except that we know these lines attract lightning. Would it be safe to take a bath? Probably, but we don't know. In short, we know nothing essential. We only know that what little research has thus far revealed is not entirely comforting — and all we can hope is that sometime soon we will know more.

Lest it be said that Los Angeles and other industrial areas are one thing and "the wide open spaces" of the West another, it might be pointed out that the city of Missoula, Montana, lies in a mountain bowl where long-term and intense weather inversions are common. Let it be added that general air pollution levels in that city have often exceeded those of Los Angeles, Chicago, and Pittsburgh. The usually reticent medical profession has of recent years asserted that health problems have been severely exacerbated by toxic chemicals in the air. The citizens have the right to ask about the *addition* of ozone, in whatever concentration. Nor is Missoula unique. Dangerous situations already exist in Kellogg, Anaconda, Butte, East Helena, and many other valley communities through the environs of which extra-high-voltage lines of *at least* 500-kilovolts are scheduled to pass. These lines cannot be buried or "undergrounded." The cost is roughly twenty times that of "overgrounding." Moreover, the lines, in spite of coolants, would heat the earth for hundreds of yards along the right-of-way with consequent environmental destruction equal to overground lines. The power industry is obviously willing to take the risks. But power company officials seem unable to understand that the risks they are willing to take with other people's welfare are inseparable from another risk. Nothing in the Constitution of the United States prevents the nation, a state, or a municipality from taking over from the so-called investor-owned public utilities.

On September 8, 1974, at a "summit meeting" of more than a dozen environmental groups at a convention center near Missoula, there was serious consideration of "taking over" the Montana Power Company on behalf of the state. In no sense of the word could the some sixty representatives all be labeled "liberal."

What *is* the responsibility of the utilities and the government in these matters? The utilities spend an absurdly small percentage of gross revenues on *any* kind of research. This percentage as of 1970 was less than one-tenth that of the average research commitment of American industry as a whole.

The federal government essentially operates on the basis of standards drawn up by the National Bureau of Standards in 1915. The National Electric Safety Code that encompasses those standards is absurdly antediluvian. It simply has no applicability at all to extra-high-voltage transmission.

The environmental impact of these huge lines is double-barreled. It consists of the obvious and the nonobvious. That the huge swaths cut through virgin forests and penetrated by innumerable access roads will despoil great tracts of magnificent land area is obvious. That erosion will be massive and that wildlife habitat will be violently disturbed are equally obvious. That the visual impact from the settled valley regions will be severe is self-evident. And that these lines may be dangerous to man, animal, and plant life both chemically and electrically is a subject to which far too little attention has been paid.

There are sometimes small blessings in large problems. Eastern and western Montana would clearly never have found common environmental cause unless a common ox were somehow gored. The huge transmission lines did it. Their construction, or proposed construction, designed to connect the huge plants at Colstrip with the Pacific Northwest for the exportation of Montana's power, also connected (and very directly) Missoula and Colstrip. Indeed, they connected any western region through which they were likely to pass with every aspect of stripping and power generation in eastern Montana.

In addition to the three 500- and 161-kilovolt lines which have earned the wrath of so many western Montanans, the Montana Power Company plans nine others ranging from 230 to 160 kilo-volts and involving an additional 300 miles, mainly in western Montana. Thus the westerners zero in on generating plants numbers 3 and 4 (700 megawatts each) at Colstrip, because without these two monstrous plants, the 500-kilovolt lines, at least, would not be built. Since the state's Department of Natural Resources has not yet issued permits for these two plants as required under the 1973 Utility Siting Act, it is the implementation of this act upon which the environmentalist concentrates. Since the act states that "it is necessary to ensure that the location, construction and operation of power or energy conversion facilities will produce minimal adverse effects on the environment and upon the citizens of the state," there is no question but that permits for the two plants will not be issued by the board or that, if they are, the matter will be dragged through every court where a cause of action might be sustained.

Two things remain deeply unsettling to many Montanans. Both in the case of the 161-kilovolt Bitterroot line and in the case of a 230-kilovolt line from Billings to Great Falls, the power company proceeded with preparations, construction, and land condemna-tions. In the former case, the preparations continued while the case was in court. In the latter case, land acquisition actually con-tinued along *their* proposed route, though the Board of Natural Resources has the power not only to deny a permit but to insist on another route.

Second, over 60 percent of the power generated at Colstrip, units 1, 2, 3 and 4, would be owned by out-of-state power com-panies. Yet all the pollution, degradation, water loss, erosion, aesthetic ruination — the virtual destruction of huge areas of a beautiful country — would be the heritage of Montana alone.

This apparent certitude on the company's part is disheartening to thousands of Montanans who see the courts and the board as the public's advocates. There is an arrogance about the company's procedures, illustrated by this kind of conduct, which both puzzles and confuses them. It could be, again, a dangerous puzzlement for the power companies.

III

A NATIONAL SACRIFICE AREA?

10

What We Don't Know "Will" Hurt Us

MONTANANS ARE VERY MUCH AWARE of "Project Independence." It is thrown constantly in their faces by oil company television ads and, at home, by the coal and power companies. Montana is not a separate nation. What right have Montanans to lock up their coal resources and tell the rest of the country to go to hell? The impression which this barrage creates — and is clearly intended to create on the local level — is that if Montanans don't cooperate, the lights will go off in Seattle, Minneapolis, and St. Paul and everyone in Bayonne, New Jersey, will freeze to death next winter. Essentially this is an appeal to patriotism and in certain respects it has been successful.

The second aspect of the campaign on the local level is that if Montana does not relax its stringent environmental standards and if its new coal tax remains in force, the coal companies will simply move to Wyoming where few of these hindrances exist and where the state administration is very friendly to development.

This would mean, say the companies, great economic loss for Montana, which would then find itself in the backwater of progress. This argument, too, has been successful in certain respects.

The "energy crisis" argument is, of course, used constantly and primitively — primitively because the argument is that only coal can save us and that *the 1.3 trillion tons under the Fort Union Coal Formation constitutes the nation's coal reserves.* This is coupled with the argument that Montana has the only low-sulfur coal available and hence the environmentalists ought not to complain.

On the coattails of these arguments is the monotonously reiterated assertion that Montana should not object to the exportation of power because it has always been an exporting state and has been greatly enriched as a consequence. As George O'Connor, then president of Montana Power Company, put it, "I think we all recognize that Montana's economy is highly dependent on the sale of beef, of grain, of metal and a host of other commodities. Without the cash commodities we sell out of state, our own financial position would suffer terribly. I submit that the export of electricity will contribute to the economic health of Montana."

All of these arguments are confusing to many Montanans because of their plausibility. The problem is, they are not really plausible at all — but it takes a little research to find that out.

One could hardly accuse Arnold Miller, president of the United Mine Workers, of opposing the mining of coal. But he and his executive board are adamantly opposed to the stripping of western coal. It can, indeed, be said that Mr. Miller has mixed motives because strip mining employs far fewer workmen than deep mining. His answer to that is, "This kind of talk [antistripping] usually gets me into trouble. Several thousand members of our union are strip-mine employees and they don't like to hear their president talking like an environmentalist." But, he says, "if I were a coal baron, I'd be heading west. And they are. . . . In the East, the general rule of thumb is that you need about two hundred men to get out a million tons a year . . . in the West you can clear the same tonnage with ten men."

Says Miller, "So the West sits there, waiting to be developed. There are huge mines in operation now, of course. But they do not represent a fraction of what is coming if the energy cartel is allowed to pursue its own timetable. The ranchers and the environmentalists who are fighting against strip mining in the Northern Plains haven't seen anything yet . . . if there is any ranchland left in Montana when Ed Phelps [president of the Peabody Coal Company] is finished, I will be very surprised."

Mr. Miller is also caustic about reclamation. "I know about 'reclamation' in Appalachia — to borrow a phrase from a former officer of our union — [it] is the small end of nothing, shaved down to a point." Before we leave Mr. Miller to get at what is really troubling him, let him speak about Montana in particular: "The moral is simple — beware of industrialists bringing gifts. Fifty years ago they promised to develop Appalachia, and they left it in wreckage. Now they promise to develop the Northern Plains. They will leave it in ruins."*

Though Arnold Miller does not dwell on the point, the fact is that the nation's coal reserves are immense and they are by no means confined to the West. The further point is that the West's coal is presumably low in sulfur content, but it is also low in BTUs per ton because it is very high in water content.

It is surprising, however, that this low-sulfur argument for the exploitation of Northern Plains coal is, in many respects, mythical. The assertion had long been accepted until the Center for Advanced Computation at the University of Illinois, the Environmental Policy Center, and the Sierra Club announced simultaneously on October 17, 1974, that while research "is only beginning," Great Plains coal varies widely in sulfur content and testing thus far does *not* warrant the generalized statement that the coal is low sulfur.† The preliminary report states: "Without question, little of the purported low sulfur coal in the Northern Plains

---

* Arnold Miller, "The Energy Crisis as the Coal Miner Sees It," *The Center Magazine*, November/December 1973.

† See *Research Office Bulletin*, Sierra Club, October 17, 1974, Mills Tower, San Francisco, California.

is, in fact, effective low sulfur coal." Research thus far completed indicates that there is such a wide variation in sulfur content in the plains area that only coal in the Montana Decker area can be positively tested as low-sulfur. While these findings are not definitive, the researchers nevertheless assert, "Eastern coal outcompetes western in terms of effective sulfur content." If definitive research bears out these initial findings, one of the really potent arguments for the strip mining of western coal will have been exploded.

Moreover, since the East has vast quantities of low-sulfur coal, and since eastern coal is much closer to the centers where the power is needed, the argument is still weaker. Still, in the West the coal men only have to deal with "eagle freaks" — and not very many of them. Big polluting power plants near the populous centers would be hard to set up. There is too much political clout there — too many environmentalists, too many highly skilled environmental lawyers, too much real expertise on the "wrong" side. The New York-based Environmental Defense Fund, for instance, has had entirely too many court victories. Moreover, even the lower courts are becoming sophisticated in environmental matters — which cannot be said of courts in the West.

The low-sulfur coal (1 percent sulfur or less) in the Central Appalachian states has four times the energy potential of the coal in the Northern Great Plains. If the reserves were tripled in Montana and Wyoming they would not equal the energy potential of the Central Appalachian *low-sulfur* coal deposits. This is one of the fallacies of talking about tonnage rather than BTUs or energy content.

If one adds medium-sulfur coal (1.1 to 1.5 percent sulfur content) in the Central Appalachian states, the tonnage would be increased by 25 billion but the energy in that tonnage would be increased by 592 quadrillion BTUs. Nor can it be said that no technology exists to process this medium-sulfur coal. Forty percent of the sulfur can be removed by a water washing process which reduces this coal to the low-sulfur category. The washing process is essentially clean.

High-sulfur coal (1.6 percent sulfur or more) is plentiful in Central Appalachia, but much of this sulfur can be removed by stack-gas scrubbing systems, and technology is rapidly developing both refinements in stack scrubbing systems and processes for removing sulfur prior to burning.

The Appalachian region, already conditioned to coal mining, would, in fact, greatly benefit from increased mining in the area. The region's poverty resulted essentially from cheap oil and a resultant depression in the coal industry. With the reverse situation now extant, both employment and wages would increase substantially if the industry returned to the area rather than moving westward. Nor, as we shall see, need deep mining be eternally dangerous and unhealthful.

There are other grossly misleading aspects to the coal and power companies' use of quantitative figures alone. It is true that about 70 percent of the nation's coal reserves in tonnage lies west of the Mississippi River. This completely overlooks the fact that in BTU value or heat content about 55 percent of the *energy* reserve lies east of the Mississippi River. Further, of the tonnage west of the Mississippi, a healthy percentage is too deep for stripping operations. For instance, Colorado and Utah respectively have 62 and 22 billion tons of low-sulfur coal. Virtually all of it is too deep for surface mining, but the coal companies don't mention that. *Nothing will alter the fact that, whether in the East, Middle West, or West, about twelve times as much coal can be reached by deep mining as by strip mining.*

In fact, if we were to believe the testimony of the National Coal Association before the Senate Public Works Committee, there is *no* low-sulfur coal east of the Mississippi River. That this assertion is flatly contradicted by detailed reports of the U.S. Geological Survey and the U.S. Bureau of Mines in no way inhibits the continuation of this blatant propaganda. Who, especially out among the "eagle freaks," reads technical reports? For that matter, who reads them in the Congress?

There is another profoundly serious effect to the sudden shift toward a reliance on western coal. Montanans should give the matter some thought because this has always been a mining state, deep mining — mostly copper. Anyone associated with that industry is aware of the fact that one does not simply shut down a mine. If one does, it is apt to be lost. The common but uninformed view of the matter is that the mineral is always there and, whenever necessary, one simply goes back in and gets it. Unfortunately, it does not work that way — with copper or with coal. As Arnold Miller put it, "You cannot turn underground coal production on and off like a light switch. If we arrive at a rational fuels policy five or six or seven years from now, and decide, as a result, to strengthen our emphasis on eastern mining, the mines will not be there and neither will the miners." Miller's primary concern is that the headlong commitment to western mining will cost between twenty-five and forty thousand lost jobs in the East. Though he does not say so, it could ultimately cost one hundred and fifty thousand jobs. Serious as that problem would be — and doubly tragic in Appalachia — its implications go beyond that.

During the period from 1903 to 1946 the copper mines at Butte underwent a series of frequent strikes, walkouts and shutdowns. On only one occasion, even when the IWW was at its most aggressive stages, did the men who manned the pumps and fans and other maintenance people leave their jobs. Mines rapidly fil with water. This is followed by massive cave-ins. The disintegration of a closed mine is swift. While it is true that the mineral is still there, the process of getting back to it is essentially akin to starting all over again. The cost is astronomical. Moreover coal mines in the East are even more subject to this swift disintegration than are such "hard rock" operations as gold, silver and copper mines in the West. Coal is soft and absorbs more water.

Few of these facts are known by the average Montanan, who

therefore sees a dilemma where, in fact, there is none. Since most Montanans recognize that solar power, wind power, and atomic power are sources that lie far in the future and since they recognize that coal is the nation's sole present resource for increased energy demands, they feel a sense of guilt in endorsing a "lockup" policy or, indeed, any policy which would harm America. At a recent meeting of concerned citizens (about 150 of them) at the small town of Bonner, Montana (through the environs of which the Montana Power Company is planning to construct two 500-kilovolt transmission lines), this sentiment was variously, if somewhat timorously, expressed by a number of people. The group was unanimously opposed to the construction of the lines. But as one young woman put it, "It worries me, though. Do we have the right? I mean, we're all Americans and we're all in the same boat. Sure, it's our state, but do we have the right to hurt America?" She and others had been taken in by the incessant propaganda.

Ironically, one of the arguments now being used by the coal industry for stripping western coal is the fact that deep mining is too dangerous. It is certainly dangerous. Since 1910 about eighty thousand coal miners have been killed. The accident rate in coal mining far exceeds that of any other major industry. It also produces a very high incidence of "black lung," an often fatal respiratory disease. In 1969 the Public Health Service announced that more than one hundred thousand miners were afflicted with "black lung."

But, as usual, behind the plausibility of the argument lie several facts the companies do not mention. Until Congress passed the Coal Mining Safety Act of 1969, federal safety legislation was scandalously inadequate and what few provisions existed were simply not enforced. While better, the act of 1969 is still grossly inadequate in terms of both content and enforcement. State legislation in the deep-mining states was even less effective than federal regulations. This was also true of western copper-mining areas, where neither federal nor state legislation of any substance existed.

Yet, this need not be. Deep mining in Europe, especially in England, gives the lie to it. In Europe, research and development as well as stringent safety regulations have reduced the incidence of deep-mining accidents to a fraction of those in the United States. Moreover, according to the Mining Enforcement and Safety Administration (MESA), U.S. Steel has drastically reduced the incidence of "black lung." More compelling, "black lung" was entirely eliminated in Australia ten years ago. It is interesting that Consolidation Coal, now much involved in Montana, is under investigation on sworn charges that it has deliberately and repeatedly falsified critical dust sampling records supplied to the U.S. government. It is even more interesting that, according to MESA, from January to April 1974 there were more strip-mining deaths than deep-mining deaths per man-hour in the United States — and this was during a coal-mining boom.

But what industry calls R & D, research and development, has hardly been impressive in United States mining. Electric utilities are the usual whipping boys because they spend less than .25 of 1 percent of their revenues on research. But they are better than the coal industry, whom they lead, oddly enough, by approximately .25 of 1 percent.

Utility and coal companies point out that they *must* mine-mouth generate on the Northern Great Plains and transport the energy to the load centers via huge transmission lines because railroads cannot carry the coal and because, even if they could, it would be too expensive. Yet about 70 percent of all coal in the United States is now carried by rail. Surveys clearly indicate that an 8 percent increase could be added without any strain on the carriers. That amounts to an increase of about 50 million tons per year. If an 8 percent increase were not sufficient, it *would be* sufficient to give the railroads adequate lead time to construct whatever new coal cars were requisite. The railroads, after all, profit from the added business.

As for cost, figures are not definitive, but what data we do have indicate that the cost of transmission lines versus rail transportation is about equal and one must bear in mind that these data do *not* include the energy loss via transmission lines.

In six western states, surface coal mining has increased sixfold since 1965, from 7.5 to 45.7 million tons annually. But one must understand that thus far this is merely a seminal operation. This is a minuscule amount of coal. By 1970 the federal government alone had already leased land under which lie 20 *billion* tons of coal — and that was as of 1970. How much more has been leased from other sources and by the government since then is a matter which involves scrambled and wildly discrepant figures. To complicate projections and present figures, many leases, particularly on Indian lands, are being challenged in various courts.

One can get a primitive idea of what is happening, however, if one bears in mind that the American Electric Power System, one of the largest electric utilities in the nation, consumed 31 million tons of coal in 1973 and by its own projections will burn 57 million tons annually by 1983. Thus, this *single* utility burned nearly as much coal as all six western coal states produced in 1974. And the American Electric Power System is very much involved in the West. It has already *purchased* 40,000 acres in Wyoming with proven reserves of 900,000,000 tons of coal; it has optioned for "additional acreage"; it has a contract with Carter Oil Company (Exxon) to supply 5,250,000 tons of Wyoming coal per year for 30 years; and it is in "final negotiations" with another "major supplier" for the delivery of 200,000,000 tons of coal over a 25-year period. It has thus far leased 4,500 acres in Montana and is negotiating for more. The American Electric Power System is only one of many utilities and coal companies now involved on the Northern Great Plains.

Thus the informed environmentalist has a massive educational job on his hands, made all the more difficult by the incessant propaganda of the companies to the effect that, after all, very little surface area will be disturbed. He must not only counteract that monotonously reiterated assertion, but he must also somehow convince a wide range of people that the eye of the beholder does not tell the truth. Man can, and fully intends to, chew up an area so vast that the eye cannot really comprehend its vastness. The eye cannot, but the machines can.

It is analogous to the sea. How could man ever pollute those endless reaches and those vast depths? But he has done and is doing so. In the mid-Atlantic, as Thor Heyerdahl and many others can attest, there are balls of plastic, globules of oil, flotsam, jetsam, junk and garbage. Vast as they are, the Northern Great Plains would make a small island in that great sea.

Though, as we have seen, the average Montanan is no stranger to great corporate power, he is now confronted with an economic power so much greater in magnitude as to strain the most ardent cynic's credibility. It is a question of visibility — or, more properly, of invisibility. The Montana Power Company is visible because Colstrip is there, its projected mine-mouth generating plants are scheduled to go into full operation no later than 1979, its transmission lines have been built, and projected routes have been given wide and continual publicity. It can be assumed that power company officials have been both shaken and nonplussed by the virulence of the very widespread attack upon them. Indeed, one need only attend a few of the very numerous public meetings called by environmental groups or the state Department of Natural Resources to witness company representatives very much on the defensive.

In a strange way the company's visibility distracts large numbers of Montanans from a far greater problem and a far greater danger. Even intimately linked, as it is, with other out-of-state utilities, the power company is small potatoes.

Those who are more familiar with the deeper problems are given to listing the coal companies whose representatives are now swarming over eastern Montana, and these people point out that this is an aggregate power of awesome dimensions. But even most of these people have not lifted the mask behind the mask behind the mask. Yet that is where the real face is. The face, quite simply, is oil.

Let us begin, however, with coal. When challenged on the basis of untoward concentration in the industry, any informed industry spokesman will point out that such charges are absurd. After all, there are about five thousand coal mines in this country and something over one thousand individual coal-mining companies. To speak of concentration or any lack of competition is a canard.

But of these some twelve hundred companies, *fifteen* produced more than 50 percent of the total tonnage of coal last year, and the top fifty of them produced two-thirds of all the coal in America. So, again, we play the quantitative game — and, playing it, we are misled.

Let us examine these top coal companies for a moment. Consolidation Coal Company is a wholly owned subsidiary of Continental Oil; Island Creek Coal Company is a wholly owned subsidiary of Occidental Oil; Old Ben Coal Company is a wholly owned subsidiary of Standard Oil of Ohio; the Pittsburgh and Midway Coal Company is a wholly owned subsidiary of Gulf Oil; the Clinchfield Company is a wholly owned subsidiary of the Pittston Company, which, among other enterprises, operates oil refineries; Eastern Associated Coal Company is a division of the Eastern Gas and Fuel Company.

Not all of the big fifteen companies are oil subsidiaries. But only North American Coal, Westmoreland Coal Company, and Utah International are independent. Of the remainder, Peabody Coal is a wholly owned subsidiary of Kennecott Copper; Ayrshire Coal is a wholly owned subsidiary of American Metal Climax (Amax); U.S. Steel and Bethlehem operate their own coal mines; and Freeman Coal and United Electric are wholly owned subsidiaries of General Dynamics. American Electric Power, which is one of the nation's largest private utility companies, owns Central Ohio Coal, Windsor Power House, Central Appalachian Coal, and Southern Ohio Coal.

Granted that there is a mix here of oil, copper, steel, and utility

companies, oil is still perversely involved. All told, with U.S.
Steel, Kennecott, Amax, and the American Electric Power deeply
involved in coal and headed for the West, or already here, the
scattered people of the Northern Great Plains are not merely dealing with "scalpers" and "deceitful leasehounds," nor do state governments have cause for comfort. In any event, since the gasoline
shortage subjected the oil industry to sudden but intense scrutiny,
we are beginning to understand that the oil companies are, in fact,
energy companies with wide-ranging interests in coal, uranium,
shale, natural gas, geothermal areas, etc. Since coal represents the
only practical substitute for rapidly dwindling petroleum reserves,
and since "Project Independence" has, in effect, given the green
light to energy companies, it is most assuredly a rational assumption that the giant oil companies are in the coal business and in it
to stay.

In President Nixon's economic message of July 26, 1974, he referred again to "Project Independence" and to the "trade-offs" that
would be necessary to make the country energy self-sufficient on
schedule. To large numbers of Montanans watching their television sets, the message was loud and clear.

Montana's senator and the Senate Majority Leader, Mike Mansfield, is slow to anger. But he has long been angry about the Montana coal problem. Along with Montana's junior senator, Lee Metcalf, Mansfield was infuriated when Secretary of the Interior
Rogers C. B. Morton refused to abide by a Senate resolution calling for a moratorium on federal leasing in Montana for one year
or until the Senate could act on stripping legislation. The senators
called Morton's decision "arrogant" and "inconceivable" — but
nothing happened.

Later Mansfield told the Senate that Montanans were being
treated "shabbily," without compassion and "without regard to the
future of this part of our nation." And he said, "If we cannot have
orderly and reasonable development of the vast coal resources in
Montana and the West, there should be no strip mining of coal."

Has the Senate Majority Leader no power? Yes, he has power — and he and Montana's congressional delegation are fighting hard. But there sits "Project Independence" and an administration committed to it. Well, say a good many Montanans, the administration will change — one way or another. Maybe. Changes in administration, however, rather rarely affect the roots of federal bureaucracy. With respect to coal leasing, the building of transmission lines or of power generating plants on federal and Indian lands, that bureaucracy can be expressed this way: D of I; D of A; BR; BLM; BIA; FEA; USFS; USGS; ACE; EPA; MESA; BPA; FPC; ICC; EMARS. Translation: Department of the Interior; Department of Agriculture; Bureau of Reclamation; Bureau of Land Management; Bureau of Indian Affairs; Federal Energy Administration; United States Forest Service; United States Geological Survey; Army Corps of Engineers; Environmental Protection Agency; Mining Enforcement Safety Administration; Bonneville Power Authority; Federal Power Commission; Interstate Commerce Commission; Energy Minerals Allocation Recommendation System.

Since most of Montana's coal is either federally or Indian owned, in some situations the involvement of *all* of these fifteen federal departments, boards, commissions, or administrations is a possibility. In *any* situation several will be involved. In most situations five or six at a minimum will be involved.

Some of these institutions are new, some are old. Some of the very important ones, such as the Forest Service, the Bureau of Reclamation, and the Bureau of Land Management, were established expressly to "serve the people's interests." It would be sheer folly to assume that that is true of *any* of these institutions today. It is certainly possible that one or several of them may become allies of the people of the Northern Great Plains over the monumental problem of strip mining. It would be more realistic to assume that they will not.

11

Montanans Fight Back

WHY HAVE MONTANANS and the citizens of Wyoming reacted to the incursions of "development" so very differently? There is an almost palpable change of attitude as one drives from the great basins of southeastern Montana up onto the rolling high plains of Wyoming.

The change is the more startling because on the surface of things the two states are so similar. Like Montana, Wyoming is huge, empty, lonely, and, depending on the eye of the beholder, malevolently ugly or breathtakingly beautiful. The topographical similarity would seem to be matched with close parallels in historical development: Indians, cowboys, cattle, sheep, homesteaders, and hardship. But, beneath the superficial similarities, profoundly different economic and hence political events occurred. Wyoming's oil boom of the 1940s and 1950s did not occur in Montana. The very powerful Wyoming Stockgrowers' Association saw no threat to land or water in the development of oil resources since neither prospecting nor drilling damages substantial land areas. Though the oil boom drastically and abruptly altered the nature of the ranch *town*, and though in hindsight we now see how that happened, it did not seem to pose a problem in the 1940s and 1950s. It was quickly, in any event, a fait accompli.

Nor had Wyoming legislators ever really dealt with vast corporate power. The legislature in Montana had so dealt since 1889 with the pervasively powerful Anaconda Company. These different events conditioned the people of the two states in different ways.

One cannot imagine Montana's governor in 1974 uttering the words of Wyoming's governor, Stanley Hathaway: "It doesn't make any difference whether you are for or against development, some of it will occur. Basically, the people of Wyoming know that they are one of the fifty states of the Union. The obligation is to help." And the governor asserted that Wyoming could support the strip mining of fifty million tons of coal annually "for the next 474 years" and "disturb less than 2 percent of the land area." The wild discrepancies of this statistical legerdemain did not disturb the governor. The point is that Hathaway is not merely some kind of aberrant political phenomenon; he represents a great many Wyomingites — perhaps a majority. A significant number of people believe that Wyoming has gone far too far along the road to industrialization in the name of oil for the people now to obstruct the changes that the exploitation of its coal will render inevitable.

Of Hathaway's nomination as Secretary of the Interior by Gerald Ford, one Montana environmentalist said: "My God, if you searched the United States for the absolutely worst Secretary of Interior you could find, Hathaway would head the list. He has one of the most abominable environmental records of any public official in this country. It's a shocking commentary on the attitude of this administration toward a large slice of America. It is an unbelievably bad appointment." Hathaway, of course, subsequently resigned due to poor health.

Historians, political scientists and sociologists have long asserted that the Great Plains is a single region. The problem has always been that it refuses to act as one. "We are at it again," said one historian at the University of Colorado recently. "If just Colorado, Wyoming, North Dakota, and Montana would stand together on this single issue, we would vastly enhance our powers." There is every indication that we will do nothing of the kind.

If what is happening in Montana is remarkable, it is the more so because the state is essentially going it alone. Montanans are not used to being in the vanguard of anything. They are cynically accustomed to being in the backwaters of nearly everything. The people, Democrats or Republicans, have, like most predominantly rural people, been deeply conservative. Montana's physical isolation has led to a kind of intellectual and even a perverse social isolation. What the rest of the country does is its own damn business and none of our own — and what it does seems to us, in any event, to be rather foolish.

When one considers that the director of the U.S. Census could find no frontier "line" in 1890, i.e., a line drawn from north to south, westward of which there was no continuous area of less than two persons per square mile, it would not be far off the mark to observe that Montana is very close to a frontier community both in terms of time and numbers of people. After all, there are only 4.7 persons per square mile in Montana today.

Historically, American frontiersmen were always profoundly suspicious of government, near or far, but particularly suspicious of government far away. They regarded the people "in the states" as effete, often supercilious, and in any event up to no good when they, the effete ones, turned their attention westward via laws pertaining to western lands or waters. These people wanted to be left alone. That is, they wanted to be left alone until they got into trouble. Then, as in the case of the Indian wars, they loudly demanded government help right now — and on their own terms. Or, as in the case of the transfer of public land into private hands, they vociferously and continuously demanded action by Congress.

But if Montanans have been consistently conservative, how does one account for the spare, clean-cut new constitution of 1972? Though it passed by less than two thousand votes, it seems very much out of character that this radical document passed at all. But that is only at first glance.

If Montanans rather typically maintained a suspicion of government, near and far, they could do little about Washington but they *could* do something about Helena. Few Montanans by 1972 were other than resentful of Helena's control, which they had come, over the years, to regard increasingly as marked by the cloven hoof of Anaconda. Moreover, though it took more than eighty years, Montanans came to recognize that that control, in turn, was corrupt — and that that corruption was expensive. It is not a conservative stance to endorse expensive government. The power at the core of Montana's environmental movement is rooted deep in the familiar ground of conservatism.

George O'Connor, a former president of the Montana Power Company and presider over Montana's largest and oldest strip-mining operation, is bright, charming, and exceedingly well informed. He is neither arrogant nor rapacious. He is a Montanan. From the beginning of his company in 1911 (which was an off-shoot of the Anaconda Company), Montana Power has enjoyed almost universal conservative support — in the legislature, the courts, and in almost all political circles. But George O'Connor and his company have been under almost ceaseless attack from almost all quarters for the past four years. It is a matter of deep concern to him. In a recent exchange of letters with him, I referred to the strong political coalition which seemed to me to have so thoroughly solidified against his company. He replied, "I guess I have had no problem during the years that I have had a certain amount of executive authority that has haunted me worse, given me more hours of concern, or found me as totally helpless to maybe determine a solution; and, if it is determined, to get an execution of it." George O'Connor is a conservative man. It must be very difficult indeed to have lost old friends so quickly.

Who and what has he lost? Who beleaguers him now and what powers do they have?

Until very recently few men or women of caliber ran for the state legislature or, for that matter, for any elective state office. Those few who did, stirred perhaps by anger or some sense of service and duty, were usually "one-termers." They found the exercise fruitless. There was little turnover in the legislature. It met for a brief sixty days every two years and no student of the history of that body could amass much evidence that it was other than "kept" in every real sense of the word. Aside from those few areas beyond the interest and purview of the Anaconda Company, the Montana Power Company, and the Northern Pacific Railroad, the legislature did what it was told.

In the early days of statehood this was accomplished by outright bribery and by the expenditure of millions of dollars by the company on the campaigns of those candidates who "feel as we do." By the 1930s, especially because the company either owned or controlled most of the press of the state, such bludgeoning techniques were unnecessary. Of the state's eight dailies, Anaconda owned seven, and it controlled most of the weeklies. Company lobbyists were everywhere; legislators knew what they were to do or not to do.

Until recently, the second- or third-generation ranchers in the legislative body went along as their forebears had. They were far removed from mining and lumbering enterprises and they had no argument with the railroads. They were ranchers, not farmers. They shipped their cattle off but once a year and had no complaints about freight rates. None of the "radicalism" of the beleaguered farmers affected them in the 1920s and 1930s, and few of those angry farmers ever sat in the legislature. There remains ample evidence, however, of growing fissures in the rancher-industrial coalition beginning in the 1950s. It is difficult to trace and document except by a close study of environmentally oriented bills which began to receive serious attention in the mid-fifties. It became more obvious in the 1960s in all legislative matters, and by the late 1960s and early 1970s all the king's men could not put the coalition together again.

Anaconda, as we have said, suffered a catastrophic international collapse in the early seventies. Moreover, the power of the Northern Pacific Railroad in the state had undergone heavy attrition as it weakened nationally. The railroad was preoccupied by its merger with the Great Northern – a merger designed to save its corporate life. The Montana Power Company, after all, was really the only corporate structure left standing in the ruins. That it was home-grown made no difference. So, once upon a time, had Anaconda been home-grown. Montana Power Company's contracts with outsiders for the construction of enormous mine-mouth coal generating plants made the company at once the center of attack. It may well be that George O'Connor's "hours of concern" and his feeling that "no problem has haunted me worse" reside in the fact that he does not understand why he is in the eye of the storm. But the reason is not obscure. Montana Power Company's Colstrip is *there;* its plans for two new massive generating units (numbers 3 and 4) are well known; its massive transmission lines are already visible; its plans for additional huge lines have been given constant publicity. But the deeper reason for the ferocity of the attack on Montana Power (which, by December 1974, had even included a crude and deplorable attempt to bomb its offices in Billings) resides in the knowledge that behind Montana Power stand Chevron, Continental, Peabody, Westmoreland, and the whole galaxy of America's largest corporations. Few environmentalists fail to understand that a victory by one means victory for all.

Though the formation and activities of numerous private environmental groups predates the passage of Montana's new constitution, these groups are best considered in the light of that constitution. That is so because in the end what they do and have done will doubtless come back to that document. Its genesis is important – as is its environmental bent.

No one could serve in the Constitutional Convention who had been a member of the previous legislature. In 1969, the legislature had referred the matter of calling the convention to Montana's voters and by an overwhelming vote of 133,482 to 71,643 the people endorsed the calling of the convention. On November 2, 1971, one hundred delegates were elected from twenty-three districts for the body which convened on January 17, 1972. These one hundred Montanans met in Helena for fifty-four long working days. They produced a document of 11,200 words, as opposed to the old document of 28,000 words.

Few of the members had ever served in the legislature or in any public capacity. They were people essentially without personal political ambition. They had nothing to trade and no constituency to hold in the pen for future political considerations.*

Moreover, the debate was almost entirely nonpartisan. The hottest issues revolved around whether or not a given proposed article was so radical as to jeopardize ratification. Since most of the members had had little political experience per se, they less often opted for compromise than for "risk." The final vote for ratification clearly indicates that they took plenty of risk.

In the third place, the people who ran for and were elected to the convention were among the best educated and civically active in the state. As one convention member put it, "My God, what if our legislators had been of this caliber over the past decade. We'd be the most progressive state in the Union."

There was, of course, intense lobbying from myriad sources. But how, in fact, do you successfully lobby a man or woman who intends never to run for anything again and could not care less whether he has your support in the future or not?

* In a state with a population as small as Montana's almost everyone knows everyone else. My brother, John Toole, was vice-chairman of the convention. I had known its president, Leo Graybill, Jr., for twenty years. I had known more than half of its members since college days. I had access not only to the public papers it produced but to many private notes, diaries and memoirs. Many members of its appointed staff were former students of mine.

Let the vice-chairman speak for *attitude* — because, in the end, that is what mattered: "It was clear to the majority of us that we would do this only once in our lives. And what we did had to be sound enough to last for maybe eighty or a hundred years. I don't like to use such a word in this context but in a way I have to. Damn it, there is a kind of immortality in this kind of thing. That's what pushes your own special interest out of it. Take _____ _____. He has spent his mature lifetime as an attorney representing the railroads, the Montana Power Company, the Anaconda Company, the banks. They did not touch him, they *could* not touch him. Hell, they couldn't even get near him.

"There may have been some that ran for the job with the idea that they would help themselves out in some way. But I doubt that they felt that way very long. If they *did* feel that way, they were soon isolated and ineffective."

Last, the convention had at its disposal the constitutions of other states and analyses thereof compiled by the Constitution Revision Commission created by the 1969 legislature. The commission also supplied the convention with all manner of model constitutions. So, the job was done.

Article IX of the constitution is deceptively simple. It reads, in part:

(1) The state and each person shall maintain and improve a clean and healthful environment in Montana for present and future generations. (2) The legislature shall provide for the administration and enforcement of this duty. (3) The legislature shall provide adequate remedies for the protection of environmental support systems from degradation and provide adequate remedies to prevent unreasonable depletion and degradation of natural resources.

All lands disturbed by the taking of natural resources shall be reclaimed. The legislature shall provide effective requirements and standards for the reclamation of lands disturbed. . . .

The use of all water that is now or may hereafter be appropriated for sale, rent, distribution, or other beneficial use, the right of way over the lands of others for all ditches, drains, flumes, canals and aqueducts necessarily used in connection therewith, and the sites for reservoirs necessary for collecting and storing water *shall be held to be a public use* [italics mine]. . . ,

All surface, underground, flood, and atmospheric waters within the boundaries of the state are the property of the state for the use of its people and are subject to appropriation for beneficial uses as provided by law. . . .

The legislature shall provide for the identification, acquisition, restoration, enhancement, preservation, and administration of scenic, historic, archeologic, scientific, cultural, and recreational areas, sites, records, objects, and for their use and enjoyment for the people.

It may well be said that all this is well and good but words, after all, are simply words. The fact remains that in the contest between private groups, state agencies, federal agencies, and the energy companies, many issues are almost certain to end up in court — and probably on constitutional grounds. It should be added that (except on civil rights matters) the Supreme Court of the United States has long demonstrated a great reluctance to declare unconstitutional what is positively asserted to be constitutional (or unconstitutional) by a state. For *either* side, it can be a long, long road to the nine men in the black robes.

One other part of the proposed new constitution was fought bitterly by what one might call Montana's establishment. This was Section 9 of Article II, which fell under the heading of a Declaration of Right. It simply reads as follows:

No person shall be deprived of the right to examine documents or *to observe the deliberations of all public bodies or agencies of state government and its subdivisions* [italics mine], except in cases in which the demand of individual privacy clearly exceeds the merits of public disclosure.

This would not seem at all remarkable, perhaps, in many states, but it was revolutionary in Montana. Legislative hearings had always been closed or, if not closed, the committee in question could and did go into executive session at the whim of a single member. Now hearings had to be public and, as construed by the courts, had to be publicly announced in advance. The Montana legislature would never be the same.

That single brief section means that whatever the committee, no environmental issue could be discussed or voted upon or determined, except in the presence of any and all persons concerned. It stripped anonymity from all legislators and it gave environmental groups an unparalleled forum. Not only could they be there, they were there. And they could and did demand to testify. The press, the new free press, was seldom absent.

The first session of the new legislature, 1973, bore about as much resemblance to previous sessions as Congress bears to the Politburo. That first session, and the second, necessitate some examination. The initial and most shocking change was immediately apparent. There was not a bookstore in the state that could keep *Robert's Rules* in stock. If legislators were fractious and undisciplined, they did not miss committee meetings or votes. They did not, as of old, read newspapers at their desks; if there was a lull, they were much more apt to be found reading their college texts. Ed Smith (age twenty-four), chief clerk of the House of Representatives, was driven nearly to distraction by house members pushing their voting buttons to be sure that they worked. The Speaker of the House (age thirty-three) wore down one side of his gavel trying to bring some semblance of proper procedure to the order of speaking and yielding.

"Will the member from Stanford yield?" shouted Tom Towe (age thirty-three) from Billings. "Yield?" shouted Paul Richards (age twenty) from Helena. "Hell, I didn't know I had the floor."

"Who has the floor?" the Speaker shouted to the clerk. Ed Smith rolled his eyes upward. "Good God, let's start all over. I don't think anybody has the floor."

But the work got done. Some 1,200 bills were passed, killed, or tabled. The committees worked far into the night. But they answered to roll calls, and sometimes the debate was scintillating. Parliamentary procedure did not long remain a mystery.

It was the committee hearings, however, that represented the most dramatic change. It was a rare committee, indeed, that did not occasionally find itself inundated by a flood of people. Those hearings by those committees which had bills pending concerning the environment were hard pressed to find space for the people who wished to attend. Often the hearings were held at night so that the entire House chamber and gallery could be used; on several occasions the hearings were moved to the auditorium of the Helena high school. Citizens quickly discovered that by a request to the chairman or by virtue of a request to a member of the committee, a place on the roster of witnesses could be reserved. They came by the dozens, sometimes by the many dozens. If their testimony was written, it was entered in the record.

It must be emphasized, of course, that the environmentalists were not the only ones at the hearings. "The Industry" was also always there, always well prepared, and usually a jump or two ahead. Industry representatives, after all, were experts. At hearing after hearing they pulled the debate into the realm of their own expertise. What, after all, does the average citizen who merely knows that his air stinks and that on most days he can't see the mountains around his town know of "scrubbers," settling ponds and the complex chemistry of manufacturing pulp? What does he really know of ambient air standards, SO_2, water coliforms, and weather inversions? And beware the emotional layman who finds himself in a debate on the law with an industry lawyer whose specialty is environmental law. It is rarely effective, even with sympathetic lawmakers, to speak only of the "quality of life," the beauty of trees, good fishing, and grass that has not been turned upside down. The English professor and the angry housewife are rarely a match for the economist and the statistician. And this brings us to the private environmental groups.

These groups began to form before the legislature underwent

its transformation and before the strip mining of coal was an issue. They formed in western and not eastern Montana. GASP (Gals Against Smog and Pollution), organized in the mid-1960s, formed in Missoula to protest the effluent from a pulp mill west of that city. CCQE (Concerned Citizens for a Quality Environment) was formed in 1974 to protest an expansion of that plant.

CCOB (Concerned Citizens of the Bitterroot) and the Hold-the-Line Committee organized to prevent a power line from cutting a swath for fifty miles down that lovely valley. They failed. CCOB was soon joined by the Rachel Carson Trust Fund, the function of which was to fight *any* degradation of the land or water in the watershed of the Clark Fork River — an immense area. They were beaten by the pulp plant in federal district court.

In addition to this very partial listing of citizens' groups, a peculiar transformation took place in the existent organizations which had deep but rather routine roots in the area — Trout Unlimited, the Wilderness Association, the Sierra Club, the League of Women Voters, and the League of Conservation Voters. The Wilderness Association and the Sierra Club did have some initial success; in concert with local organizations they completely stopped the practice of forest clear-cutting on the semiarid slopes of the Bitterroot Valley.

Initially, these early groups in western Montana were mostly sound and fury. They held mass meetings and mimeographed notices. They were great petitioners and picketers, but they had only the vaguest idea of whom to petition except the congressional delegation. Except for the clear-cutting issue, they lost and lost and lost again. In retrospect, their losses are understandable. It was more than that the powers arrayed against them were great; it was that they were full of passion but short on facts. And there was another factor.

It is easy to hate the Forest Service, the Bureau of Land Management, the Bureau of Reclamation, and the Bureau of Indian Affairs when one deals with them in the abstract, and in the huge marble edifices in Washington from which their garbled memoranda spew forth. It is quite another matter to deal with the district forester in Missoula or the BIA area director in Billings, or Ed Zaidlick of the BLM in Helena. For these are human beings in rumpled suits or worn boots and they are worried, knowledgeable, helpful, and somehow quietly seeking compromise and peace. It is another thing to sit quietly with a man who seems to be caught in the middle but who seems also clearly to love what you love.

So, for the most part, the early efforts of the environmental groups failed. But they were tenacious and they learned. In many cases, all but the hard core deserted, but the hard core remained.

It would be too much to say that when the pervasive issue of coal burst upon the scene in 1971, the new groups which quickly formed in eastern Montana avoided all the mistakes of their predecessors to the west. It would also be too much to say that they sent an emissary westward to find out how it was done. But it would not be too much to say that a kind of cross-fertilization took place. This occurred because, in the interim, the new constitution had been adopted, and in the confusion of the first legislature to convene under its aegis (1973) the groups came together — after a fashion.

Early in the session a furrow-browed Don Aldrich, lobbyist for the Montana Wilderness Association, sat in a threadbare motel room in Helena and talked to some young and eager environmentalists who had come to "lobby."

"But, you see," he said, "we cannot go off in all directions. We have to funnel things. We must know who is doing what." He stopped and grinned. "Now that is quite an order when you consider that even the legislature does not know what it is doing." Aldrich, an old hand and a former legislator, looked thoughtfully at the floor.

"You see, pretty much, industry knows what it is doing. Oh, not completely. Sometimes we grant them too much in that respect. They have weaknesses, very grave weaknesses. In this case two of them. First, they are in a great hurry to get what they want. It is expensive to wait — and it is nervous; and nervous people sometimes make mistakes.

"In the second place," and he raised his head and grinned widely, "if *we* don't know what is going to make the legislature tick, neither do they. They have money but otherwise we start even, I think. And that has never happened in my experience before. That is why it is so important for us to funnel our efforts and not go off in all directions."

This was the effective genesis of the Environmental Information Center and it was soon ensconced in an ancient room in the ragtag Placer Hotel. There, night or day, one could always find Phil Tawney, William Bryant, or some other person, usually young, pounding a typewriter, surrounded by lists, proposed bills, bills, analyses, fliers from other states, pamphlets, booklets, statistics and copies of testimony. Nor did the center end with the session. It is still very much in existence, and publishes a fact-filled legislative *News Letter* to alert all concerned to pending environmental hearings.

One could often find Kit Muller there — the legman, the mover and the doer of the Northern Plains Resource Council; headquarters, Billings. The NPRC, of all the dozens of environmental groups, is perhaps the most effective — and this is in no small part due to Muller. He is a Harvard graduate, a native Montanan, a quiet, almost taciturn twenty-eight-year-old who, in addition to being unflappable, is massively well informed on all matters pertaining to strip mining.

The NPRC is, in fact, a kind of holding company or, as Muller puts it, "a coordinating umbrella for affiliate organizations," each of which has one member on NPRC's board. Among them are the Rosebud Protective Association, the Powder River Basin Resource Council, the Tri County Ranchers Association, the Central Yellowstone Valley Association, and AERO (Alternate Energy Resources Organization).

NPRC was formed by ranchers; it is largely supported by ranchers, and it is by no means a "youth" organization. Some of its most active members are in their sixties or seventies.

It publishes a monthly newsletter called the *Plains Truth,* which is more of a small magazine than a newsletter. While the *Plains Truth* has a circulation of only about 2,500, that figure does not measure its influence. Most legislators subscribe to it, as do most elected officials. Moreover, it has a jealously guarded reputation for accuracy. It has, admittedly, an ax to grind and its editorials are often caustic. But it carries reprinted federal documents, verbatim testimony at hearings, and much statistical material that would be most difficult to obtain elsewhere.

It should be remarked at the outset that none of these organizations is "radical." Listen for a moment to Muller and bear in mind the inherent conservatism of Montanans: "While many people in the state are upset with investor-owned utilities, I'm not inclined to think that they feel public ownership would solve our problems. This distrust of public utilities is partly due to a general mistrust of public ownership and 'government,' partly due to the history of such outfits as the Bureau of Reclamation, Bonneville Power Administration, and TVA, and partly due to a mistrust of bigness. . . . [Our board] is inclined to feel that the central question is not one of ownership but rather is one of size and feel that the electrical system in the country needs to be decentralized."

As for what these myriad environmental organizations *do,* the question is rather easily answered. They no longer send passionate members to public or legislative hearings: they send lawyers to contend with lawyers, geologists with geologists, hydrologists with hydrologists, and agronomists with agronomists. They rarely attend any hearing without press releases already carefully prepared. They have their own lobbyists, usually paid (but not very well). They present slide shows on strip mining to civic clubs, high schools, and colleges. They organize and conduct public debates on a statewide basis and they draw on their own pool of expertise, largely academic. The NPRC maintains its own full-time, paid lobbyist in Washington, D.C.

The CCQE, for instance, arranges for a public debate with officials of the Hoerner-Waldorf pulp plant at Missoula, but they no longer send angry laymen; they send Dr. Ronald Erickson, a nationally known ecological chemist from the University of Montana.

The NPRC will arrange for a public debate with the Montana Power Company — but they do not send a furious rancher, they send Dr. Arnold Silverman, a geologist and a member of the National Academy of Sciences.

Most of the organizations have speakers' bureaus. Most issue press releases "grading" legislators on environmental issues. While the NPRC can hardly match the Montana Power Company's expenditure of $100,000 a year for television advertising in support of the construction of units numbers 3 and 4, it does run repeated radio spots in opposition to the units.

Again the question: How powerful and how effective are these organizations? The race is simply not run yet, and no one can prophesy. But speculation is essentially empty unless put in the broad context of what *underlying* powers are involved or what balances and imbalances exist in terms of *ultimate* power. Opposition can be loud, obviously informed, sustained — and misleading. Form is by no means necessarily substance.

First of all, do the many private environmental groups have a solid ally in state agencies now operating under the aegis of a new constitution and a rejuvenated legislature?

The three agencies essentially involved are the Energy Advisory Council, the Environmental Quality Council, and the Department of Natural Resources and Conservation. These agencies have some potent statutes at their disposal: a tough Clean Air Act; a tightly drawn Utility Siting Act, and a strong Strip Mining and Reclamation Act. The Department of Natural Resources and Conservation, for instance, presumably has the power to prevent the building of any power generating plants or high-voltage transmission lines in Montana. Moreover, all three of these state agencies are now staffed with well-trained experts in all the complex fields involved in the process of mining, power generation, and transmission.

As an example of the activities in which they have been involved, the latter department has commissioned dozens of studies itself (one took 600 days to complete) and it has also participated actively in a massive study of the entire Fort Union Coal Formation area which involved intensive examination by seven work groups under the aegis of the Northern Great Plains Resources Program. This study was a cooperative venture involving Montana, Nebraska, North Dakota, South Dakota, Wyoming, the Environmental Protection Agency, the Department of Agriculture, and the Department of the Interior. When this huge report was delivered to the state, the Department of Natural Resources and Conservation prepared a program from the information therein which was presented in nineteen Montana communities. Part slide show, part commentary, the program was designed to elicit popular response, encourage debate, and solicit testimony. These programs jammed auditoriums and did, indeed, result in debate. If the environmentalists missed none of these programs, neither did industry. It was an impressive demonstration of "education on the road," and it may be a tribute to the evenhandedness of the department that both industry and environmentalists found much in it to criticize. Neither, however, seemed to find much of a key in the program to the ultimate stand of the Department of Natural Resources. But it may be very revealing that the Department of Natural Resources *staff* formally and unequivocally announced on January 27, 1975, their unqualified opposition to the construction of Colstrip plants numbers 3 and 4.

It is certainly no secret that the several other staffs of the Montana environmental agencies are hostile to the construction of mine-mouth generating plants and extra-high-voltage transmission

lines in Montana. They oppose strip mining except under rigid
and tightly controlled circumstances. But staff recommendations
must be passed on to a mixture of appointed and elected boards
and, ultimately, to the legislature and perhaps the courts. The acid
tests have yet to come.

There is an almost pervasive dubiety in Montana concerning
federal environmental policies — a jaundiced focus, in this case, on
the Bureau of Land Management and the Bureau of Reclamation.
If this attitude is, indeed, a part of the frontier heritage, environmentalists, nevertheless, have no lack of evidence that the policies
pursued by both bureaus have at best been irrationally vacillating
and at worst downright devious, secretive and dishonest. More
generally, they mistrust the parent, the entire Department of the
Interior.

While the fact that federal regulatory agencies of all kinds have
for years been peopled by representatives of the industries to be
regulated comes as no surprise to much of anyone, it remains
deeply unsettling to Montanans that the men in high places in the
Mineral Resources Section of the Department of the Interior
come almost exclusively from the minerals or petroleum industries.
They not only come from those industries, but having come and
"served" they return to the industrial fold, usually with better-
paying jobs. John Kenneth Galbraith calls it "bureaucratic symbi-
osis." Montanans, perhaps simplistically, are more inclined to call
it simply "crooked."

And then, of course, there is Congress, which, in the view of
most Montanans, labored mightily on strip-mining legislation only
to bring forth from a conference committee a mishmash of a bill
which, in any event, was pocket-vetoed by Gerald Ford.

So to the question, how goes the battle?, the wary Wally McRae
squinted off over his rolling hills and said, "Well, I'll tell you,
looking inward, not bad, not bad at all. But if you look outward,
eastward, maybe not so good."

Still, the fact is that the Wally McRaes of this giant land have *never* liked what they saw when they looked eastward. McRae's father and his grandfather would have said much the same. The fact is, also, that Wally McRae is a very hard man to move — as are all of his kind.

12

Montana as a
National Heritage

IN OUR RUSH AND PLUNGE across the huge continent, the manner in which we "used" its resources has, in retrospect, come to seem like exploitation and plunder. That is the reading of the present into the past — but without recognizing that then the resources seemed truly limitless. Contemporaries have left us abundant evidence that they did not believe this monstrous land could *ever* be really "tamed" or "civilized."

So when the land and its infinite abundance suddenly (and in a very real sense it *was* sudden, or at least the comprehension of it was sudden) revealed itself to be nearly "used up," the reaction set in. Land, and often land for land's sake, became first a value and then an ethic. That, too, is understandable. Because if we have become a great nation by dedicating ourselves to intensive "use," we can hardly avoid a sense of deep loss when we find ourselves running out of much more to use. What do we do now? What, as a matter of fact, *are* we now?

That is the core of the environmental issue. It is the clash of an old and essentially honored ethic and a new and often strange one. And the clash, of course, lends itself admirably to hyperbole, polarization and great hostilities.

In most areas of America the form of this conflict, the ribs of its

body, the edges and parameters of its substance, are obscured by
its complexity. This is so because in most areas of America environmental degradation is not only many-faceted, it rises from
almost countless sources — and, above all, it is *there;* it is part of
everything else. To untie the knots, to undo it, is therefore to
undo everything else.

It is no real credit to Montana or Montanans that the issue is
clearest here. No conscious political or economic policy pursued
by Montanans resulted in the fact that today the body's ribs can
be starkly seen and the shadow cast by the substance can be etched
on the land. The reasons are historical and geographical.

It is not quite true that conservation and environmentalism are
solely the products of the mid-twentieth century. For instance, the
cutting of timber on public land was an issue as early as 1831,
though this was more a matter of revenue for the federal coffers
than an issue of conservation. But conservation was a genuine issue
by 1877, when Carl Schurz was appointed Secretary of the Interior. It was a hot issue during the first administration of Grover
Cleveland; and in his second administration (1897) Cleveland established thirteen new Forest Reserves, encompassing 21,379,840
acres in the West. Of these reserves more than 8,000,000 acres
were in Montana.

The essential lack of response from Montanans to the locking up
of timber reserves is merely illustrative of Montanans' attitude toward later and increasing land reserves of other types. Who cared?
After all, by 1900 the huge state still had only 1.7 persons per
square mile. If it had 3,000 miles of railroad, the average Montanan
was little involved because he lived a long way from the track.
There were less than 15,000 miles of so-called public roads, and
even by 1910 there were only .16 miles of road per square mile in
the state. There were only 1,300 miles of telephone lines and less
than 5,000 "sets" in use, and "use" was more an adventure than a
reliable means of communication.

The point is that the westering American either passed far to the south of this remote, rugged, frigid, hot, northern exclave of the great West or he hurried through its dangers — both real and presumed — to get quickly to the salubrious Pacific slope. The point also is that Montana is still bypassed today.

The creation of Cleveland's reserves and vast additions to those reserves under Theodore Roosevelt did, indeed, bring screams of anguish from nearly all western senators and congressmen, including Montana's. But the anguish of Montana's lumbermen and miners was subdued. In point of fact, it did not really matter greatly to them.

In the first place, under the Land Grant Act of 1864, the Northern Pacific Railroad had been granted 14,740,000 acres in Montana (16 percent of the total area of the state), much of it heavily timbered. The railroad, in turn, sold or leased stumpage to the mining magnates.

In spite of the reserves, there was plenty of timber to go around. By 1910, the Anaconda Company alone owned 1,116,000 acres of timberland which it had purchased either from the railroad or from private owners who had obtained timberland through various land grant laws. The company also acquired large tracts by fraud and "dummy entrymen," i.e., individuals who filed on small tracts of timberland presumably for themselves, but actually for the company.

The result was that land and what it could produce always existed in great abundance, but the area was "people poor." Even in the 1950s, scholars were writing of the high cost to Montana of her great spaces and, as a matter of firm policy dating back to the turn of the century, the several departments of state which were concerned with economic development thought almost exclusively in terms of "peopling this place." What *kind* of people they were and whether they might do this environment good or bad mattered not at all. The unremitting labors of those assigned the responsibility of attracting people to Montana went largely unrewarded except for the catastrophic homestead boom.

It is little wonder, then, that when a million acres were carved from the state to form Glacier National Park, there was not a murmur of dissent from lumbermen, miners, or anyone else. Indeed, on the contrary, this would produce a splendid tourist boom.

A better illustration of attitudes is the fact that when the federal government began to carve huge chunks out of Montana to create "wilderness" and "wild areas," Montanans responded with little interest except for a small minority of sportsmen. Officially, the state was pleased. Again, it might bring tourists. "Wilderness areas" were defined as encompassing 100,000 acres or more while "wild areas" ranged from 5,000 to 99,999 acres. By 1960, nine such areas had been carved out of the state, involving a total of 1,984,000 acres. More have been added since 1960.

While it is true that Montana sportsmen were much interested in the preservation of these pristine areas, what was actually happening was a kind of nascent, even perhaps subliminal, *national* recognition that something important, something even vital was vanishing, and some part of it should be saved to remind America of something. This "recognition" dates back to the 1930s.

A neighbor of mine, who owns many acres of ponderosa pine land to the west of me, last year encountered a group of young people from New Jersey. For a rather nominal rent they wanted to "set up housekeeping" in "his forest." An old-time Montanan, my neighbor was nonplussed. What did they mean? What the hell would they want to do that for? It also struck him as funny, but he was intrigued; because in spite of somewhat exotic clothing, long hair, and some confusion as to which female "belonged" to which male my neighbor is a decent man, and he remarked to me, "You know, by God, I like these people. I'm not using that property and they are welcome. *But what the hell for?*"

In any event, I came to know them. There were a dozen of them, the oldest twenty-nine, the youngest nineteen, and they were from Bayonne. None had college degrees but all save two had had some college education. Only one couple was married. What they wanted was very simple. They wanted to live "close to the land." They wanted to be "self-sufficient." They were not dropouts, they assured me. They believed in hard work and cooperative endeavor. They would build log cabins; they would garden (organically) and perhaps raise sheep, chickens, and have milk cows. They had bused and hitchhiked all over America. This was the place. You could not really "live" in Bayonne — or in much of the rest of America for that matter. Values were all fouled up. Nobody loved anyone. No one was really "productive." Americans did not know how to work with their hands. What had happened, said the twenty-nine-year-old (and, after a fashion, the leader), was that Americans had lost the land; they therefore could not live in harmony with nature and therefore could not, in turn, live in harmony with each other.

All that, of course, made very good sense, basic sense. The trouble was that it made sense only philosophically. Pragmatically it was senseless. Of this, in due course, I convinced them — and they left. I think of them now with a certain sense of sadness. You cannot grow gardens in ponderosa pine forests because the land is impregnated with turpentine; cows and other animals abort when they eat pine needles. The water table was perhaps five hundred to one thousand feet beneath the land they had chosen. What would they do for water? They had come in summer but what would they and their animals do when the snow banked up in drifts of four or five feet in their forest in the winter? There were no jobs in their valley except for highly skilled millworkers and woodsmen — and they had no money. How would they sustain themselves in the meantime? They had never seen a double-bitted ax, or cut down a tree, or notched a log. They had intended to hunt in the wild Selway a few miles westward — but they had never fired a rifle, gutted an elk, seen a trap or a snowshoe. And they did not know that even the most experienced natives of the

valley approached the Selway in the fall with extreme caution, perhaps a thousand dollars' worth of equipment, and years of experience – and even then the elk usually got away.

It was a warm and lovely August day when I drove them in the
truck down to the highway. The valley was exceedingly beautiful
and quiet. They were going to split up and hitchhike – eastward.

"Will you go back to Bayonne?"

"We don't know yet, but I suppose we will." A long pause.

"Maybe there isn't anyplace else. Maybe there is only Bayonne."

When we arrived at the highway, one of the girls (I never
learned her name) took her packsack out of the back of the
pickup, turned around several times looking at the valley, and
then looked rather somberly at me. "Well, Max and I will never
go back to Bayonne. There has *got* to be more than Bayonne. We
will go and learn some more about places like this. And then we'll
be back . . ." and she gave me a rather brilliant smile and said,
"with snowshoes." I very much hope they will be back.

I have another neighbor. He is a well-paid foreman at a sawmill some thirty miles south of his ranch. He cannot make a living
on the ranch, and the sawmill is in trouble because the trees on
the high slopes of the valley have been drastically overcut. He is
a native; he hunts in the Selway; he loves Montana. About a week
after the "commune people" had left, he and I were working on
a small dam in Mill Creek, a blue-green and whitely rushing stream
that rises deep in the wilderness and finally spills onto our pas-
tures. I asked him about conditions at the mill. He straightened
up, put his hands on his hips, and arched a little to take the crook
out of his back. He is not a young man.

"Funny thing. I was just thinking about that. Here we are,
we've got water in August – clean, cold water in August. And
we've got it because of the trees up there." And he nodded toward
the Selway. "Wilderness or not, if my mill doesn't get the trees up
there, a hell of a lot of good this clean, cold water is going to do

me. And if my mill does get the trees up there, I'll be goddammed if I want to live here anymore at all. It's a goddam mess."

As for the owner of my neighbor's mill, who lives in Missoula, there is no problem at all. That is, there is no problem that could not be solved by a big dose of good old American common sense.

"For Christ's sake, nobody tells a farmer to plant his wheat and then leave it there so some goddam tourist can say how pretty it is. Well, trees are a crop. Anyhow, who the hell but a few hunters and a few rich bastards from the East ever see the trees in the Selway? I tell you, you got to use land. It's not there to look at — it's there to use."

What are the gradients — and it makes little difference if we talk of trees or water or coal? Are we talking about total use, multiple use (a favorite Forest Service term), some use, little use, no use? It may seem that the sentimentality of the group from Bayonne was so naïve that in the end such an attitude can have no lasting influence on what happens. But that might be the very gravest of errors — at least in Montana. The fact is that their experience here was not a rarity; it has become rather commonplace. The further fact is that not everybody *has* gone back to Bayonne. A surprising number with the same philosophy, the same intent, but simply more determination have come and stayed — or have come, left, and returned to stay. If they are not zealots, they are close to it. They are, in short, determined not to bring Bayonne to Montana.

A mere twenty miles north of where the Bayonne group found and lost its forest is the Bass Creek commune. It is no faddish commune such as those spawned all across the country by the raw discontent of the 1960s. It has been there, as a small stable community, since 1967. Its members are extraordinarily active in community and state affairs. At the moment, the commune is preparing to sue the United States Forest Service for basic changes in a Forest Service plan to extend logging higher up the westward slopes of the Bitterroot Valley.

Listen to a commune member for a moment: "I am not interested in tilting at windmills. None of us is. None of us likes conflict. But I testify on these matters not merely because I am an economist who believes that growth for growth's sake is economically unsound and, in fact, disastrous, but also because I came to Montana by choice. We all did. We do not want to see happen here what, in fact, we fled elsewhere. We can still stop it here. It will be hard but it can be done. There are not many places left in America where that can be said. We do not hide in the commune. That should be obvious. We recharge our batteries there. From the land, hard work, and the country? Indeed, how else?"

This man is far from alone and his allies are by no means simply commune dwellers or recent arrivals. It is, however, significant that of the 8,000 students at the University of Montana, 25 percent (and growing) are from out of state. This is a matter of neither low tuition nor low entrance standards — it is overwhelmingly a matter of calculated choice. These young men and women found something very basic lacking in the communities from which they came. They are aggressively seeking something else. Some of them express it with great clarity and vigor. What it boils down to is some kind of relationship with some kind of *real* national heritage — and, yes, it is rooted in land, space — and in something that this presumably inhospitable place has not yet lost.* The majority of these students intend to stay — if they can, if only the jobs are here. A startling number indicate that they intend to stay even if they find themselves underpaid, overeducated and overtrained for what they must do. This is a peculiar view for college students

* For a decade I have taught a course entitled "Montana and the West." It was and is designed primarily to acquaint out-of-state students with the peculiarities of the state to which they have come. It is not designed for history majors. The enrollment runs between 400 and 500 students per quarter. For the past five years I have made it a point to interview as many out-of-state students as possible. The similarity of their views and their reasons for coming here is striking. Indeed, I should long since have formalized the process with written questionnaires. But until very recently I felt no need to quantify the obvious.

who are now, once again, career-oriented. And this, too, this view contrary to national studies of presumed student attitudes, is another straw in the wind that something unusual is afoot in Montana.

Is there an appreciable difference between these young people and young Montana natives? There is, indeed, some difference, but it is in degree rather than in kind. And it should be reemphasized that while youth are usually more articulate about what they want and why, the philosophy is by no means subscribed to merely by the young. The difference between the young and the older people is predominantly that the young want "into" this way of life and their elders are already there — and wish to stay.

Is Montana the *only* place where this "something" exists? Of course not. It exists in greater abundance in Alaska. And what of New Mexico, Nevada, Idaho? Montana does not exist in some fundamentally separate kind of a way either from its neighbors or from the country. But it still has this "something." Montana has been a vastly rich state, but not in terms of minerals, timber and agriculture. Its long-range wealth, though long considered a curse, was, in fact, its blessing: space and elbow room — quality space. It *has* maintained a direct link with the American past in that abiding sense. America *was* "the beautiful, the spacious skies" and the wind-bent grasses and the great rivers and the tumultuous mountains and wild forests — the land unspoiled.

If Montanans cursed the loneliness and fretted over the high cost of emptiness, what a terrible irony if we were now to turn what was once a curse into a blessing and then back into a curse — because we failed to understand the true nature of our wealth. As for "use," real use is the maintenance, in essence, of what we have, and that means that those "resources" (in the usual sense of the word), must be used, *if at all*, carefully, slowly, and thoughtfully.

Montana's heritage is national. It is here that the real argument against the "national sacrifice area" (for coal) rests. And it is here that pro-development logic breaks down.

The argument is simple. In the larger interests of the greater number we must swiftly convert oil-burning power generating plants to coal-fired generating plants. It makes no sense to put polluting plants in populous areas. The sensible thing to do is to follow the "Farmington System." Via transmission lines the power generated comes cleanly into the populous areas. After all, the giant Four Corners plant in New Mexico is out in the desert. True, some people and land will be damaged — and that is regrettable. But in Montana or New Mexico, for instance, there are far fewer people than elsewhere and much more land — and people are more important than land. "Speak to us not of profit. We are acting for the greater good."

Part of the fallacy of that argument we have already considered. Invisibly the poison of these plants travels vast distances in the high winds of the upper atmosphere. Another aspect of the fallacy lies in the fact that foreign as the Northern Plains may seem to the people of New Orleans, they are irrevocably hitched to those plains by a giant umbilical cord, the Mississippi River. Down the Tongue to the Yellowstone, down the Yellowstone to the Missouri, down the Missouri to the Mississippi.

And what shall we say of the Platte, the Arkansas, the Canadian, the Colorado, the Pecos, the Rio Grande? What of Natchez, Memphis, St. Louis, Omaha, and Kansas City? There are people there. They cannot drink acid; they cannot pump salt and alkali onto their fields or into their factories and feed lots. Out here we are already dumping arsenic, cadmium, lead and salt into our rivers. Not very much yet, but wait a few years.

If you say, "Speak to us not of profit. We are acting for the greater good," then serious consideration should be given to the fact that today there are only slightly over eight million farmers and ranchers on the American land. They are feeding over two hundred million people in America — and an unknown but significant number abroad. And those eight million are dwindling by the year — and so is the land they work. The government no longer has vast food stocks. The reserve of wheat alone is down to about a month's supply.

All this is quantifiable. All this really gives the lie to the assertion that a "national sacrifice area" can be confined, that it can be sacrificed, fenced in and forgotten. But what of the "unquantifiable," which in the long run may be the most pernicious sacrifice of all. When these last reaches have gone, where will America go to see what it has been?

What is involved is a loss of memory, a loss of continuity, a loss of roots, a loss of tradition, a loss of parenthood, a loss of experience, a loss of maturity, a loss of rudder — and a loss of direction.

But are all these things preserved only in faraway and empty places? Are these things solely possessed by rural people? Are they in only one place? Of course not. It is, nevertheless, historically accurate to say that for the much greater part of the two-hundred-year existence of our nation, the most compelling and influential conditioner of our values, our stability, and our national *direction* was our intimate relationship with and discovery of the meaning of the land. That is, indeed, no less true of Russia, China, or Afghanistan. That does not make it less important to America.

But, you say, the frontier is gone. Our problems now are urban and technological. We have no need to ask where we have been except in those terms. Well, then, no man has a need to ask questions of his father or his own childhood. As the twig is bent . . .

There remains a crisis, a very real and awesome energy crisis. Is the stripping of coal in Montana and on the Northern Plains a necessary activity? Will it, in an interim period, genuinely alleviate our pains until alternate sources of energy are developed? That that is more than simply questionable has been demonstrated in the previous pages. There remains something to be added — the self-evident things. Statistics are not dramatic. Nevertheless, consider carefully the fact that with 6 percent of the world's population, America consumes one-third of its energy.

Since energy wastage in America is so egregious that it is not a matter of finding it but rather of avoiding it, let the matter stand there, except for the asking of these questions — all of which are rhetorical.

Would the American "life-style" and the country's position as a world power be essentially altered if we had not *doubled* the use of electricity between 1960 and 1970? (This with only an 11 percent increase in population.)

Is our technology really advanced and has industry really spent adequately for "research and development" when it remains a fact that in the conversion and transmission of coal-produced electricity there is a loss of 65 percent of the actual energy in the coal?

Could we return to the "pioneer" year of 1960 in terms of energy consumed without undue discomfort or loss of national, political and economic power?

Is the weakening of our antipollution laws necessary in this crisis in view of the fact that the Environmental Protection Agency calculated in 1968 that the cost to the nation of polluted air and water was $16.1 *billion?*

Since $8 billion of this damage is attributed to SO_2 and since $4 billion of *that* is attributed to SO_2 from coal-fired plants, is coal really the "cheap" fuel it is billed as being by the electric industry?

Is it necessary to rush westward to mine coal when most of the reserves in BTUs are in the East and in deep mines?

In view of the resultant heavy unemployment in deep mining in already depressed areas in the East, does western strip mining help the general economy of America simply because it is cheaper for the energy companies to strip-mine western coal?

The sole reason for the coal industry's westward rush is profit. The overall question is: Can America as a whole really afford that kind of profit?

In 1970, the Bureau of Business Research at the University of Montana produced a document entitled *The Montana Economic Study*, edited by a young economist, Samuel B. Chase, Jr., a man extraordinarily talented and perspicacious.* It was also a grim document with grim projections. Not only was Montana's personal per capita income 14 percent below the national average, it was destined to plunge to 21 percent below that average by 1980. Montana's "bellwether industries" — agriculture, mining, railroading, and lumbering — were all in decline and destined to continue to decline (strip mining in 1970 was not the subject of the frantic analysis which arose after 1971's *North Central Power Study*).

Young Montanans between the ages of nineteen and twenty-four were outmigrating at a discouraging rate because of the poor job market. There were no indications of a reversal in the trend. *The Montana Economic Study* made no recommendations; it had not been Chase's charge to do so.

In a series of debates, both formal and informal, Professor Chase and I belabored the merits and demerits of statistical analysis — and the quantifiable versus the unquantifiable — over a period of several months.

It was Chase's contention that however lyrical about space, beauty and heritage I might become, I could not controvert the facts. Montana *could* improve its economic status if it were willing to pay the price. (This was *not* part of his study.) That price was pollution, in effect. We could, for instance, in view of our vast water resources, sustain many, many pulp mills rather than the single mill at Missoula. Pulp mills, after all, could use all the wastage in our forest products industry. Such mills could use timber which in no other respect was commercial — down timber, rotten timber, crooked timber, diseased timber, stumps, branches, bark — everything. But the price would be pollution from the pulp mills. I could argue for a pristine country but I could not have that

---

* Professor Chase is now one of the principal advisers to the Federal Reserve Board in Washington.

country and jobs, too. He, Chase, did not argue that Montana should pay that price. He was, after all, a Montanan and he loved the state the way it was. But he argued that I should recognize that space, beauty, clean air, and water were *still* Montana's economic curse.

I have no doubt that he would employ the same argument today with respect to strip mining. And I have no doubt that he would grin at me again and ask me that loaded question: "Will you be sitting there at noon when the worker opens his lunch box and finds no sandwich therein but only a paper scroll with your lyrics to an unspoiled land inscribed thereon?"

I could never really answer that question satisfactorily then and I suppose I cannot now. One cannot endorse one man's hunger today for his grandson's contentment and peace of mind thirty-five years from now. No, I do not want to sit by that man when he opens that lunch box.

But if it were really that simple, and I had the courage, I would rather suffer the anger and resentment in that man's eyes today than to know that I had purchased today with all of his grandson's tomorrows.

We have our monuments, Williamsburgs, vast museums, historic houses, even our tombs, to remind us of our heritage. In spite of the skill and research which have gone into them, in spite of their beauty, they are, in some root kind of way, sterile. The House of Seven Gables does not speak a single word of Hawthorne. However carefully one listens, there are no whispers there.

The artifacts of the past which lie in our great museums are peculiarly mute. However skillfully displayed, however informative their labels, these things have been lifted from an old context and they have left their essence in the vanished places from which they were taken. To commemorate, let alone to "recreate," our heritage is somehow synthetic. It is certainly educational and worthwhile — but unfortunately it is in the very nature of monuments to be dead.

On the Missouri River a few miles east of Great Falls, Montana, lies the sleepy little town of Fort Benton. Once, in the 1860s, because it was the headwaters of steamboat navigation on the river, it was a roaring hub of empire. Trails radiated outward from it, westward and northward, carrying men and goods to the Pacific Coast, the inland Rocky Mountain mining towns, and the Canadian West. The town itself was a roaring mixture of bullwhackers, cowboys, soldiers, traders, French voyagers, Indians, and merchants.

Let me drive you a few miles northward on a narrow pitted road and then let us leave the car and walk a few hundred yards through the sparse grass. There you will see ruts, and if you look carefully you will see that the rutted area is fifty or sixty yards wide. You are looking at the Whoopup Trail over which oxen and horses hauled the mighty wheeled freight wagons from Fort Benton to Fort McLeod in Alberta. They hauled whiskey for the Indians, traps for the trapper, tobacco, flour, coffee, rifles, and a thousand commodities. But I ask you to stand very still and listen to the soft hush of the wind in the grass. After a moment, in the wind, you will hear the creak of leather, dim curses, the crunching sound of heavy wheels on rocks, and, far away, the lowing of cattle. This place is no monument; it bears no marker. Yet here are the ruts made by the passing of the men of an American empire — still speaking if we will listen.

Let us move to the rotting boardwalks of Elkhorn; again, no monument — a ghost town perched high on a mountain above the Boulder Valley, empty. If there is a mournful sound to this wind it is because it moves through emptiness, around the sagging buildings, into the silent rooms of the opera house, out again, to brush against the old mill's beams and rusted hoists. But listen carefully and you will hear with your inner ear, quite clearly, the sound of boots on the boardwalks, the sound of a piano, and everywhere the murmuring of voices. Now squint your eyes, blur things a little, and Elkhorn will suddenly jump into the roaring life of still another American empire.

But, you say, these things and places are few and far between. That is true. Man made them and left them and so they will vanish unless he makes them into monuments — and ghosts always desert monuments. When now Americans come with tennis shoes, pink shorts, golf hats, and cameras, their noise destroys the capacity really to hear and they cannot see for the seeing of their own day and their own kind.

So let us consider what else is left here in Montana — things and places that need no restoration, no making of monuments, no pointing arrows leading you down neatly white-graveled pathways to see something dead.

You are very short of time? So, the clatter notwithstanding, let us take a small airplane and fly, quite low, across the length of this land, Montana. We shall begin in the west, steeply climbing up out of this valley and, leveling off, we shall head eastward.

Surprisingly, you will rarely see the neat geometric patterns of the towns. They will look odd, superimposed and fragile, and you will quickly lose sight of the roads and rails that connect them. They will appear as tiny and insignificant ribbons buried in the folds of gigantic mountains. In all directions that is what you will see — a vast, jumbled, jagged tumult. But that is not enough to say. These monstrous mountains swell, rear up, fall off into valleys and white rivers; they are haired with trees or they are bald. They jam and crash into each other. They curve as gently as breasts or bristle like turrets and towers.

And they *move*, as surely as great waves move on the sea but not as regularly, for they move in all directions at once. With every move their color changes — black, red, purple, green, blue, all shifting and shading off into each other.

It is true that in the valleys you will see farms. Not many. But lakes you will see everywhere. Large, small, hidden, round, snake-

like, ineffably lonely, glinting and somber — and from them, sometimes, white water falling in mist down cliffs.

You will see roads. Ugly scars, zigzagging sharply, mostly
abandoned, the logs having come out. And here and there patches
like skin disease, clear-cutting. Some places the gray spars of trees
left by the fires. Other places the webs of fallen timber blown
down by fearsome winds — all fallen in the same direction, an
impenetrable mat.

But where, really, is man? In all these years has he *still* left only
these few scars? Have you ever flown from Boston to Washington? Have you ever flown from San Diego to Los Angeles?

And then the mountains drop away, shelving down, sliding out,
treelessly rolling, dropping down to the plains. They are a surprise,
the plains. They are not level; they are not flat. Again the
occasional town, transient, fragile and looking lost in what is now
seen to be the constant motion of the land. Across the rolling,
often broken, sometimes gullied and canyoned plains, the shadows
of the clouds speed eastward and the grass ripples and shimmers.
The plains roll in constant, silent motion.

The rivers. They glint — curving, looping, splitting around
islands, spilling over banks, or dwindling into brown trickles, having been drunk up by the gigantic thirst of this land.

There are not many fences. The few main roads cut straight and
incongruously across the hugeness. The gravel roads follow section
lines, marking off squares and rectangles as if to render motionless
the motion — as if timorously to measure the imperious measure-
lessness. This land ceaselessly laps at the structures of man — so that
the towns, the roads, the rails, and the fences seem not so much
pretentious as weakly anchored. It is as if the builders had said, we
know that none of this will hold or last but let us borrow one
month from your agelessness so that we can measure out our lives
and tell ourselves that we are here.

Once, with variations, that was all of America. And reduced to
the irreducible, that is the American heritage. For, in truth, no

American on any frontier East or West believed that he could triumph over the land — or make it lie still and obey him as the humble servant. He knew better, far better. He did not seek to "still the restless wave"; he rose and fell with it. Whatever he used of the land or, however, in truth, he abused the land, he was not filled with the ultimate arrogance of believing that he had the power, to say nothing of the right, to use it all up. *He was no eater of carrion.*

You cannot drive across America today and say that it is all used up. Far from it. But neither can you drive across America today without knowing that we have used up vast reaches of it. Much more sadly, you cannot look at America today without recognizing that great numbers of us *do* believe that we have not merely the power to consume it all — but the right. We have become gluttons.

No, Montana's still predominant and triumphant land is not America's only heritage. But it represents a very important root of America's first, oldest, and deepest feeling about ourselves and our land. As such, it, and a drastically dwindling number of other places, *is* a national heritage. And the heritage is not spelled C-O-A-L.

13

Of Mirrors and Idols

THERE IS A STORY, doubtless apocryphal, attributed to Plenty Coups, one of the few chiefs of the Crow who was genuinely revered by his people. Among the many items which the white trappers and traders employed to obtain furs from the Indians, none save knives, guns, and whiskey were more in demand than mirrors. The myth has it, of course, that this was because these "primitive" people thus saw themselves for the first time. It was not really a myth, because the whites believed it. This, according to the story, vastly amused Plenty Coups, who knew why his people really wanted mirrors.

The Indians had long since developed a *long-range* signal system consisting of sign language (from which our own deaf and dumb sign language has been clearly adapted). They also used drums and smoke signals. They at once recognized that the mirror would be most valuable for long-range signaling. Plenty Coups, who was present at one of these late "rendezvous" when mirrors were going for pelts worth five hundred times the value of the mirrors, was sitting cross-legged beside a trader who remarked to him that it was a fine thing that his people could now see themselves. The amused chief turned to the trader and said, allegedly (and the versions vary): "The mirrors are valuable to my people.

We do not have your wires to talk upon. But you do not understand that we have always seen ourselves. How can you drink from a still pool and not see your face? The mirrors are fine but they break very easily. The pools and the lakes never break. It is true that if the wind comes, I cannot see my face in the water. But what kind of man am I if between today when there is no wind and tomorrow when there is a wind, I forget who I am?"

The story is, I think, a parable for the subject of this book. Like a mirror, an institution is man-made, an artifact; and like a mirror, it reflects. Not, of course, faces, but wishes, intentions. We can use our institutions as the Crow used their mirrors: to get something done. Or we can become idolators, taking the reflection for the reality, as if the fleeting, two-dimensional image were our very selves. Eisenhower's Secretary of Defense, Mr. Wilson, was, on the surface of things, misquoted when he allegedly said, "What is good for General Motors is good for the country." The saddening thing is that in explaining how he had been misquoted, he affirmed very honestly and conscientiously that he *did* believe what, in fact, he had not said. A man who can confound the welfare of his company with that of his nation is, in the sense I intend, an idolator.

And in this sense the mirror takes on an eerie life of its own, as an idol does, as does any man-made device which masters man. We confer this life upon our creation. It is our folly to believe that a mirror can tell us who we are, or that the idol demands our sacrifices. "The American way of life," largely a man-made institution, now in its insatiable demands for energy requires the sacrifice of the American earth, and with it, I fear, much of what makes us American. And we are doubly idolators to confound the profit-seeking of the energy corporations with our life-style as a nation, and that life-style with our national soul. What makes us American is not our electric toothbrushes, it is our home. Not our houses, but our land; our country, not our possessions.

I was lying on my back on a brown grass hill behind Bud Redding's house. It was a late September afternoon. I could hear the steady sibilance of a small wind in the box elder leaves and the barely perceptible ringing of crickets wearied by a long, hot summer. In the enormous sky, great puffs of cumulus clouds rose like bulbous fists, the wrists shaved off and flattened by some high and silent wind. I could hear the muted sound of quiet voices from below, and the grass around me rustled dryly in its old age. A lone grasshopper, like a small rod of dust, clacked into the air fitfully and then fell back into the grass upside down. He was properly dying. Across the valley I could see fat cattle, mostly somnolent, a few grazing in a desultory way. All around me another fall had come, cool, brown, yellow, blue, subdued, and somehow very quietly and peacefully old.

Suddenly there was a tremendous explosion. The earth beneath me shook and shifted. Very abruptly I sat up. I saw a huge brown piece of earth rise into the sky, disintegrate, and turn into an enormous yellow-gray cloud which swiftly began to spread across the entire field of my vision. Westmoreland Coal Company was breaking up the overburden.

When the hard, flat echo of the blast ended there was a silence so profound, it was as if the earth itself had stopped breathing. No motion, no leaves whispered, the grass stood still. Across the valley, though I could not hear them, I saw the cattle running in panic through the mist of falling dust. Then I saw the small figure of my son running up the hill toward me, his yellow hair flying behind him, his small legs pumping like pistons. When he came up to me I saw his intense blue eyes and I saw that he was angry. He turned around and looked through the filtering dust. The cattle were still running and now the air was heavy with the acrid smell of cordite. I heard my son say, "They've got no right, they've just got no right." His fists were clenched.

No, they've got no right. And I have no right to tell my son to give it to them. I have no right to say to the ranchers, what the hell, sell and get out. My son is eleven, most of the holdout ranchers are in their seventies. The difference is more than half a century. My son must be fighting as hard sixty years from now as they are today. Above all, my son. He *has* the right to his time on a whole earth — and whatever our time may be, so do we all.

Bibliography

This is a highly selective bibliography and is intended merely as a guide to topic literature. Exhaustive bibliographies can be found especially in the listing under Documents.

BOOKS

Abbott, E. C., and Smith, Helena Huntington. *We Pointed Them North.* Norman: University of Oklahoma Press, 1955.

Adams, Andy. *The Log of a Cowboy.* Lincoln: University of Nebraska Press, 1964.

Athearn, Robert G. *High Country Empire.* New York: McGraw-Hill, 1960.

Berkman, Richard L., and Viscusi, W. Kip. *Damming the West: The Report on the Bureau of Reclamation.* New York: Grossman Publishers, 1975.

Carson, Rachel. *Silent Spring.* Boston: Houghton Mifflin, 1962.

Dale, Edward Everett. *Cow Country.* Norman: University of Oklahoma Press, 1965.

De Roos, Robert. *The Thirsty Land.* Palo Alto, Calif.: Stanford University Press, 1948.

Dick, Everett. *Tales of the Frontier.* Lincoln: University of Nebraska Press, 1970.

Dimsdale, Thomas. *The Vigilantes of Montana.* Butte: McKee Press, 1929.

Doty, Russell L., Jr. *Poles Apart.* Missoula: University of Montana Press, 1970.

Ewers, John C. *The Horse in Blackfoot Indian Culture.* Washington, D.C.: U.S. Government Printing Office, 1955.

Gaffney, Mason, ed. *Extractive Resources and Taxation.* Madison: University of Wisconsin Press, 1967.

Gard, Wayne. *The Great Buffalo Hunt.* Lincoln: University of Nebraska Press, 1968.

Gates, Paul W. *Landlords and Tenants on the Frontier.* Ithaca, N.Y.: Cornell University Press, 1973.

Glasscock, C. B. *The War of the Copper Kings.* New York: Grosset & Dunlap, 1935.

Gregg, Josiah. *The Commerce of the Prairies.* Lincoln: University of Nebraska Press, 1967.

Gressley, Gene M. *Bankers and Cattlemen.* Lincoln: University of Nebraska Press, 1966.

Hamilton, W. T. *My Sixty Years on the Plains.* Norman: University of Oklahoma Press, 1960.

Hill, R. T. *Public Domain and Democracy.* New Haven: Yale University Press, 1970.

Howard, Joseph K., ed. *Montana Margins: A State Anthology.* New Haven: Yale University Press, 1946.

Ise, John. *United States Forest Policy.* New Haven: Yale University Press, 1920.

Kraenzel, Carl F. *The Great Plains in Transition.* Norman: University of Oklahoma Press, 1955.

Levine, Louis. *The Taxation of Mines in Montana.* New York: B. W. Huebsch, 1919.

Malone, Michael, and Roeder, Richard. *The Montana Past: An Anthology.* Missoula: University of Montana Press, 1969.

Metcalf, Lee, and Reissemer, Vic. *Overcharge.* New York: David McKay, 1967.

The Montana Almanac. Missoula: University of Montana Press, 1957, 1958, 1959, 1960.

Osgood, E. S. *The Day of the Cattleman.* Chicago: University of Chicago Press, 1968.

Ottoson, Howard W., et al. *Land and People in the Northern Plains Transition Area.* Lincoln: University of Nebraska Press, 1966.

Pomeroy, Earl. *In Search of the Golden West.* New York: Alfred A. Knopf, 1957.

Riegel, Robert E. *America Moves West.* New York: Henry Holt and Co., 1947.

Robbins, Roy. *Our Landed Heritage: The Public Domain.* Lincoln: University of Nebraska Press, 1962.

Russell, Charles M. *Good Medicine.* New York: Doubleday, Doran and Co., 1930.

————. *Trails Plowed Under.* Garden City, N.Y.: Doubleday, Page, 1927.

Sharp, Paul F. *Whoop-Up Country.* Minneapolis: University of Minnesota Press, 1955.

Smith, Henry Nash. *Virgin Land: The American West as Symbol and Myth.* Cambridge: Harvard University Press, 1970.

Smurr, J. W., and Toole, K. Ross, eds. *Historical Essays on Montana and the Northwest.* Helena, Mont.: Western Press, 1957.

Toole, K. Ross. *Montana: An Uncommon Land.* Norman: University of Oklahoma Press, 1959.

————. *Twentieth Century Montana: A State of Extremes.* Norman: University of Oklahoma Press, 1972.

Webb, Walter Prescott. *The Great Plains*. New York: Grosset & Dunlap, 1931.

Young, Louise B. *Power over People*. New York: Oxford Press, 1973.

ARTICLES

Anderson, David H. "Strip Mining on Reservation Lands: Protecting the Environment and the Rights of Indian Allotment Owners." *Montana Law Review*, Summer 1974.

Benton, Lee. "The Mini Oils: The Davids That May Beat Out the Goliaths." *Financial World*, June 1974.

Clinch, Thomas A. "The Northern Pacific Railroad and Montana's Mineral Lands." *Pacific Historical Review*, September 1965.

Christiansen, William. "Energy *vs*. Environment." *Montana Rural Electric News*, September 1973.

Conway, James. "The Last of the West: At Home with the Strippers." *The Atlantic*, September 1973.

Crowley, John M. "Water and Electric Power in Montana." *Montana Business Quarterly*, Autumn 1971.

Davison, Stanley. "Hopes and Fancies of the Early Reclamationists." In *Historical Essays on Montana and the Northwest*, edited by W. Smurr and K. Ross Toole. Helena, Mont.: Western Press, 1957.

Dietz, Donald R. "Strip Mining for Western Coal: Not Necessarily Bad." *Journal of Range Management*, May 1975.

Dye, Harold V. "Taxation of Minerals under Article XII, Section 3, of the Montana Constitution." *Montana Law Review*, Winter 1971.

Evans, William B., and Peterson, Robert L. "Decision at Colstrip." *Pacific Northwest Quarterly*, July 1970.

Ford, Collier. "Montana: Giant Grab Bag." *America*, December 23, 1972.

France, Tom. "The Disturbing Lack of Competition." *Montana Journalism Review*, No. 18, 1975.

Gates, Paul Wallace. "The Homestead Law in an Incongruous Land System." *American Historical Review*, October 1935.

Gillespie, Marie. "Coal Mining Taxes in Montana." *Montana Business Quarterly*, Winter 1974.

Guthrie, A. B., Jr. "A Plea to Halt Reckless Progress." *Montana Journalism Review*, No. 18, 1975.

Johnson, James H. "State and Local Taxation of the Bituminous Coal Industry." *West Virginia Law Review*, 1973–74.

Josephy, Alvin M., Jr. "Agony of the Northern Great Plains." *Audubon: Magazine of the National Audubon Society*, July 1973.

Leidnitz, Larry, and Hertoguard, Thomas A. "Coal Development in North Dakota: Effects on Agriculture and Rural Communities." *North Dakota Farm Research*, September–October 1973.

McDowell, Edwin. "The Shoot-out over Western Coal." *Wall Street Journal*, June 21, 1974.

Miller, Arnold. "The Energy Crisis as the Coal Miner Sees It." *Saturday Review–World*, December 1973.

Muller, Kit. "The National Importance of Regional Energy Development."
     Western Wildlands, Autumn 1974.
Northern Plains Resource Council. *The Plains Truth*. Monthly, 1972–1975.
O'Connor, George. "Problems in News Coverage." *Montana Journalism Re-
     view*, No. 18, 1975.
Smith, Annick. "Property Tax Reform in Montana." *Montana Business
     Quarterly*, Winter 1974.
Toole, K. Ross, and Butcher, Edward. "Timber Depredations on the Public
     Domain: 1885–1918." *Journal of the West*, July 1968.
Toole, K. Ross. "What History Teaches Us About Land Misuse." *Montana
     Outdoors*, May–June 1974.
Walcheck, Ken. "Weep for the Roche Jaune" (Yellowstone). *Montana
     Outdoors*, July–August 1974.
Webb, Walter Prescott. "The American West: Perpetual Mirage." *Harper's*,
     September 1957.
————. "The West and the Desert." *Montana: The Magazine of Western
     History*, Winter 1958.
Wicks, Garry, et al. "A Look at Coal-Related Legislation Enacted by the
     Forty-third Legislative Assembly." *Montana Business Quarterly*, Summer
     1973.

DOCUMENTS AND MANUSCRIPTS

Alwin, John A. "Patterns of Montana Towns: 1860–1920." Unpublished M.A.
     thesis, University of Montana, 1972.
Bahls, Loren L., and Miller, Marvin R. *Saline Seep in Montana*. Environ-
     mental Quality Council, Second Annual Report, 1973.
Brown, Paul L., and Ferguson, Hayden. *Crop and Soil Management for
     Possible Control of Saline Seep in Montana*. Bozeman: Cooperative Ex-
     tension Service, Montana State University, June 1973.
Coal and the Energy Shortage. Presented by Continental Oil Company to
     Security Analysts, December 1973.
Department of the Interior, Office of the Secretary. *Decision on Northern
     Cheyenne Coal Lands*. June 4, 1974.
Donaldson, Thomas, ed. *The Public Domain: Report of Public Land Com-
     mission Codification*. Washington, D.C., 1884.
Council on Economic Priorities. *Leased and Lost: A Study of Public and
     Indian Coal Leasing in the West*. Vol. 5, No. 2, 1973.
Environmental Quality Council (Montana). *First Annual Report*. October
     1972.
Environmental Policy Center (Washington, D.C.). *Facts About Coal in the
     United States*. April 1974.
Ford Foundation. *Exploring Energy Choices: Preliminary Report of the Ford
     Foundation's Energy Policy Project*. Washington, D.C., 1974.
Gold, Raymond. *A Comparative Case Study of the Impact of Coal Devel-
     opment on the Way of Life of People in the Coal Areas of Eastern Mon-

tana and North Eastern Wyoming. Final Report, Institute for Social Science Research, University of Montana, Missoula, June 1974.

Grant, Frank R. "Robert N. Sutherlin: Prophet for the People." Unpublished M.A. thesis, University of Montana, 1971.

Joint Interim Subcommittee on Fossil Fuel Taxation (Montana). *Analysis of Fossil Fuel Taxation*. Legislative Council Staff, July 1974.

Jovick, Robert L. *Critique of Prospective Coal Development in Eastern Montana*. Economic Development Association of Eastern and Western Montana Interstate Commission for Higher Education, 1972.

Judge, Thomas L. *Testimony Given Before the Congress, House Interior Committee*. Governor's File (Montana), March 19, 1973.

————. Letter to Gordon McOmber and Harold Gerke on Yellowstone River Moratorium. Governor's File (Montana), January 28, 1974.

League of Women Voters. *Coal Development in North Dakota*. Bismarck, 1974.

Montana Agricultural Experiment Station. *An Economic Analysis of Alternative Technologies for Cooling Thermal-Electric Generating Plants in the Fort Union Coal Region*. Research Report 49, January 1974.

Montana Department of Natural Resources and Conservation. *A Resource Inventory Method for Land Use Planning in Montana*. December 1973.

Montana Energy Advisory Council. *Coal Development*. December 1974.

————. *A Proposed Series of Projects to Evaluate the Potential Physical, Biological and Water Use Impacts of Water Withdrawals and Water Development on the Middle and Lower Portions of the Yellowstone River Drainage*. December 1973.

Montana Energy Advisory Council and Department of Natural Resources and Conservation. *A Study of Filed and Use-Appropriated Water Rights in Portions of the Yellowstone Basin in Montana*. January 9, 1974.

Montana Legislative Council. *Water Resources*. Report 53 to the 43rd Legislative Assembly, Helena, 1972.

National Academy of Sciences–National Academy of Engineering. *Rehabilitation of Western Coal Lands, A Report to the Energy Policy Project of the Ford Foundation by the Study Committee on the Potential for Rehabilitating Land Surface Mined for Coal in the Western United States*. Washington, D.C., 1973.

National Governors' Council. *Testimony Given by Western Governors of the Major Coal Producing States*. Wheeling, W. Va., 1973.

Northern Plains Resource Council. *The Western Low Sulphur Coal Myth*. May 1975.

United States Department of the Interior, Bureau of Reclamation. *Report on the Yellowstone Division of the Missouri River Basin Project, Montana and North Dakota*. 1964.

United States Corps of Army Engineers, U.S. Army Safeguard System Command. *Community Impact Report, Malmstrom Deployment Area*. Prepared by Wilsey and Ham, Foster City, California, July 1970.

Ziontz, Pirtle, Morrissett and Ernstoff. *A Petition and Legal Analysis of the Northern Cheyenne Indian Tribe to Rogers C. B. Morton, Secretary of the Interior, Concerning Coal Leases and Permits* (2 vols.). Submitted January 7, 1974.

Index

BIA. *See* Indian Affairs, U.S. Bureau of (BIA)

Bighorn River, 163

Big Musky, Ohio, 4

Big Sky Mine, 100–101

Billings, Montana, 94, 95, 111, 149, 213; area director in, 58, 59, 65; power plant, 100, 191

Birney, Montana, 100, 115, 122

Bitterroot power line, 178–182, 191

Bitterroot-Selway Wilderness Area, 179, 181; and "the Selway," 231–233

Bitterroot Valley, 178, 179, 219, 233

Black Hills, 41

"black lung," 100, 201, 202

Black Mesa area, 62–63

"Black Power," 68

Bones Brothers Ranch, 122

Bonner, Montana, 201

Bonneville Power Authority (BPA), 183, 207, 222

bonus, coal. *See* royalties, coal

Boulder Valley, 241

Box Elder reservoir (proposed), 165

Boyson reservoir, 166

Breeder's Gazette, 72

Brewster, Burton C., 115

Bryant, William, 221

buffaloes, 26, 35, 71, 72, 73, 76

Bull Mountain area, 111, 121, 122

Bull Mountain Landowners' Association, 113, 149

Burlington Northern Railroad, 121, 145

Business Research, Bureau of, 239

Butte, Montana, 86, 146, 178, 182, 200

Cady, Bruce, 121, 123

Campbell, Hardy Webster, and "Campbell system," 135–137. *See also* homesteading

Canan, James F., 47, 51–52, 53

Cardozo, Benjamin N., 50

Carter Oil Company (Exxon), 97, 203

Casper, Wyoming, 94, 165

Catlin, George, 27

cattle-raising: acreage for, 115; beef prices and, 72, 139; vs. coal production, 115; cost of, 123; drought and, 74, 139–140; and eminent domain, 146–147; vs. homesteading, 31, 70–79, 141; and Indians vs. ranchers, 48; longhorns, 71; losses in, 75–76; market, 70–77; in Montana, 29, 70, 72, 74–75, 77, 114, 115, 123; nutrition (grass) and, 30, 122–123; and overgrazing, 74–77; and politics, 124–125, 178, 211, 212–213; and public domain, 73–74, 76, 118; and ranchers' associations, 46, 73, 111–113, 117, 121, 124, 144, 149, 208, 221 (*see also* Northern Plains Resource Council); and ranchers vs. industry, 48, 69, 114, 115–122, 124–125, 141–142, 145; and ranch traditions and philosophy, 69, 78–79, 83, 93–95, 103–104, 114, 116–125, 143, 178; vs. sheep-raising, 77; "shrinkage" in, 122–123; sociological study of, 78–79; speculation and exploitation in, 69–79; and Texas drives, 71–72; and "trespass," 102, 119–122, 124; in Wyoming, 72, 75, 77

CCOB (Concerned Citizens of the Bitterroot), 219

CCQE (Concerned Citizens for a Quality Environment), 219, 223

census, and U.S. Bureau of, 135, 210. *See also* population

Center for Advanced Computation, University of Illinois, 197

Central Appalachian Coal Company, 205

Central Ohio Coal Company, 205

Central Yellowstone Valley Association, 221

Charter, Boyd, 122, 123, 143, 149–150

Charter, Mrs. Boyd, 111, 113, 149–150

Chase, Samuel B., Jr., 239–240

Cherokee Indians, 71

Chevron Corporation, 46, 63, 213